THE STATES AND THE NATION SERIES, of which this volume is a part, is designed to assist the American people in a serious look at the ideals they have espoused and the experiences they have undergone in the history of the nation. The content of every volume represents the scholarship, experience, and opinions of its author. The costs of writing and editing were met mainly by grants from the National Endowment for the Humanities, a federal agency. The project was administered by the American Association for State and Local History, a nonprofit learned society, working with an Editorial Board of distinguished editors, authors, and historians, whose names are listed below.

Kentucky

A Bicentennial History

Steven A. Channing

W. W. Norton & Company, Inc.
New York

American Association for State and Local History
Nashville

Author and publishers make grateful acknowledgment to the following for permission to quote from archival material:

The Department of Special Collections, Margaret I. King Library, the University of Kentucky, for permission to quote from the Alben W. Barkley Papers, the A. O. Stanley Papers, and the Ollie J. Bowen Interview in the A. B. Chandler Oral History Project.

The Southern Historical Collection of the University of North Carolina Library, Chapel Hill, North Carolina, for permission to quote from the Alexander and Hillhouse Family Papers, Alexander Series, No. 11.

The State Historical Society of Wisconsin, Madison, Wisconsin, for permission to quote from Series "S" of the Draper Manuscripts.

Library of Congress Cataloguing-in-Publication Data

Channing, Steven A
  Kentucky: a Bicentennial history.

  (The States and the Nation series)
  Bibliography: p.
  Includes index.
  1. Kentucky—History. I. Title. II. Series.
F451.C49   976.9   77–24635
ISBN 0–393–05654–8

Published and distributed by
W. W. Norton & Company, Inc.
500 Fifth Avenue
New York, New York 10036

Printed in the United States of America
1 2 3 4 5 6 7 8 9 0

To my darlin' Laura Hope—
our own native Kentuckian

Contents

Invitation to the Reader   ix

Preface   xiii

Acknowledgments   xvii

1 The Promised Land   3

2 Serpents in Eden   36

3 Era of Bad Feelings:
    Banks, Slaves, War   76

4 The Age of Feudalism   119

5 "As Ye Sow . . . "   164

Suggestions for Further Reading   213

Index   216

Illustrations

A Photographer's Essay by Joe Clark   Following Page 110

Original Maps by Harold Faye
    Kentucky, Contemporary Map Keyed to Text   Facing Page ix
    Nineteenth-Century Kentucky: Natural Divisions,
      Resources   Facing Page 54

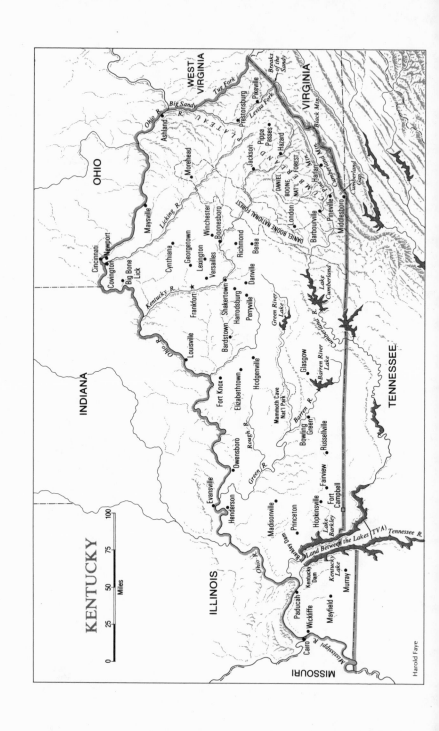

KENTUCKY

Miles
0 25 50 75 100

ILLINOIS
INDIANA
OHIO
WEST VIRGINIA
VIRGINIA
TENNESSEE
MISSOURI

Cairo
Wickliffe
Paducah
Mayfield
Murray
Kentucky Dam
Kentucky Lake
Lake Barkley
Barkley Dam
Land Between the Lakes (TVA)
Tennessee R.
Mississippi R.
Ohio R.
Fort Campbell
Fairview
Hopkinsville
Princeton
Madisonville
Henderson
Evansville
Owensboro
Green R.
Rough R.
Bowling Green
Russellville
Barren R.
Barren River Lake
Mammoth Cave Nat'l Park
Green River Lake
Glasgow
Hodgenville
Elizabethtown
Fort Knox
Louisville
Bardstown
Shakertown
Harrodsburg
Perryville
Danville
Frankfort
Kentucky R.
Lake Cumberland
Cumberland R.
Berea
Richmond
Versailles
Lexington
Georgetown
Winchester
Boonesborough
Cynthiana
Big Bone Lick
Covington
Newport
Cincinnati
Maysville
Licking R.
Morehead
Ashland
Big Sandy R.
Ohio R.
Tug Fork
Prestonsburg
Pikeville
Levisa Fork
Breaks of the Sandy
PLATEAU
Jackson
Pippa Passes
Hazard
London
DANIEL BOONE NAT'L FOREST
DANIEL BOONE NAT'L FOREST
Barbourville
Pineville
Middlesboro
Cumberland Gap
Black Mtn.
Cumberland Mtn.
Pine Mtn.
Harlan
CUMBERLAND

Harold Faye

Invitation to the Reader

IN 1807, former President John Adams argued that a complete history of the American Revolution could not be written until the history of change in each state was known, because the principles of the Revolution were as various as the states that went through it. Two hundred years after the Declaration of Independence, the American nation has spread over a continent and beyond. The states have grown in number from thirteen to fifty. And democratic principles have been interpreted differently in every one of them.

We therefore invite you to consider that the history of your state may have more to do with the bicentennial review of the American Revolution than does the story of Bunker Hill or Valley Forge. The Revolution has continued as Americans extended liberty and democracy over a vast territory. John Adams was right: the states are part of that story, and the story is incomplete without an account of their diversity.

The Declaration of Independence stressed life, liberty, and the pursuit of happiness; accordingly, it shattered the notion of holding new territories in the subordinate status of colonies. The Northwest Ordinance of 1787 set forth a procedure for new states to enter the Union on an equal footing with the old. The Federal Constitution shortly confirmed this novel means of building a nation out of equal states. The step-by-step process through which territories have achieved self-government and national representation is among the most important of the Founding Fathers' legacies.

The method of state-making reconciled the ancient conflict between liberty and empire, resulting in what Thomas Jefferson called an empire for liberty. The system has worked and remains unaltered, despite enormous changes that have taken place in the nation. The country's extent and variety now surpass anything the patriots of '76 could likely have imagined. The United States has changed from an agrarian republic into a highly industrial and urban democracy, from a fledgling nation into a major world power. As Oliver Wendell Holmes remarked in 1920, the creators of the nation could not have seen completely how it and its constitution and its states would develop. Any meaningful review in the bicentennial era must consider what the country has become, as well as what it was.

The new nation of equal states took as its motto *E Pluribus Unum*—"out of many, one." But just as many peoples have become Americans without complete loss of ethnic and cultural identities, so have the states retained differences of character. Some have been superficial, expressed in stereotyped images— big, boastful Texas, "sophisticated" New York, "hillbilly" Arkansas. Other differences have been more real, sometimes instructively, sometimes amusingly; democracy has embraced Huey Long's Louisiana, bilingual New Mexico, unicameral Nebraska, and a Texas that once taxed fortunetellers and spawned politicians called "Woodpecker Republicans" and "Skunk Democrats." Some differences have been profound, as when South Carolina secessionists led other states out of the Union in opposition to abolitionists in Massachusetts and Ohio. The result was a bitter Civil War.

The Revolution's first shots may have sounded in Lexington and Concord; but fights over what democracy should mean and who should have independence have erupted from Pennsylvania's Gettysburg to the "Bleeding Kansas" of John Brown, from the Alamo in Texas to the Indian battles at Montana's Little Bighorn. Utah Mormons have known the strain of isolation; Hawaiians at Pearl Harbor, the terror of attack; Georgians during Sherman's march, the sadness of defeat and devastation. Each state's experience differs instructively; each adds understanding to the whole.

The purpose of this series of books is to make that kind of understanding accessible, in a way that will last in value far beyond the bicentennial fireworks. The series offers a volume on every state, plus the District of Columbia—fifty-one, in all. Each book contains, besides the text, a view of the state through eyes other than the author's—a "photographer's essay," in which a skilled photographer presents his own personal perceptions of the state's contemporary flavor.

We have asked authors not for comprehensive chronicles, nor for research monographs or new data for scholars. Bibliographies and footnotes are minimal. We have asked each author for a summing up—interpretive, sensitive, thoughtful, individual, even personal—of what seems significant about his or her state's history. What distinguishes it? What has mattered about it, to its own people and to the rest of the nation? What has it come to now?

To interpret the states in all their variety, we have sought a variety of backgrounds in authors themselves and have encouraged variety in the approaches they take. They have in common only these things: historical knowledge, writing skill, and strong personal feelings about a particular state. Each has wide latitude for the use of the short space. And if each succeeds, it will be by offering you, in your capacity as a *citizen* of a state *and* of a nation, stimulating insights to test against your own.

James Morton Smith
General Editor

Preface

*After reading a great deal about bussing, I once had a
crazy idea while teaching at Murray: wouldn't it be
wonderful if people from this area could be bussed across
Kentucky to our region? Then people from my East
Kentucky, many of whom have never seen cotton grow,
could be bussed to see the Jackson Purchase. Thus
Kentuckians from the extreme ends of this Commonwealth
could get to know one another.*

Actually, we are strangers to one another.

Jesse Stuart, My World

IN his gentle way, Kentucky's foremost storyteller, Jesse
Stuart, illustrates the guiding theme of this book.
Kentuckians have shared an extraordinary history. From
the beginning, they exhibited a fierce pride in their name, a
powerful devotion to the magnificent estate they had acquired.
At the same time, their unique geography and their all-
too-familiar distinctions of wealth and power generated a sharp
regional consciousness within the state—eastern mountains and
Bluegrass, Knobs, Pennyroyal, and Purchase. The Cumberland
Plateau of the Appalachians forms natural barriers in eastern
Kentucky. Westward, the plateau breaks into modest tablelands
and many small peaks called knobs. The north-central heart of
Kentucky, the Bluegrass, is surrounded by the Knobs. To the
southwest, below the western coal fields, are rocky hillsides and
random hills laced with small streams whose banks are covered
with the wild mint called pennyroyal that gives this area its
name, locally pronounced "the Pennyrile." At the extreme
western tip, separated from the rest of the state by the vast
impoundments of Kentucky Lake on the Tennessee River and
Lake Barkley on the Cumberland, is the Purchase—more

properly, the Jackson Purchase, named for Andrew Jackson, who purchased it for the United States from the Chickasaws in 1818.

Each area developed a characteristic accent, crop, and historic sense of grievance. Rugged individualism, clan loyalty, and localism increased the problem of creating a sense of community. Kentucky's fabled passion for politics did not reduce the division, for it was largely a politics of particularism, of *us* against *them*. Then, over the past half-century, powerful economic and social changes began to alter the lives of Kentuckians, even in the remotest hollows. Regionalism and the rural values that thrived in those provinces became imperiled by the intrusion of new ways of getting and spending.

Kentuckians are uneasy about the trade-off between their conservative rural values and the demands of the fast-approaching twenty-first century. It may be a very good moment to consider the roots of their modern predicament. This brief history makes no attempt at presenting a comprehensive account of this state's experience of more than two hundred years. Recently, the leading student of Kentucky's past reminded us that "The Kentucky story and society fall into parts which no one so far has been clever enough to mold into a single piece." [1] Recognizing that wisdom, this bicentennial history is an interpretation of some of the principal themes and events that together shaped the distinctive, contrary, vexatious, and often admirable character of the natives of this commonwealth. No attempt is made at comprehensive coverage, particularly with regard to the unsettled modern era. I have followed the advice implied in Henry Watterson's recipe for a mint julep. The Louisville editor of two generations ago told us to "pour whiskey into a well-frosted silver cup, throw [all] the other ingredients away and drink the whiskey." [2] Similarly, space requirements have compelled me to try to identify the truly

1. Thomas D. Clark, *Kentucky: Land of Contrast* (New York, Evanston, London: Harper & Row, 1968), p. 259.

2. Richard Barksdale Harwell, *The Mint Julep* (Savannah: The Beehive Press, 1975), p. 50.

important and stick to the main road. I can only hope that this volume may lead readers to deeper explorations in Kentucky history; for their guidance, a list of recommended readings is presented at the conclusion of the narrative.

ACKNOWLEDGMENTS

Although acknowledgments come at the beginning of a book, they are, of course, written at the end of the long road of research and writing. For me, that road was made easier because of the assistance I received all along the way from many talented and dedicated people. I wish to thank the board of the American Association for State and Local History for inviting me to write this bicentennial state history of Kentucky. The unflagging encouragement and valuable criticism of the two fine editors of the series, Gerald George and Timothy Jacobson, were of great benefit. I am grateful for the kindness shown by Hambleton Tapp, James Klotter, Robert Sexton, Terry Birdwhistell, and Professor Lathel Duffield in facilitating use of their writings. The critique kindly provided by my colleague Carl B. Cone saved me from many errors. I have also benefited immensely from the insights provided into the political and cultural processes in the state by Al Smith, Edward Pritchard, Don Wheeler, and professors John B. Stephenson and Bennett Wall. Naturally, errors of fact or judgment that remain are solely my responsibility. For essential typing assistance, I thank Louise Rodgers and Natalie Schick. And, first and last, I am beholden to my most ardent critic and supporter, my dear wife Rhoda.

Kentucky

1

The Promised Land

Can anything be more Absurd than the Conduct of Man,
here is hundreds Travelling hundreds of Miles, they know
not for what Nor Whither, except its to Kentuckey, passing
land almost as good and easy obtained . . . but it will not
do [,] its not Kentuckey [,] its not the Promised land [,] its
not the goodly inheratence [,] the land of Milk and Honey.
          Moses Austin, "A Memorandum . . . 1796–1797"

OR a century and a half, the emotional and physical
heart of English settlement on the North American continent lay in the seaboard communities. The colonists
looked eastward across the vast Atlantic to the Old World for
their social and political inspiration, for their economic suste-
nance and enrichment. By the middle of the eighteenth century,
Europeans had made substantial adjustment to the rough, novel
American environment. Not yet fully new kinds of men, they
had nonetheless been compelled to learn much from relentless
teachers: nature and the Indian. The secrets of corn and game,
of deerskins and trails, were already part of the lore of survival
in the strange land. Yet, in the long decades since the planting
of their first permanent community at Jamestown in 1607, Englishmen and their later fellow settlers, the Scotch-Irish, Germans, and others, had, by 1750, stepped barely a few hundred
miles westward from the security of their original coastal towns,
inland villages, and plantations. Physically, the new land was
theirs; psychologically, ideally, they clung to the harbors linking them to Europe.

3

During the next fifty years—the last half of the eighteenth century—all that changed radically. In an astonishing leap of faith and action, the newcomers would chart and settle the valleys of the eastern Allegheny mountains, overcome the obstacles of the high Appalachian ridge, and claim and counterclaim the fabled Lands of the Western Waters. That great era in American history was powerfully symbolized by a revolutionary war against colonialism and for national identity and independence. And that turbulent period also marked—appropriately—the origin and founding of the first transmontane state, the first far-western frontier: Kentucky.

Kentucky was no mere child of an age of expansion, incidentally spawned in the westering floodtide. The land wistfully styled *Ken-tah-teh* by the Cherokee occupied a central role in the frontier drama of the Revolutionary era. To the Cherokee, and then more fiercely to the whites of the eastern colonies and states, *Ken-tah-teh* meant *tomorrow,* "the land where we will live." [1] Above all, it was Kentucky that became the focus of the growing appetite for new lands, an ambition apparently frustrated by British imperial plans. It was Kentucky that witnessed the first important English settlements beyond the mountains. It was Kentucky that channelled the great movement of peoples into the Mississippi Valley. And it was in and of Kentucky that some of the most persistent and characteristic myths of frontier America were shaped. The period covered in this initial chapter concerns not so much Kentucky as it actually was, for until the 1780s, the area called Kentucky was mainly wilderness, a few hastily constructed forts huddled against the threatening forest, with a total population hardly numbering in the hundreds. But Kentucky as idea, as coveted prize, occupies a remarkable place in the story of the origins of the American nation.

During much of the 1600s, the first century of English colonial settlement, images of Kentucky blurred indistinguishably into larger, vague notions about the vast western lands. But by the last decades, more specific reports about the trans-Allegheny frontier had begun to filter eastward. The pool of information

    1. William E. Connelley and E. Merton Coulter, *History of Kentucky* 5 vols. (Chicago: The American Historical Society, 1922), 1, 1–2.

grew slowly, fed by a mixture of reliable and inaccurate eyewitness and second-hand accounts passed from red man to white, from Frenchman to Englishman. These tales spoke ambiguously of delights and dangers, of an environment both inviting and threatening, yet clearly gigantic in its potential wealth. But who could or would attempt to claim such a kingdom? Certainly not the hesitant English. So, for a long while, stories about it lay dormant. With eastern homesteads still there for the taking and relatively secure from danger, the lands beyond the mountains would have to wait.

During the early eighteenth century, however, the population of the American colonies steadily increased. Not only Englishmen came now, but so did German, Dutch, French, and Swedish Protestants, eager for new homes and religious freedom. With them came those most relentless of American pioneers, the Scotch-Irish, fleeing political turmoil at home. They all traveled west and south into Pennsylvania and down the Allegheny valleys to settle back-country Maryland, Virginia, and the two Carolinas. So vigorous was the filling-in process that, by the early 1740s, talk of overpopulation was commonplace. Though these regions might very well have looked thinly settled to the modern observer, contemporaries were undeniably experiencing a sense of diminishing resources and opportunities. It was not only that feeling of restlessness and confinement so nicely phrased by Daniel Boone—the dread of being able to see the smoke from a neighbor's chimney—though there was enough of that. There were other portents of unwanted change. The abundant animal population had noticeably thinned and been forced to move into rougher terrain. Game that had helped feed and clothe generations of early pioneers and, in the vagaries of the hunt, had helped educate them in the lore of the woods was no longer abundant. In addition, the harshness of colonial agricultural practices, particularly in the world of the tidewater tobacco plantations, had begun to deplete and erode the relatively thin topsoils; southern planters hungrily eyed the supposedly richer soils to the west. And through all of that, new European settlers continued to come down the Shenandoah and other valley conduits, pushing ever southward, westward, and upward into the mountain valleys.

The American population had fully entered a prolonged and

spectacular growth phase that would see it double every twenty-five years. That, combined with its exploitative and expansive agricultural ways, made a contest for possession of the continent seem inevitable. But the roots of Kentucky settlement went far beyond mere statistics. The land called Kentucky did not simply happen to be in the path of the coming wave. By the middle of the eighteenth century, the image of Kentucky as a positive western Eden had become the focus of reports about the west, and during the next five decades, that image—part myth, part reality—would become a bright, alluring magnet for easterners and Europeans.

Somewhere out there, in the land beyond the mountains, was said to be a country to delight every pastoral heart. In the seaboard colonies, from New England to the South, the best lands seemed already largely possessed, used, and abused by farmers and planters; but out to the west, the land still lay unbroken, stretching out in rolling plains, rich and unclaimed. There, the earth was lush and verdant, great with trees, deep soils, and delicious grasses. It was said to be ribbed with fresh, cool streams and salt licks that surely nourished marvelous supplies of fish and game of every description. Once begun, the cycle of storytelling could not be checked. *There* was the dreamed-of Eden of the West, a place without winter, the pot of gold for any man with the will to claim it. The image of Kentucky that emerged into American consciousness in the later colonial period was, in fact, the myth of America itself: a place of boundless land, perfect opportunity, stirring adventure—in short, the perpetual frontier. The truth was that the country called Kentucky would soon prove to possess few of those idyllic qualities. Its pioneers would be punished by the hardships of the westward trek, nipped by frostbite, killed by hostile Indians, and relatively few of the many who arrived would ever come to own an unchallenged piece of good farm land; but the image of Kentucky as a "bright pastoral thought" would prove impervious to such realities.[2]

That image, however, only begins to explain the origins of

2. Arthur K. Moore, *The Frontier Mind: A Cultural Analysis of the Kentucky Frontiersman* (Lexington: University of Kentucky Press, 1957), p. 5.

Kentucky settlement, for those origins were bound up within a complex web of economic and political rivalries. Desire for possession of Kentucky gradually expanded to involve fur traders, land speculators, ambitious colonial leaders, and, on the broadest scale, the struggle between England 'and France for mastery of the North American continent. For more than a century, England and France had fought for domination, both in the Old World and the New. In the mid-eighteenth century, France moved aggressively to solidify her position in North America. She sent her agents, Indian traders, Jesuit priests, and soldiers into the Appalachian frontier from Canada to the Ohio Valley to construct and improve forts and firm up alliances with powerful Indian nations—especially the Iroquois—all along the frontier. Although England lagged in such efforts, it was clear that both nations laid claim to identical western regions and that further conflict was inevitable. By seizing the initiative, France not only exposed the entire frontier to increasingly bold Indian raids, but challenged the expansionist dreams of British Americans just when those dreams were growing especially vivid.

If the question of expansion seemed less than urgent to English politicians in London, that certainly was not true among the colonials. Indian affairs and the land question were the most troublesome issues in the provincial assemblies. Of paramount importance to the future of Kentucky were the ambitions of certain great land speculators, particularly those identified with and aided by the royal governors and the assembly of Virginia. By the 1740s, various groups of eager speculators were working to secure enormous parcels of western land for settlement and sale. Once begun, the fever of speculation spread rapidly. Between the spring of 1745 and May 1754, more than two and a half million acres of land, mainly in western Virginia, were granted to various promoters. Such schemes ultimately had little practical result; the grandest proposals proved entirely stillborn. The whole phenomenon did have two consequences of great significance, however, for the future of both Kentucky and the United States: the beginning of thorough exploration of the Appalachian Plateau, and the beginning of events that would lead to war over the future of America.

Under the auspices of two principal land promotion companies, the land beyond western Virginia began to be visited, explored, and eventually hunted systematically by the English. In March 1750, a party sponsored by the Loyal Land Company and headed by the highly regarded surveyor, Dr. Thomas Walker, set out southwestward up the valley of Virginia on the first expedition of any real consequence. On April 17, the party reached the great opening in the Allegheny rise, through which tens of thousands of western pioneers would journey throughout the next century. The party passed through the Cumberland Gap (so named by Walker) and spent the next two months exploring the mountains and rivers of what was to be eastern Kentucky as far north as the Levisa Fork of the Big Sandy River in present-day Johnson and Lawrence counties, before returning southward back into Virginia. Although the group never reached the flatter, more fertile bluegrass region, Walker and his party would carry back important information about the geography and potential riches of the area. The following year, Christopher Gist, agent for the Ohio Company, another group interested in land speculation, paralleled Walker's route. Entering the area from the northeast, Gist visited Shawnee towns on the Ohio River, crossed over to the south bank at the mouth of the Scioto, and started downstream toward the Falls of the Ohio. In mid-March 1751, upon learning that a party of hostile French Indians had encamped at the falls, he reversed his plan and went back across the mountains to his home in the Yadkin Valley of western North Carolina, bearing abundant new details about the country.[3]

The adventures of Walker and Gist and the tales they told of the beautiful country beyond the mountains excited the ambitions of Virginians still further. When Robert Dinwiddie, himself an eager land speculator, became governor of the colony it was certain that Virginia would move to assert her ancient claim to the lands beyond the mountains, a claim dating back to the founding of Virginia itself. In 1753 Dinwiddie dispatched a young surveyor named George Washington to feel out French intentions on the frontier. It soon became clear that the French

---

3. Thomas D. Clark, *A History of Kentucky* (Lexington: The John Bradford Press, 1960), pp. 22–23.

would not yield their claims voluntarily. Here was a situation beyond the capacity of private land companies or individual colonies. Although an official declaration of war was delayed until 1756, the English sent General Edward Braddock to Virginia with two regiments to contest the French claims.

The French and Indian War, as it came to be called in the colonies, was a bitter nine-year struggle, for the French with their thousands of native allies proved formidable adversaries. The first years of the war were a disaster for the English. In 1755 the arrogant Braddock, well-schooled in European techniques of fighting but ignorant of the dangers in the forests of America, combined his force with colonial militia under Lt. Col. Washington. On July 9 the army marched headlong into a bloody ambush near Fort Duquesne, by the forks of the Ohio River. Braddock and many others were killed, and Washington led a defeated army eastward. The experience was a shocking introduction to frontier warfare for such woodsmen as Thomas Walker, serving as principal commissary; Christopher Gist, a scout in the ill-fated expedition; and John Finley, Indian trader, wagoner, and Kentucky explorer. Also along, as teamster and blacksmith, was a young North Carolina farmer named Daniel Boone. The Braddock "slaughter pen" was followed over the next three years by further setbacks that exposed the western frontier communities to relentless attack. It was only after British minister William Pitt took charge of the war effort that the course of events was changed. The empire-minded Pitt redirected the focus of military efforts upon North America; and, by 1762, the campaigns he initiated had exhausted French resources for waging a two-front war. In the Treaty of Paris, signed in February 1763, France ceded virtually the entire territory east of the Mississippi River to the English and the area west of the river to the Spanish.

The English had acquired the greatest colonial empire of the age, and they looked ahead to limitless wealth and power. For the colonists, peace meant the apparent end of an ancient threat and rivalry and the prospect of rapid movement onto the lush plains and valleys beyond the Alleghenies. Yet, countless obstacles to settlement in Kentucky remained. Most ominous was the continuing problem of Indian resistance. Far from being reconciled to the collapse of New France, many western tribes harbored deep hostility to the idea of an expanding English empire in the Mississippi Valley. Since the French had always been more interested in trade than in settlement, their presence had never been oppressive to native culture. But Indian leaders knew very well that the English perception of empire was different. British America was a place to live, to occupy fully by the tens of thousands. Such occupation had already meant either the annihilation or forced removal of many eastern Indian nations, and the Treaty of Paris seemed to signal the coming of just that kind of overwhelming, smothering invasion of the West. The result was an era of mutually barbaric warfare unmatched until the full-scale warfare directed by the United States Army against the trans-Mississippi tribes after the Civil War.

Indian hostility to the idea of unlimited, uncompensated white occupation of their land was undeniable. Just as certain was the fact that the British, having expended millions of pounds sterling and thousands of lives to acquire the Mississippi Valley, were not about to keep it as a natural reservation either for red men or game. It must be exploited by American settlers, preferably in a way that enriched Englishmen. But what was the hurry? Why permit squatter settlement free from British control, contributing nothing to British profit? And why excite the fears and animosities of the aborigines? The result of that thinking in London, four thousand miles from the frontier, was King George III's Proclamation of 1763 aimed at temporarily barring permanent white settlement beyond the crest of the Appalachian chain. The proclamation also sought to draw pioneers away from the mountain frontier line by encouraging migration to newly acquired Nova Scotia and Florida.

The British government, however, could not hold back American expansion forever. Ambitious speculators demanded it. Men of the colonial militia who had served in the late war and been pledged land warrants in the western territory demanded it. Thousands of ordinary folk, both newly arriving immigrants and restless easterners, expected it. Resident British agents wrote to the home government warning of the dangers of renewed Indian conflict; significantly, the Indians themselves were eager to enter into better understandings with their long-time adversaries to fix a permanant boundary for white settlement.

The result of these converging interests was a series of wilderness congresses between Indians and whites. The grandest of these was held in the fall of 1768 at Fort Stanwix in the upper Mohawk Valley of New York. Here gathered perhaps three thousand Indians and thirty of their chiefs, representing most importantly the Six Nations of the Iroquois Confederacy, and an equally distinguished body of colonial governors and agents of the royal government formed the English delegation. A vast grant of western territory possessed or claimed by the Iroquois was granted to the whites. In return, a line was drawn absolutely (or so the red men hoped) separating Indian country from white. The significance for future Kentucky settlement was immediately apparent: the Fort Stanwix Treaty line ran the entire length of the Ohio River from Fort Pitt (Pittsburgh) to its confluence with the Tennessee River. Territory to the north of the line was reserved to the Indian. Momentously, any Iroquois claim to Kentucky was extinguished. At about the same time, Cherokee leaders in the Carolinas agreed to a similar treaty line that seemed to relinquish any Cherokee claim to the region that included northern and eastern Kentucky. The Indian barrier to Kentucky settlement was apparently gone.

These important treaties served as a starting signal for the next great wave of transmontane migration. Beginning in the spring and summer of 1769, thousands of pioneer folk began to reoccupy abandoned settlements and found new communities at the forks of the Ohio, the upper valleys of Allegheny Virginia, and, to the south, the valley of the Watauga River in what would be northeastern Tennessee. Lush valleys all along the sprawling mountain frontier were rapidly filling up. The next grand leap westward was about to begin.

Accounts of Kentucky history traditionally now turn to consider the activities of the man popularly assumed to be the great central figure, not only in the pioneer settlement of this state, but of the entire frontier, one Daniel Boone. Yet who was he? Shrouded in legends and folklore that have multiplied ceaselessly over the past two centuries, the D. Boone who killed a "bar" now stalks across the stage of American history and mythology as one of our singularly gigantic figures. All modern-day professional accounts about that period have attempted to place the exploits of the man in proper perspective; we now surely know nearly everything of consequence and a great deal of inconsequence about him, and we have a sound notion of his accomplishments. Yet it is likely that all of these balanced accounts will do little more than place a small dent in his popular image. While the ghostly shade of ole Daniel has probably chuckled over the absurd inflations of his contributions and winced over the ridiculous distortions of his life and times in television shows and earlier fiction, the Boone legend itself simply is beyond revision. Like images of Kentucky and the West, Daniel Boone as idea has long since become part of an almost sacred and certainly meaningful American folklore.[4]

In the popular imagination, Boone is credited above all as the first explorer of Kentucky and the leader of its first permanent white settlement. Most of us can probably bring to mind's eye the luminous painting by the nineteenth-century western artist George Caleb Bingham, *Daniel Boone Escorting a Band of Pioneers into the Western Country*. There is the sturdy Daniel, striding confidently toward us, through Cumberland Gap and into history; his wife Rebecca and the rest of the party follow, all secure from the natural dangers around them because Boone is with them. We know that he did lead such groups of Yadkin Valley farmers along that route—though they were far from being impervious to misadventure. We also know that Boone was neither first explorer nor settler and that he was, in fact, but one among a number of equally ambitious and courageous pioneer leaders. In 1766, at least four parties of adventure-loving North Carolina and Virginia farmers and former scouts had crossed the mountains and spent considerable time on long hunts in the eastern Kentucky hills.

---

4. The genesis of the Boone legend owes much the writings of John Filson, schoolteacher, land promoter, and a friend of Boone. The so-called *Autobiography* was largely penned by Filson and became, through many editions in English and other languages, the principal source for the marvelous tales about Boone's exploits and character.

Boone's first journey to Kentucky was in no respects different from these other wandering hunts. Like most of the others, he lived in the upper Yadkin Valley of North Carolina, where rainbow talk of unexcelled game and land just beyond the next plateau was common in conversation around the homey cabins. Like the others, the Boone family had marched a long trail ahead of substantial settlement, their own move beginning in Berks County, Pennsylvania, in 1750 and ending with the purchase of land in what is now Davidson County, North Carolina, in December 1753. Boone differed from many of his fellow woodsmen in that his family had been English Quaker in origin, rather than Scotch-Irish, but he otherwise shared the characteristics of the typical "long hunter." Like most, he had a lifelong antipathy to the drudgeries of farming and the confinements of a well-settled community. He shared with them a profound love for the hunting life, with its natural beauties and freedoms, the delights of freshly killed bear meat and venison, and the monies to be gained for skins and furs. Partly for these reasons, he also shared ambivalent feelings about the natives of the land, at once profoundly admiring and copying many of the red man's ways of living and killing, and at the same time being forced into bloody conflict with them. These men were early, raw-boned representatives of a whole class of eighteenth- and nine-teenth-century frontiersmen who marched ahead of the main body of pioneer settlers all the way across the continent, men who, in their flight from the main settlement areas, ironically hastened the relentless conquest of the West.

Daniel Boone himself was much more than just a scratching, antisocial mountain man. He was to remain in central Kentucky for many years and play an instrumental role in founding and securing its first permanent settlements; but that lay ahead. In the fall of 1767, Boone, weary from a season of plowing and reaping, determined to treat himself to the refreshment of a western hunt. Then nearing his thirty-third birthday, Daniel had been listening to tales of Kentucky since as early as 1755 from such men as John Finley, the western adventurer who had served as chief scout to General Edward Braddock's army. Now Boone eagerly set out across the Cumberland Plateau with one or two companions; but as winter set in, they found themselves wandering through the dense thickets of the hills of eastern Kentucky and Tennessee, becoming lost, or as Boone preferred to recall, "confused," and never reaching the much-talked-of Great Meadow beyond the mountains. Boone returned to domestic life on the Yadkin in the spring, but clearly he yearned to participate in a more effective hunt. He also chafed under the discontents of life in western North Carolina, which at that time was marked by increasing conflict between backcountry folk and an overbearing eastern royal government. Good fortune came knocking when, early the next year, old John Finley, now an itinerant peddler, entered the valley. Plans evolved rapidly to launch another hunt, and on May 1, 1768, Finley, Boone, John Stewart—Daniel's brother-in-law—and three others mounted their horses and set out for the western country. Adventure was on their minds, but more important was the lure of anticipated fur profits; the possibility of land speculation also glimmered on the horizon.

Rebecca Boone would not see her husband again for two years. It was during that long hunt that Daniel was to be involved in a seemingly endless sequence of adventures that, told, embellished, and retold, emerged as part of the basis not only for the Boone legend, but for the larger mystique of the American frontiersman. Finley led the party through the Cumberland Gap to the Red River and then quickly to the valley of the Kentucky River. At long last, Boone was able to stand atop a rise and look out across a splendid rolling plain stretching far to the north and west—the thickly caned "Great Meadow." The party soon set themselves to hunting, and throughout the summer and fall the stacks of skins and peltry grew. Pleased with themselves and lulled into carelessness by the swift, quiet passage of the seasons, the men failed to notice that increasing numbers of Shawnee hunting parties were moving about in their vicinity. They had also incautiously made camp near the famed Warrior's Path, the principal north-south trail used by the Ohio-based Shawnee, by the Cherokee, and by themselves during their own journey. In late December, Boone and Stewart were captured by Shawnee braves who forced them to hand over the entire store of pelts.

"The time of our sorrow was now arrived," Boone later

recalled.[5] They had lost the fruits of a year's planning and labor. Though Daniel and his companions were unharmed and only warned to leave the territory, a number in the group, Finley included, were badly frightened and determined on departing Kentucky at once. As they straggled eastward, the party fortuitously encountered Squire Boone, Daniel's younger brother, along with a companion, journeying out to meet them with fresh supplies and ammunition. The two Boones, Stewart, and the fourth man, Alexander Neely, bitter over the recent loss of their stock of pelts, chose to return to the hunt. That proved a terrible mistake. During their first encounter, the Shawnee had preferred to ''rob'' and warn off the intrusive whites. After all, the pelts were really theirs, the Indians reasoned, since the land and game were theirs; still, western Indians were at peace with the British colonists, so bloodshed was to be avoided. Future meetings were destined to be far less agreeable. Over the coming months, the Boone brothers narrowly escaped a number of attacks. John Stewart, separated from the others, was definitely killed by braves; Neely finally fled, but much later he, too, was found dead, probably of starvation. The Boones continued to hunt during the rest of 1770, however, and on into the following spring. They began to build up a second rich stock of skins and furs.

Despite hazards and troubles, that period included some of Daniel's happiest days. During this summery spell there occurred the oft-told story of a party of hunters who, startled by the unexpected sound of a white man's voice in what they assumed was Indian wilderness, discovered Daniel Boone, bursting with good feelings, warbling away alone in the middle of a meadow! In March 1771, the Boone brothers finally loaded their pack horses with the catch and moved southeastward, passing through Cumberland Gap and reaching the fringes of settlement in the Powell River valley in western North Carolina. There, one night in May, while settling into camp, they were visited and robbed by a party of Cherokee. Although Squire managed to save some of the skins and pelts, he and Daniel were forced to trudge back to

5. John Bakeless, *Daniel Boone, Master of the Wilderness* (1939; reprint edition, Harrisburg, Pa.: Stackpole Company, 1965), p. 51.

the Yadkin with little tangible to show for two years of labor. What did show was their love for the land they had lived in and hunted and their desire to return one day and possess a piece of it. Meanwhile, Daniel Boone's reputation as a scout and hunter knowledgeable about the Indians and the geography of Kentucky had grown enormously. He and the other North Carolina and Virginia long hunters were to stimulate still further the interest in settling the unclaimed country.

So the region known as "Kaintuckee" became the principal target for land-hungry easterners, from ordinary folk restless for their dreamed-of small pot of gold to the grander schemes of the ambitious speculators and politicians of the seaboard and England. Still, by the end of 1772, not a single permanent white habitation existed anywhere in the region. Virginia officials and land speculators, however, were about to move aggressively again to seize control of western claims.

These plans received encouragement from the highest sources of provincial government, including a gentleman named John Murray, Earl of Dunmore, now Royal Governor of Virginia. Lord Dunmore was an unscrupulous man, determined to sustain the ancient Virginia claim to Kentucky, eager to grasp a share of those lands for himself and his allies, and coldly indifferent to the plight of western Indians. Against the foil of Dunmore's ambitions, Kentucky in 1773 took its most serious step yet toward settlement.

The best-organized and most determined of these schemes was carried out by a party led by Captain Thomas Bullitt, who represented Dunmore himself. Bullitt's group, which descended the Ohio River to Kentucky in June, had been joined by two other parties of Virginians, one including James Harrod, also representing the governor's interests, and the other led by the McAfee brothers, James, George, and Robert, of Botetourt County. For the next two months, these men alternatively separated and rejoined, exploring and hunting lands along the Ohio and beyond, into the beautiful cane-covered meadows of the central and eastern bluegrass plains. While still together in early July, the men delighted at the astounding sight along Big Bone Lick of the prehistoric bones and teeth of mastodons and other

Glacial Age creatures. Later that month, the McAfee brothers directed a survey of splendid lands along the Kentucky River on what is today the site of the city of Frankfort. August found the Bullitt party marking off town lots at the Falls of the Ohio, now the city of Louisville. Before September, all of these surveyors had begun their return to Virginia, eager to launch settlement on a fuller scale the following spring.

News of their activities soon reached Daniel Boone and the Yadkin Valley people. Concerned that the prime lands would soon be taken up by wealthy land speculators and having already nursed his heart's desire to settle in Kentucky for two years now, Boone was not long in deciding on a bold plan: he would jump the gun on the Virginians by leading, not a party of hunters or surveyors, but actual settlers, with wives and children, intent on building new homes in the wilderness. Lacking legal sanction but inspired by the Boone reputation, a substantial party assembled and, in September 1773, set off for the Cumberland Gap, the first true migration of white settlers to Kentucky. But the fates had not smiled on Daniel this time. While encamped at the Gap, a small party, including Boone's son James, became separated three miles from the main group. Early the next morning, they were suddenly attacked by Shawnee. Hearing gunfire, Daniel hurried to the rescue—too late. All but two were killed. Among the dead was young James, who had suffered dreadful torture before being allowed to die. Horrified, the group rejected the elder Boone's urgings to go on and withdrew eastward. Once again, the morning sun found Daniel Boone marching away from Kentucky, despondent, and, for the moment, defeated.

To the north, however, Dunmore and his people went forward. With the melting of the winter snows and the full flowering of spring in 1774, the Virginians resumed their push down the Ohio River into Kentucky. Most important was a party led by James Harrod. Journeying south and east of the Kentucky River, members of the Harrod party drew lots and dispersed to found Harrodsburg—first named Harrodstown; later, the vicinities of Danville, Big Springs, and Boiling Springs were surveyed. Log dwellings were built, land was cleared and corn planted. The permanent white settlement of the region appeared

to have begun at last. But wild Kentucky was still unready to be
subdued. One hot July day, the quiet of the settlements was
broken by a surprise attack from Shawnee braves. Unfortunately, that was no isolated venture. Soon thereafter, Harrod
and his associates were visited by two men from the east, agents
commissioned by Governor Dunmore to carry a chilling warning to each of the surveying parties in the wilderness: a full-
scale Indian war was about to begin again. Ironically, one of the
messengers was Daniel Boone—who managed to find time to
admire Harrod's community and purchase a piece of property
there.

Time and again frontier settlers had suffered Indian attacks,
violent and ultimately futile attempts at retribution for the cru-
elty inflicted on red men, efforts to compel an honoring of the
peace treaties ignored by most whites, or attempts to stem the
flood of European immigration onto Indian lands. Only humane
statesmanship could have cooled the fiery ill feelings that
burned on both sides. The Pennsylvanians, with their traditions
of Quaker justice to native Americans, had possessed those
qualities and were trusted accordingly by the Indians; Virginians, on the other hand, were justifiably feared and despised for
their land-grabbing and their flagrantly racist dealings. On that
basis, the Englishman Lord Dunmore was the ideal representative leader of the province. A willful man "fond of his bottle," [6] Dunmore saw no distinction between the pursuit of his
growing private interest in Kentucky lands and the interests of
all would-be western settlers.

Although the only major battle of the brief Dunmore's War
was not even fought on its soil, Kentucky and control of the
land there were paramount issues. Impatient with the attempts
of Pennsylvanians to maintain an even-handed policy and
frankly determined to precipitate war, Dunmore seized Fort Pitt
in the spring of 1774 and claimed the region south and west of it
for Virginia. The war quickly reached its climax in the Battle of
Point Pleasant, fought at the confluence of the Kanawha and

6. So said Virginian Richard Henry Lee, First Continental Congress Debates, October 6, 1775, as recorded in the *Diary and Autobiography of John Adams,* edited by
L. H. Butterfield, 4 vols. (New York: Atheneum, 1964), 2:194.

Ohio rivers on October 10, 1774. The Indian force, ably led by Chief Cornstalk of the Shawnees, inflicted substantial casualties, but failed to drive the English from their position and so withdrew. Dunmore soon arrived with additional forces and compelled Cornstalk to accept the Treaty of Camp Charlotte, yielding hunting rights in Kentucky and agreeing to allow whites to travel unmolested down the Ohio. Once again, the illusion of a secure and peaceful Kentucky glimmered on the western horizon.

Although the fright bred by Dunmore's War had inspired a near total evacuation of Kentucky by whites, the Camp Charlotte Treaty clearly signaled renewed efforts for 1775. And that year did prove to be momentous. With the Indian menace apparently ended, speculation and settlement in Kentucky lands were now more inviting than ever. In early March, James Harrod and his party returned and constructed a fort that became an anchor for settlers coming out from Virginia. Soon there were several hundred central-Kentucky pioneers, all hoping to establish claims, lay in corn, and return home to gather up their families and possessions for the great move across the mountains.

Back in the Yadkin and other western Carolina valleys, the appetite for a piece of Kentucky soil was rising again, fueled not only by land hunger and local discontents, but by the last and best-conceived of the great land-promotion schemes. From the time of the origin and collapse of that plan, the Transylvania Company and its founding genius, Richard Henderson, who proposed the plan, have been objects of controversy among contemporaries and historians alike. Yet some basic points are undeniable. The Transylvania Company was simply the most recent in a long line of privately sponsored schemes to encourage western settlement for personal profit. The idea was as old and honored as the London Company, which had created the very first British mainland colony of Virginia as a private venture; and it was as recent and dishonored as Lord Dunmore's plottings. Where there was land and clouded title, entrepreneurship would seek to fill the vacuum. In addition, whatever the flaws of Henderson's land title and leadership—and they were real—

the Transylvania Company did have an extremely important and beneficial impact on early Kentucky history.

Most people who knew Richard Henderson saw him as a hard-driving man of great ambition. Kentucky had a way of attracting such men. Born in Virginia, Henderson grew up in the Yadkin Valley, became a self-educated lawyer of high reputation, and in 1769 was named to the Superior Court of North Carolina. Four years later, following the legal and political turmoil precipitated by angry westerners—the Regulators—Henderson was denied reappointment to the bench. Finding himself unoccupied and financially depressed, he soon turned his attention westward. It would have been remarkable if he had avoided infection by the Kentucky fever, but Richard Henderson would never be content with the ordinary life of a farmer or backwoods barrister. In August 1774, he joined with five similarly ambitious friends to form a land company designed to purchase a vast tract from the Cherokee and to oversee its settlement. By autumn, he had visited Cherokee chiefs in eastern Tennessee and made substantial arrangements for a great parley to be held the following spring.

The western settlements were ablaze with anticipation late that winter, as the Henderson entourage crossed the mountains, their long train of wagons loaded with goods for trading with the Indians. Word also spread that Henderson had hired Daniel Boone to assist in the treaty-making and to help mark a trail and lead the first settlers to the prospective new lands in Kentucky. For nearly three weeks, a vast assembly of whites and Cherokee created a colorful pageant of feasting and bartering on the banks of the Watauga River near present-day Elizabethton in eastern Tennessee. At first, it appears that the Indians had neither expected nor intended to relinquish any considerable portion of their Kentucky claim, but in the end they did accept Henderson's attractive offer. On March 17, 1775, the Treaty of Sycamore Shoals was agreed to; the Transylvania Company was to pay the Indians goods and sterling worth ten thousand pounds for an immense tract comprising much of modern Kentucky west and south of the Kentucky River to the Cumberland River. Henderson then negotiated the "Path Deed," acquiring a strip of land connecting the western North Carolina settlements with the new Kentucky tract through the Cumberland Gap.

Regardless of the enticements offered by the Transylvania Company, the Cherokee decision seems astonishing. Here was a great Indian people voluntarily trading away extensive hunting rights for goods that amounted, as one tribesman later discovered, to a single shirt per person. Perhaps even a shirt was better than forced expulsion and expropriation. Still, not all those present at the Watauga conference welcomed the bargain. Oconostota, among the foremost chiefs, passionately warned that his proud nation would one day find itself pushed deeper and deeper into the wilderness until, one day, the insatiable Europeans, "not being able to point out any further retreat for the miserable Cherokees, would then proclaim the extinction of the whole race." [7] But the true Cassandra proved to be not one of the elders, but the great Chief Attakullakulla's own son, Dragging Canoe. Bitter over the action of his people, but powerless to thwart it, Dragging Canoe delivered the famous prophecy that, while the country called Kentucky was fair, "a dark cloud hung over that land." [8]

From the perspective of two centuries, the Cherokee's warning seems understandable enough. The next twenty years were to be marred by repeated conflict between white men and Indians for control of central Kentucky. Young Dragging Canoe himself was killed only the year after the conference, during an attack upon white settlers in Tennessee. But the phrase "dark and bloody ground," as it was misquoted and recopied over the years, soon came to signify a quite different notion. Settlers and land promoters seized upon the reported remark and exploited it as a rationale both to encourage settlement and to disparage the culture and claims of contemporary Indians. According to these

7. Quoted in William Stewart Lester, *The Transylvania Colony* (Spencer, Ind.: Samuel R. Guard & Co., 1935), pp. 34–35. Lester's source is John Haywood, *The Civil and Political History of the State of Tennessee* (Knoxville: Heiskell and Brown, 1803), pp. 58–59.

8. Draper Manuscripts, the State Historical Society of Wisconsin, Madison, Wisconsin, 12 S 110 (microfilm ed.).

whites, the land allegedly was darkened by savage disputations among the Indians; none of them had actually lived in Kentucky, but most of them had fought over it. That piece of propaganda would presumably make it easier for white settlement, since it meant that they were not really taking anyone else's land. Any observant white could quickly see in the great earthen mounds scattered across the region evidence that a substantial people had, at one time, long ago, occupied these parts; but builders of such mounds as those surely were unrelated to the contemporary "savages." Myths began to circulate suggesting that the entire upper Mississippi Valley had in fact been peopled by a great nation of "white Indians," or non-Indians. These great mounds and other earthworks could not have been produced by mere redskins. So-called mummies—preserved, desiccated corpses reminiscent of old Egypt—were discovered in the cave region of Kentucky and seemed to confirm that. Picts, Welshmen, Israelites—a host of legendary nationalities were envisioned as stalking across the ancient fields of Kentucky—anything but Indians.[9]

Most of this was nonsense. The mound builders were native Americans whose activities dated back nearly a millennium; the peoples of various prehistoric Indian cultures had occupied the rock shelters and valley bottoms of eastern and central Kentucky for thousands of years. One astonishing fact, however, must have influenced the attitudes of incoming whites greatly: the bluegrass region and the areas to the south and west of it were unoccupied by any permanent Indian settlements by the time of the influx of the white pioneers. Indian people were not actually living in the region, nor had they been doing so in any numbers for perhaps a century or more prior to the 1770s. Considering the much-touted beauties of the bluegrass country, that is amazing. Here, apparently, was a fertile, well-watered region with abundant grasses, cane and trees—and the red man declined to live in it. Explanations came readily to hand, usually based upon Dragging Canoe's "prophecy." Some believed the power of the Iroquois Confederacy so great, the fear of their warriors

9. Douglas W. Schwartz, *Conceptions of Kentucky Prehistory* (Lexington: The University of Kentucky Press, 1967), pp. 7–17.

so strong, that other tribes were prevented from dwelling in Kentucky by some mysterious ban exercised by that nation. Also, the area was supposedly contested by the northern Shawnee and the southern Cherokee, with neither able to gain the upper hand. Another popular idea held that Kentucky was the heart's delight of all Indian hunters and was preserved by them as a kind of national park, a mutual hunting ground for all tribes.

Though they have persisted until hoary with age, these answers do not wholly stand up to scrutiny. If the bluegrass region was such an Eden, why had Indians apparently deserted it by the time of white entrance? If the fish, game, and fowl were superior, why had they not moved there, to save the considerable energies expended in prolonged hunting trips? And why were the Indian nations around the perimeter of the region in fact *not* in active conflict with one another in the eighteenth century? On the contrary, their general behavior, particularly those north of the Ohio, had been one of co-operation, the better to harass the advancing white horde. Finally, even if Iroquois chiefs had desired to wield authority over Kentucky and prevent its occupation, they would have been hard put to do so, considering the vast distances involved. The Iroquois Confederacy was powerful in its own spheres of influence, but their home grounds were hundreds of miles away, in Pennsylvania, and in upper New York. In any event, they had readily signed away any claim to rights in Kentucky in the Fort Stanwix Treaty of 1768.

These older explanations have some validity, but there is another important point that helps to explain the absence of permanent Indian residents in Kentucky. Studies made of the life and health of the natives who lived in the bluegrass region in the earlier era—A.D. 1100–1650—have revealed a startling incidence of a deadly bone pathology. These populations are called the Fort Ancient and are believed to have been the ancestors of the Shawnee. Examinations of skeletons taken from Fort Ancient burial sites indicate a very high incidence of mortifying bone disease. Occasionally found in skeleton populations elsewhere in the state, the disease is clearly concentrated in the bluegrass region. The effects of the illness are visible as swelling, softening, and lesions of the longer bones, and evidently it afflicted both sexes and all ages, although it intensified with age. In addition, the pathology was not confined to the Fort Ancient people, but had also affected their central Kentucky predecessors, the Adena culture, which had occupied the same area approximately during the period from 800 B.C. to A.D. 800.

Anthropologists who have studied the phenomenon have concluded that the source of the problem lay in some peculiarity of the physical environment. They have tentatively linked the bone disease to the deficiency of certain metallic trace elements in the soil and water, particularly manganese, trace elements that are essential to healthy bone growth. If that be true, it may partially explain the reluctance of native Americans actually to stay and live in central Kentucky.

There was an old story, circulated by whites, about a mighty battle held at the forks of the Ohio sometime in the distant past. It was said that the unburied bones of the warriors were piled high, and the land called Kentucky was afterwards haunted by a multitude of restless spirits whose "bad medicine" repelled future Indian settlement. Perhaps the story was only symbolic of the message of warning transmitted by the unfortunate experiences of the Adena and Fort Ancient peoples. To the Indian, with his limited corn, squash, and game diet, Kentucky for all its apparent abundance might well have been a "dark and bloody ground." [10]

Richard Henderson and his North Carolinians, however, were not about to be turned away from their ambitions for Kentucky land, regardless of the origins or substance of Dragging Canoe's warning. Even before the Sycamore Shoals agreement, Henderson dispatched Daniel Boone and a party of woodsmen to blaze a trail to the south bank of the Kentucky River. At first, the expedition went smoothly and by late March had reached the rolling plain in the heart of present-day Madison County, close

10. Lathel Duffield and Louise M. Robbins, "A Proposal to National Science Foundation for a Research Grant in Support of 'Environmental Influences on Bone Pathology: A Study of the Fort Ancient in the Kentucky Inner Blue Grass Region,' December 1971"; and Louise M. Robbins, "The High Incidence of Bone Pathologies in Fort Ancient Peoples of Kentucky" (paper presented at the Fortieth Annual Meeting of the American Association of Physical Anthropologists, Boston, Mass., April 1971).

to their goal. Suddenly, Dragging Canoe's prophecy took on terrible meaning. Early on the morning of March 25, the sleeping company was attacked. One of the black slaves was killed in the opening volley, and some of the whites were badly wounded. Once the red men were driven off, Boone was again placed in the unhappy position of attempting to persuade his comrades to remain in dangerous country. This time he only half failed; some remained, though many chose to return to the security of the eastern settlements.

That was hardly what Richard Henderson had planned. The Cherokee Nation had abandoned its ancient legitimate claim to the region; what, then, was the problem? Simply that Boone's party had been attacked not by Cherokee, but Shawnee. These braves were unaware of the Sycamore Shoals agreement, although it would have mattered little enough to the feisty Shawnee, had they known. Their own Chief Cornstalk had supposedly signed away Shawnee hunting rights after Dunmore's War. But the Shawnee were like the hated Europeans in one respect—they were not easily persuaded to abide by paper treaties. It is certain that the Shawnee claimed hunting rights in Kentucky. It was they who had robbed and warned off Boone back in 1769; they had similarly threatened other groups of whites, and it was they who had killed Boone's son in 1773. But this time, the intrepid Boone held fast, and with a small group of comrades, hastily constructed a fort and dispatched an appeal to Henderson to hurry on with his larger party, stores, and ammunition. Daniel then tried to reach his goal, Otter's Creek, just south of the Kentucky River.

That was one of the many dark times in Kentucky pioneer history. Henderson received Boone's plaintive letter as he was reaching Cumberland Gap, and at nearly the same moment the trail ahead grew noisy with erstwhile pioneers rushing eastward. Henderson's energies were sorely tested. Almost a hundred men fled past them during these days, as they attempted to move into Kentucky. "The general panic that had seized the men we were continually meeting was contagious," Henderson vividly recalled, "it ran like wildfire; and, notwithstanding every effort against its progress, it was presently discovered in our camp; some hesitated and stole back, privately; others saw the necessity of returning to convince their friends that they were still alive, in too strong a light to be resisted.'' [11] Henderson labored mightily to quell their fears, using promises of larger grants of land to hold the loyal remnant. At length, his party of forty reached Boone's camp and by the twenty-second of April 1775, Fort Boonesborough—so named by the grateful Henderson— was under construction, and parcels of land were being laid out and distributed.

That spring and summer were the only tranquil times the Transylvania Company was to know. Immigrants continued to trickle in from the east, ground was cleared, and corn planted. By May, there were four small but sturdy settlements in central Kentucky, and a number of lesser bands of whites to the north and east, totaling, in all, about three hundred men. Seeking to firm up his claim to authority and land, Henderson organized the first political meeting of whites ever held in Kentucky. The men met under a great elm near the Boonesborough fort on May 23. Joining the Transylvania representatives were delegates chosen from the previously re-established Harrodstown and related Boiling Springs settlements, and the new community at Saint Asaph's Springs (near modern Stanford) founded by another Virginian, Benjamin Logan. The convention adopted a crude constitution providing for executive rule by the Transylvania Company Proprietors, along with a representative legislature elected annually. Nine laws were passed, concerning such essentials as courts, militia, and land distribution, as well as one protecting the fast-disappearing wild game from being recklessly hunted out before the first frost. In September, the Transylvania Proprietors meeting in North Carolina commissioned James Hogg to represent their interests at the Continental Congress, then meeting in Philadelphia. If they could get "official" congressional recognition of the company as the new western colony, their claim to land and political authority would be dramatically reinforced.

But Kentucky simply was not to be born a private proprietary colony. Despite Hogg's appeals, the Continental Congress re-

11. James Hall, *Sketches of the West*, 2 vols. (Philadelphia: Harrison Hall, 1835), 2:260–265.

fused to act in his favor. Virginia delegates, backed by their new governor Patrick Henry, were unwavering: Virginia's claim to Kentucky as its rightful western property must be upheld. Indeed, from the moment Henderson's land company was launched, back in 1774, officials of Virginia and North Carolina had been denouncing his schemes as illegal and dangerous. Legally, he erred in failing to obtain necessary permissions from crown and provincial officers to treat with the Indians and offer land for sale beyond the mountains. With the revolt against England fast approaching, Henderson hoped to get such sanction after the fact from the Continental Congress. A more important defect in the Transylvania idea, however, was that it flew in the face of Virginia's determination to possess the land called Kentucky. No private land promoter, certainly no Tar Heel Carolinian, was going to thwart those ambitions. Hogg returned home empty-handed.

Meanwhile, in Kentucky, disaffection with Transylvania rule was slowly brewing, particularly amongst the Virginia-oriented men of Harrodstown and Saint Asaph's. The cause of discord was no mere emotional attachment to the Old Dominion. The price of land would have been less, under Virginia law, than that decreed by Richard Henderson and Associates. In addition, many settlers had not only come to Kentucky for land, but for freedom from the law and organization of the settled east; they disliked Transylvania government, and they resented the diminished influence of Harrodstown and the Virginians. The catalyst for this embroglio arrived in the summer of 1775 in the person of George Rogers Clark. Clark was one of the fascinating personalities in the early history of Kentucky and the nation. To some historians he is a western patriot-hero, leader of brilliant maneuvers against Indian and white British forces in Indiana. To others, he remains an intemperate self-seeker. Certainly he was the equal of Richard Henderson in ambition. After spending the summer in central Kentucky and returning home to Virginia for the winter, Clark came back in 1776, determined to destroy the power of the Transylvania Company and gain a dominant influence for himself.

Before arriving, Clark had written to suggest that a convention be held at Harrodstown on June 6. Although he had not yet reached the settlement, the meeting was held and named Clark and a man called Gabriel Jones as delegates to Williamsburg to seek protection and incorporation by Virginia. While Clark had evidently held grander ideas about declaring Kentucky independent at once, he abided by the decision and journeyed eastward. Arriving too late to address the Virginia assembly, Clark was able to wrest from the new state council a promise of five hundred pounds of gunpowder for the Kentucky settlers—an implicit promise of the Virginians' intention to assert jurisdiction over Kentucky.

Here was one of the truly momentous events in Kentucky history, a decision that would control the area's political future and influence its social and economic patterns for a generation; yet it occurred incidentally, almost accidentally. Far bigger events were taking place, overshadowing, yet profoundly influencing the status of the little Kentucky settlement. A Declaration of Independence had been signed in Philadelphia by representatives of the newly rebellious thirteen colonies. Virginia was no longer a province, bound by English law—she was now a state, with much broader powers. If the experiment in revolution could be sustained, if British loyalism and British military power could be subdued, Virginia would appear at last to be able to exercise her will over her long-sought western territory of Kentucky. Indeed, the appetite for land and the wealth and power land could give was surely part of the motivation behind the American Revolution itself. Kentucky was at once a cause of the Revolution and its child. In October, the Virginia Assembly met at Williamsburg and heard the arguments of both Henderson and Clark. Though the Carolinian was able to stave off the verdict for awhile, the bill endorsing incorporation—guided through the House by an able young legislator named Thomas Jefferson—was finally agreed to on December 7, 1776. The County of Kentucky was officially created by Virginia, with Harrodstown as the seat of government. Kentucky and the new nation of the United States were created together and grew up together.

Richard Henderson, incidentally, never really suffered from that series of events in 1776. After two years of agitation, the Virginia Assembly granted him compensation in the form of two hundred thousand acres of land in Kentucky near the Green

River, site of the county and city of Henderson today, while
North Carolina bestowed on him an enormous parcel of land
nearly the same size, in the vicinity of modern-day Nashville.
Henderson lived to be elected a North Carolina legislator and
died wealthy and honored in the state that had denounced him.

Whether county or nation would survive the Revolutionary
War to do any growing remained to be seen. Although the British regarded the wilderness territories as of secondary military
importance, the peculiar nature of the conflict in Kentucky and
the West made for a mutual brutality largely unknown in the
seaboard states. British authorities moved rapidly to formulate
plans for a western offensive. The vast region from the Appalachians to the Mississippi River must be held for the king and
potential rebel soldiers pinned down and destroyed before they
could aid or be aided by the eastern armies. As early as the
spring of 1776, alliances were struck with the principal
northwestern tribes. In effect, the Mingos, the fierce Wyandottes, and the Shawnee were being groomed as assault forces
to attack the scattered and vulnerable white settlements in Kentucky.

The prospect of increased attacks was terrifying to the settlers, and with reason: even before the spring of 1777, sporadic
Indian raids had already largely depopulated Kentucky. Those
whites who had not fled had entered the relative security of the
more substantial forts in the Bluegrass; hardly 150 men altogether remained when the initial major invasions occurred.
Following skirmishes at Boonesborough in early March, a
Shawnee force attacked Harrod's and Logan's forts repeatedly.
During an attack on Boonesborough in April, Daniel himself
was badly hurt by a musket ball that smashed into his ankle.
The Indian forces, however, were not large, and they had no
cannon to smash the log walls of the forts, so the forts held.
Their occupants suffered throughout the summer from persistent, troublesome, and often murderous ambushes. In the fall,
the weary pioneers were reinforced by the arrival of a hundred
Virginia militiamen, soon followed by a contingent of Carolina
troops from the Yadkin Valley. Kentucky County had weath-
ered a year of war. Two elected burgesses now represented its

interests in the Virginia Assembly, and in September the first
court was convened. Perhaps the best sign of the emerging confidence of the region is reflected in the first census, taken in
Harrodstown. The figures showed that there were, among the
fort's 217 souls, 24 women—an indication of the coming stability of family life—and 19 slaves, an omen of economic stability
and future problems.

But events again assumed the false appearance of peace; and
Daniel Boone became involved in one of his most astonishing
adventures. In January 1778, thirty men marched northeast from
Fort Boonesborough to make precious salt at the Lower Blue
Licks. While the men worked, boiling down the salty spring
water, Boone hunted the woods to supply venison for the camp.
Suddenly, in early February, Shawnee warriors sprang upon
him, forced him back to the camp, and captured nearly the
whole party. Boone surely had a most remarkable relationship
with the Shawnee. Though they had been fighting one another
for nearly a decade, there had developed between Boone and the
Shawnee a mutual respect and, in a strange way, even an affection that now helped save Boone's life, the lives of his companions, and the inhabitants of the fort. Boone was able to
prevent bloodshed in the capture at the salt lick, and he de-
ceived the Shawnee into abandoning any intentions of attacking
the now virtually helpless Boonesborough. The Indians were
evidently so delighted with their famous prisoner and so eager
to ransom their captives for British goods that they returned at
once to their homes across the Ohio River at Old Chillicothe.

The impact of the capture on those back at the fort was immediate and stunning. They felt that the men were lost forever, for
the British were believed to be "hair buyers," paying Indians
for American scalps. The blow was too much. Even Daniel's
own Rebecca joined the flight back to the security of the Carolina and Virginia settlements. But none could have guessed
what actually lay in store for Boone. By the time he was
marched north to British headquarters in Detroit, he had so
ingratiated himself with the Shawnee that they refused even five
times the normal ransom and returned to the Ohio with their
prize. Soon he was being initiated into the rites of the tribe
under the affectionate eye of Chief Blackfish, who claimed him

as an adopted son. Hair plucked, skin scrubbed, decked out in finery and a new name—Big Turtle, because of his diminutive height and ample waist-line—Boone became a contented prisoner. Although the guard was relaxed, Daniel tarried on, clearly relishing the joys of this springtime interlude, hunting and living with the Shawnee. Perhaps he also nurtured the hope that, while he lived among them, no attack would be launched on the white settlements. On June 16, however, the spell was broken, for he learned that a major assault had been initiated by the British; he left the village and fled south to warn and rejoin his friends at Boonesborough.

Needless to say, his welcome was not unmixed with suspicion. Not only did he bear the physical imprint of the Shawnee, but it was subsequently charged by some that he had conspired with the British and was in fact a Trojan horse sent to betray the fort. Amid these recriminations, the settlement prepared for attack. In early September, a substantial force arrived, numbering several hundred Indians and ten experienced white French Canadian officers serving the British; they surrounded the fort and demanded its surrender. Parleys with Boone and the other leaders within revealed that the Indians expected the Kentuckians to give up without bloodshed. The red men had misjudged Boone and his fellows, who used a two-day grace period negotiated by Daniel to complete preparations for the siege, while the unsuspecting Indians strolled about the settlement. At the end of the waiting period, the occupants of the fort announced to the astonished redskins that they rejected the surrender demand. Soon thereafter fighting began in earnest, and for the next nine days the Indians sustained a furious but largely harmless attack, hurling torches and firing muskets and arrows at the fort without inflicting much damage. The cabin roofs, damp with rain, would not burn; the warriors proved to be poor marksmen; and the spirit within the fort was not to be broken. On September 20, 1778, the siege was abandoned. The survival of Boonesborough had dramatically assured the survival of Kentucky itself for the duration of the Revolutionary War.

While the bluegrass region continued to be harassed by bloody skirmishes, the next three years were a time of relative security and welcome growth. Encouraged by the news from

Boonesborough, by George Rogers Clark's successful compaigns on the northwestern frontier and his founding of Fort Nelson at the Falls of the Ohio, the trickle of pioneer settlers became a steady stream. Lulled into a false sense of security, they established many new farm communities or "stations." So vigorous was immigration that not even the dreadful scarcities of game and corn inflicted by the memorable "Hard Winter" of 1779–1780 could restrict the flow; even in early spring, with the rivers frozen and the ground still lying chill under the exceptional winter snows, hundreds of eastern families were already arriving. And that was only the curtain-raiser for 1780, which proved to be the greatest year of immigration yet seen. The rich lands of central Kentucky were rapidly being cleared, plowed, and fenced off.

Although the fact of immigration is not surprising, its timing and nature were noteworthy. The Indian menace, still very real, had been neutralized in the popular imagination. More remarkable was the fact that the Revolutionary War was being waged all this while. It was during these fateful months in the war that thousands of easterners decided to migrate beyond the mountains and—so they thought—beyond personal danger. The unprecedented immigration gave rise to a suspicion that the settlers of Kentucky were not overimbued with patriotic revolutionary fervor, that the Kentucky population was, indeed, streaked with pro-British loyalism. No doubt many of those frontiersmen and women who chose that moment to flee westward were hostile to the Patriot leaders. After all, Washington and his associates, who were to become noble Founding Fathers only much later on, were rebel leaders against the age-old authority of king and Parliament. Many who came were Virginia and North Carolina Tories deprived of their lands or otherwise mistreated by overzealous Patriots. The Indian menace also worked both ways, for there was bitterness against the new nation's failure to provide better protection; loyalty to the crown might produce an end to the Indian invasions. The fairest evaluation, however, would seem to be that most Kentuckians were preoccupied with their personal struggles and were indifferent to the greater struggle either for or against the abstract idea of national independence. Monarchy, Republicanism—few Kentuckians seemed interested in warring over these symbols; but speak of redcoats or redskins threatening the fragile security of the new settlements, and there was ardor and bravery enough.

None could have realized how quickly that spirit would be tested. In the fall of 1781, newspapers from the East brought amazing news of the surrender of Lord Cornwallis and his army at Yorktown, evidently marking the collapse of the British war effort. Instead, it was to be the signal for a last desperate assault on Kentucky. Unable to hold the East, the English appeared determined to protect Canada and the Great Lakes and to secure the western regions before the beginning of peace negotiations. Pioneers migrating to Kentucky had been feeling the sting of Indian warriors throughout these years, and the spring of 1782 brought dreadful evidence that security was still an illusion. At Little Mountain (Mount Sterling), Captain James Estill and thirty-four men engaged a smaller party of Wyandotte braves in the most sustained battle yet fought in these parts. While there were about as few Indians as whites left, by the time the hand-to-hand struggle was over, word of the disastrous encounter spread like wildfire and created a deep sense of foreboding among the forts and stations.

These apprehensions were well justified, for another large-scale Indian assault upon Kentucky was already being plotted. At Old Chillicothe, in the village where Boone had once cavorted with his admiring Shawnee captors, three hundred braves—including an especially determined core of Wyandottes—met in early August to complete plans for an invasion of the Bluegrass. The triumph of Patriot arms in the Revolution was lamented by native Americans, for an independent United States would surely make the position of red men even more perilous. Now was the time to strike. By August 15, 1782, the army led by British officers had penetrated deep into central Kentucky, and a portion of it laid siege to the fort at Bryan's Station just north of the new village of Lexington. Meanwhile, others attacked a smaller station in Madison County and, withdrawing, defeated a party of pursuers in an ambush near Upper Blue Licks on the Licking River.

The real testing time lay ahead. At Bryan's Station, the Indians and their British officers showed that they had in no way improved either their patience or their techniques for siege warfare, and within a few days they began to withdraw, having burned the surrounding cabins and fields and killed the livestock. By then, a considerable relief force was on the way, and by the evening of August 17, a war council determined on relentless pursuit of the departing Indian army. Throughout the next day, Kentucky militiamen followed them northeast toward the Licking River along a path well marked by signs of the Indians' passage. Whether these signs were evidence of haste, arrogant indifference, or deliberate lure was unclear. Early on the nineteenth, as the Kentuckians reached the banks of the Licking, a party of Indians was glimpsed slowly retreating over the hills beyond the river. Were they the last stragglers of the retreating army, or bait for an ambush? Another council hastily assembled. Daniel Boone knew the dangers of the terrain ahead and warned against precipitous movement. Scouts were dispatched across the river and returned with the good news that the way was clear; the redskins had evidently continued their withdrawal. At once the men were eager to resume the chase. Plans were made for a division into three attacking groups should the Indians be encountered, and men and horses soon splashed across the stream and began to ascend the other side of the valley.

Suddenly, from well-concealed hiding places, the waiting Indians unleashed a terrible volley. The advance group under Colonel Richard Todd was nearly annihilated at once. The Kentuckians had blundered into a superbly executed ambush. Within minutes the right flank under Stephen Trigg was turned; and on the left, Boone, nearly surrounded by howling braves, called the retreat. Tomahawks replaced muskets; the battle became a screaming, stumbling rout, and the waters of the Licking ran blood-red toward the Ohio. Fortunately, the braves were satisfied with their victory on the battlefield and did not pursue the fleeing whites. With a second and much larger force gathering under Benjamin Logan at Bryan's Station, that proved wise. Still, the field of battle was fully the Indians', and the emotional impact on Kentuckians was for a time devastating. More than a third of the original number of 182 men, including some of the brightest pioneer settlement leaders, had been killed or captured.

Ironically, that greatest triumph of red arms was fated to represent not first things, but last. The Battle of Blue Licks marked the high tide of Indian hostility in Kentucky. Though real security still lay ahead, never again would the region be visited by such a red host. Perhaps the main reason for that lay in activities taking place thousands of miles from the Kentucky frontier. Exactly one month after the disaster on the Licking River, the British formally opened peace negotiations with American commissioners waiting in Paris. The War for American Independence was over. In effect, the tragedy at Blue Licks was the last battle of the Revolution, and the peace treaty would declare to all the world that the western boundary of the new republic—and of Kentucky—was to be the Mississippi River.

So, in a sense, the carnage at Blue Licks marked a kind of dividing line between two epochs in the history of Kentucky and the new nation. As a glittering western idea and as frontier reality, Kentucky had already played an instrumental role in the larger American drama of expansion, private and official ambition, and national independence. More than just illustrating the principal themes of the American colonial and Revolutionary experience, the rich prize of Kentucky was among the principal issues involved in that experience. Now many of its own founding fathers were either dead or on the wane. New men, new issues, new modes of behavior, and the problems of a fast-maturing agricultural society were already assuming stage center.

2

Serpents in Eden

*And when arrived at this Heaven in Idea, what do they
find? A goodly land I will allow but to them forbiden Land.
exhausted and worn down with distress and
disappointment they are at last obliged to become hewers
of wood and Drawers of water.*
    Moses Austin, "A Memorandum . . . 1796–1797"

$\mathcal{T}$HE realities of life for the first generations of Kentuckians
continue to be obscured by myths and rose-colored recollections, images that proved impervious to time and the rigors of
frontier life. Such tales were so pervasive in the Revolutionary
era that they even took the form of ironic misconceptions about
the place. There was that Pennsylvania German, for example,
who refused to migrate to Kentucky because he understood its
climate was a perpetual summer. In such an Eden, farmers must
labor all year long, he reasoned, "and that was not his fancy;
winter, with a warm stove and sluggish days, being indispensable to his happiness." [1] Later, the memories of older settlers
would scour smooth their remembrances of times past, and the
myth of Kentucky as a western democratic paradise fast became
part of the gospel of American nationalism. It is difficult to go

---

1. *Travels in the Confederation from the German of Johann David Shoepf,* translated
and edited by Alfred J. Morrison, 2 vols. (Philadelphia: W. J. Campbell, 1911), 2:5.

beyond these Arcadian images and see the evolving patterns of life in all their variety and vitality. Yet it is valuable, for the past has always been prologue in conservative Kentucky. Peering closely at those folkways, we find not strangers, but shadows of ourselves.

The pluck of those immigrants who made the fearful Atlantic crossing by the tens of thousands is indeed impressive. Forsaking friends, families, and familiar surroundings, drawn by hopes for a more bountiful and spiritual life, they cast themselves on the seas for a harrowing voyage and an uncertain fate in a new world. On a smaller scale, Kentucky's settlers re-enacted that adventure, for to cross the mountain plateau implied an isolation, a cutting off reminiscent of the Atlantic experience. Across ocean or mountains, the move called for nerve and motivation. Like early America itself, the new world of Kentucky threatened more than isolation. It meant exposure, physical, social, and psychological. Exposure to hostile Indians, exposure to a new agricultural environment and economic liabilities, exposure to loneliness and the corrosive effects of the frontier upon community life.[2]

Why would so many engage in an uprooting and immigration so troublesome? A few, of course, were Christian true believers, millennialists, such as the Shakers or the main-stream Protestant evangelicals who craved remoteness to work out their private dreams of salvation. And later, in the wake of the general settlement, there would inevitably arrive the perpetually rootless, the thieves and speculators, drummers and day laborers, along with an eager retinue of lawyers and politicians. But the great mass of people who gave life to Kentucky—who were they, and why had they come? Economics, broadly construed?—to be sure. Above all, for land, better and cheaper than what one could hope for in the eastern states. The leading edge of hunters and trappers was already moving on, as the wildlife retreated or dwindled. But the land remained: for the Revolutionary War soldiers who had been promised homesteads, for

2. Otis K. Rice, *The Allegheny Frontier: West Virginia Beginnings, 1730–1830* (Lexington: University Press of Kentucky, 1970), p. 19.

the younger sons of Old Dominion planters, for those who believed Virginia soil fertility was diminishing, and for all the rest
lured on by the illusion of a garden paradise. Possession of land
meant a great deal more to those eighteenth- and nineteenth-
century folk than mere acreage. Of course, there was truth to the
old saw that the typical American farmer did not want an unreasonable amount of land—only all that adjoined his own farm.
More important, land was the principal source of wealth, indicator of social status, and guarantor of personal and family security to a degree difficult to imagine in our urban, bureaucratic
age. That had been true in the Old Country, and, in the seemingly boundless terrain of the New World, land hunger was insatiable.

The desire for personal advancement, however, gives us only
a part of the answer. Virginia and Carolina Tories certainly had
different incentives for moving on; so did many others. Fascination about the unexplored West was undeniable. There was a
restlessness in the country, a persistent urge to cross the next
mountain, inspired partly by the materialist dream that the valley on the other side would at last prove to be the land of ease
and plenty. Yet that mobility sprang from more than romantic
optimism. In a sense, the Kentucky frontier also marked the advance edge of western European civilization. Though still
largely agrarian, the European immigrants and their American
offspring had long since begun to embrace more progressive or
capitalistic economic and cultural values. British America itself
existed because of individual and national restlessness, probing
secularism, avarice, impatience with traditional forms of authority that marked the emerging "modern" personality. The men
and women of the Kentucky pioneer family may have believed
that all they wanted was a stable farm community; but in their
eagerness to uproot themselves and seek a new destiny in the
western woods, they became new actors in a centuries-old
drama of social change.

Finally, it would be foolish to underestimate the influence on
Kentucky immigration of rising American national self-
consciousness and confidence. The splendid Mississippi Valley
now lay open. Americans were beginning to perceive theirs as a
western, perhaps even a continental destiny. The rapid settle-

ment of Kentucky, Tennessee, and the North and Southwest territories just after the Revolution was a testament to the American desire for national expansion.

America as a narrow band of settlements tightly hugging the coastal plain was at an end. A new America was arising, and Kentucky played a significant role in that epochal movement of people. Geography gave Kentucky County a fateful position. The rivers of the eastern states flowed to the Atlantic; Kentucky's pointed westward, toward the interior, toward the Mississippi. The region was also centrally located, jutting into the west like some great arrow. Over the coming decades, the commonwealth became a major conduit for thousands who would eventually move on, they or their children, into the northwest and southwestern states. Kentucky was also a melting pot for eastern folk. By the 1780s, most immigrants were no longer Virginians, but men and women from the middle Atlantic states—Pennsylvania, New Jersey, Maryland—moving down the Ohio River, along with a continuing train of North Carolinians retracing the steps of the Boones through the Cumberland Gap.

They all followed well-worn roads to the Bluegrass. Buffalo traces and Indian trails, such as the Warrior's Path, were the basis for those early roads, with Lexington, an ancient crossing-ground for bison, already the principal hub by 1790. The settlement of Kentucky seeped outward slowly, embracing the fertile central bluegrass region before moving toward the southern and western areas of the state. The total population, which had numbered in the mere hundreds in 1780 and had leapt to twelve thousand three years later, was to reach a hundred thousand by the early 1790s, and continued climbing rapidly.

Despite the appearance of tranquillity that dominates the general image of early Kentucky, the place was in fact one of the classic arenas of aggressive settlement—a future-oriented society, characterized by anticipation, mobility, speculation. In that, it was typical of America. Unfortunately, special circumstances arose in this part of Eden that began to channel its legal, social, and economic life in deplorable directions. Fiercely acquisitive agrarian capitalism was by no means the private preserve of the bright-eyed pioneer family. It was shared and realized more fully by those who already possessed some wealth, knowledge, and power. The ideal of egalitarianism, of abundance, of secure, sturdy, prosperous homesteads—the ideal, in short, of yeoman democracy—was severely undermined in Kentucky from its earliest days.

The root of the problem was land. In other transmontane territories and states, particularly to the north and west, the land was to undergo systematic public surveys before being distributed under various orderly disbursement schemes. Unfortunately, that was not true in Kentucky. The haphazard, madly disorganized fashion in which land was acquired here was fraught with unanticipated evils. The inequitable "system" that arose may have resulted in part from that prolonged period of uncertainty about who ruled the region—Indians, the French, private land companies, the British, or the Virginians. Certainly the Virginia tradition of land to the powerful was deeply influential. The system was also perhaps the unavoidable fruit of Kentucky's being the first region settled beyond the mountains. While there were few precedents, however, there was no lack of men hungry for a stake in paradise.

By the eve of the Revolution, when Virginia asserted her ancient land claim by annihilating the Transylvania Company and establishing Kentucky County in 1776, some equitable and systematic arrangement should have been made for the survey and sale of the western lands. Such an orderly legal instrument might have worked against the ambitions of avaricious planters, speculators, and public officials. But there was available no experience, no familiarity with such a radical notion as democratic land distribution. Land—the life blood of wealth, status, and power—was there to be seized with both hands, and devil take the hindmost. The lessons of the preceding two centuries of plotting, warring, speculating, and despoiling all spoke to that point.

The land problem went far beyond errors of omission. Legislation adopted by the new Virginia state government too often added to the growing confusion. In 1777 the Virginia Assembly adopted an act that had the ring of fairness. By that so-called "ancient cultivation law," individual settlers had their land claims assured on the basis of prior occupation. But since the vast wilderness territory had never been officially surveyed and divided off, a great question mark hung over the boundaries of older claims. In addition, the potential for fraud was considerable; many speculators came west merely to construct hasty cabins, record a claim, and depart. That was only the beginning. The next two years were momentous ones in the East. The war against Britain had created desperate financial circumstances, for both Virginia and the Continental Congress. Where was the money to come from to finance the war, to pay for supplies and compensate the soldiers? The fate of the Revolution itself seemed to hang on that issue. Paper money had been printed by the barrel and was depreciating as fast as the presses churned out the bills. The public was hostile to taxation, and public officials were eager to avoid testing their uncertain patriotism that way. Virginia was critical to the outcome of the Revolution, and she fortunately had an attractive alternative enjoyed by no other state: the rich lands of Kentucky. Aside from all the other benefits expected to flow eastward from the Kentucky cornucopia, it was now hoped that Kentucky would help save Virginia for the Revolution.

By Act of 1779, the Assembly sought to correct some of the abuses of the "ancient cultivation" law of 1777, and, more important, sought to make Kentucky land pay a part of the costs of war. Under the new law, only those actually living in Kentucky County could have their "ancient" claims assured. And two new devices were added to establish claims—soldier bounties and direct purchase. The bounties were aimed at encouraging and rewarding military enlistment and service, and they came in the form of warrants guaranteeing from fifty to five thousand acres of Kentucky land, depending upon rank and length of service. Direct purchase promised a source of revenue for the embattled Virginia state government and its militia. Finally, a system was set up—needlessly and dishearteningly complex—to establish *bona fide* claims to specific parcels of land.

The Kentucky land question, which had teetered on the edge of chaos for a generation, now tumbled headlong into pandemonium. Inspired by desperation, acquisitive cunning, lack of foresight, and incompetence, the Law of 1779 opened the gates to a wild flurry of speculation and abuse. Soldier warrants issued by the thousands quickly came to be valued, exchanged, and sold virtually as pieces of currency.

Kentucky immigration had increased dramatically during the war. Many were drawn west by newly acquired land warrants; others hoped to capture their piece of paradise under the "ancient cultivation" idea as squatters, often encouraged to move west by legitimate landowners eager to have neighbors for protection and fellowship. With the close of the Revolution, immigration accelerated, fueled by peace and by the expectations of former soldiers with precious land warrants. And all of that before any detailed public survey had been made.

The result was total disorganization in the pattern of land claims and a demoralizing defeat for countless thousands of lesser folk who had believed that they possessed a secure home in the promised land. The pattern of Kentucky land claims became a crazy-quilt design of varying sizes and shapes, more often than not overlapping with other equally untidy tracts. As land regulations came and went, newcomers arrived, often speculators or "locators" paid by wealthier residents or easterners to establish still more recent claims that might hold up in subsequent litigation. And lawsuits there were, hundreds upon thousands of cases involving an army of claimants, counterclaimants, and a retinue of ravenous lawyers. Kentucky became a hothouse of litigation, aswarm with contests for possession of the best lands.

What had gone wrong? The reasons did not altogether involve fraud, greed, and power. In the early decades, the business of locating and recording claims often fell to men as honest and ambitious as they were illiterate and ignorant of the law. Being early residents, hunters and farmers, they seemed logical choices as surveyors; they were eager for the work, since they took a substantial portion of the land warrant as payment for their services. Thus did Daniel Boone and others acquire vast tracts for themselves. The results for Boone and many others were frequently disastrous. "They strewed the locations over the face of the country as autumn distributes its falling leaves, heedless of those which had previously fallen . . . destitute of design . . . regardless of consequences." Humphrey Marshall, a contemporary lawyer, politician, and chronicler of those times gives us a choice example of the problem: "George Smith enters 500 acres of land on a treasury warrant, lying on the north side of Kentucky [River], a mile below a creek, beginning about twenty poles below a lick, running down the river, westerly, and northwesterly, for quantity." That looks well enough, until we recall that the north side of the river was all of Fayette County, then more than a third of the entire region of Kentucky. And which of the five hundred northside creeks flowing into the river is intended? The bounteous potential for honest error and subsequent fraud delighted the eye of every speculator and lawyer.[3]

The resulting plague of litigation was mortifying for thousands victimized by misappropriation, forced to vacate, or reduced to much smaller claims or outright tenantry. Among them were the many families of squatters who had hoped to establish claims under the earlier "ancient cultivation law," as well as those who were unable to sustain concrete claims because of procedural and financial obstacles. Men of wealth, gentry speculators, sons of planters and the like possessed the tools to manipulate the legal tangle to their advantage. The best lands fell into their hands and the hands of absentee owners. Many true pioneers ultimately lost their estates to speculators and the wealthier landowners because they "had neither the craft nor the foresight necessary for eluding the legal net woven by the avaricious or unskilful legislators, cunning lawyers, and metaphysical courts." [4] Many smaller farmers soon migrated to regions of more secure ownership out of the state; many others were reduced to the status of landless renters. Thus the serpent in Eden. At an incredibly early stage in its development, Kentucky became a place of landlords and tenants, of rich estates for the few and second- or third-rate smaller farms for the many. Humphrey Marshall lamented in 1808 that the abuse of land titles "more than Indian wars, or any thing else, has re-

3. Humphrey Marshall, *The History of Kentucky* . . . 2 vols. (Frankfort: Henry Gore, 1812), 1:173–174.
4. George Robertson, *Scrap Book on Law and Politics, Men and Times* (Lexington: A. W. Elder, 1855), p. 273.

tarded the population; obstructed the improvement; distracted
the people; and depreciated the value of the soil, in the country.'' [5]

Agricultural and social patterns in the first generations of
Kentucky life reflect these realities. The place that had been the
most vivid symbol of frontier paradise, opportunity, and a level-
ing of social distinctions proved a fickle friend to many farmers
of ordinary means. In one sense, that was perhaps inevitable.
The personal qualities that enabled such figures as Boone,
Simon Kenton, Benjamin Logan, and other pioneer leaders to
enter the true wilderness and endure privation and Indian troubles often made them incapable of remaining as prominent personalities in a maturing society. Not all these men died in
Boone's unhappy circumstances, without a parcel of the land he
had fought for; some, like James Harrod and Logan himself,
were clever and careful enough to preserve their estates. But
more broadly speaking, an almost generational type of change
seemed to occur within the first twenty years of Kentucky settlement. Those who had led frontier migration seemed suddenly
aged and spent. By the mid-1780s, the country appeared suf-
ficiently subdued to invite a vigorous occupation by the genteel
classes and their black bondsmen. New men were rapidly arriving to fill the social and political vacuum.
    The familiar names of many of those families suggests certain
critical facts. They were principally Virginians, these Breckinridges, Todds, Bullitts, McDowells, and the rest. Kentucky
society and politics soon came to feel the stamp of such dominant families. Studiously intermarrying, interweaving fortunes
and influence, these family lines and clusters extended during
the next century to shape the character and direction of life in
the commonwealth profoundly. Their founding patriarchs were,
often as not, young men of some wealth and social pretension,
tobacco and grain planters or sons of middle- and upper-class
farmers of tidewater or piedmont Virginia. They came because
of the traditional attachment to the idea of primogeniture, which
encouraged the male progeny of Old Dominion families to move

5. Marshall, *History of Kentucky,* 1:178.

on. They came because of the depressed state of the eastern tobacco market. They came for the land, and, by legal means and otherwise, they soon engrossed much of the best acreage in the Bluegrass.

While incoming yeoman immigrants had the numbers, then, the gentry possessed skills and advantages that gave them at least a higher plateau from which to launch their race for wealth, status, and power. Oratory, book-learning, the Virginia tradition of government by gentlemen—these proved valuable weapons against the egalitarian atmosphere of the frontier. Just as important, however, was the fact that most new Kentuckians did not reject a stratified society; rather, they craved a higher rung on its ladder and a chance to make the climb. Few would reach the top, but nearly all seemed to accept the need for a top, bottom, and places between.

There the appeal of the eastern Virginia life-style became crucial. The tidewater model of society was itself an impression of English gentle-country society, as seen through an American glass: not toiling peasants, but African slaves; not immense rural homes and estates, but usually cruder plantations; not blooded aristocracy, but First Families and more openness. That was a prestigious example of the way a society could organize itself and distribute its material prizes and badges of status. Ironically, most of the Virginia emigrés were not even natives of the eastern lowland counties, but rather came from the Piedmont and the Valley. Perhaps that made them only the more eager to recreate their second-hand image in Kentucky. The reproduction could never be perfect and had to bend to the new circumstances of a rougher, more expansive western country; but the tidewater model presented itself to Kentucky when its own relationships were especially plastic and so proved very influential.

The story of an emergent Kentucky elite is all the more fascinating because it anticipated by as many as two generations some of the same adjustments that were to occur in much of the nineteenth-century South. Slaveholding, large, landed estates, the cultural and political values of the aristocratic tidewater were all inherently hostile to democracy. In order for slave-owners, especially the larger planters, to retain security for their property and position, a disproportionate influence in their states was essential. That had not been difficult in the tight little world of colonial Virginia. The real challenge came when those values and social arrangements were subjected to the strain of westward expansion and a rising adulation for democratic reform. As the first western slave state, Kentucky experienced the tug between free labor and slave, between popular and plutocratic rule long before those stresses preoccupied statesmen to the south. And except for the occasional protests of a few critics, wealth easily triumphed in Kentucky, as everywhere else. Land disputes created a buzz, but engrossment of the best soils proved irresistible. And why worry? There always seemed so much more available.

The slavery question was likewise resolved in favor of the gentry minority. Of course, Kentucky was never a land truly dominated by plantation slavery. But neither was it the promised haven for poor men. Slaves had accompanied whites from the beginning of the settlement, and the black population had grown very rapidly after the Revolution. From bearing supplies and leading wagons, hundreds and then thousands of Negro bondsmen had graduated to clearing fields, planting and harvesting, and helping to construct homes for their masters and themselves. As early as the first federal census in 1790, there were 12,430 Kentucky slaves. Within ten years, that number had increased 230 percent, representing a fifth of the total population. The number of blacks in the state continued to grow, chiefly by importation, at a greater rate than the whites until the 1830s, making up nearly a quarter of the total population throughout most of the period prior to the Civil War. Moreover, black people tended to be concentrated in the distinctive regions of more fertile soil, most noticeably in the Bluegrass. In 1833, however, a law was enacted forbidding further importations, and that, combined with various economic factors, initiated a slowing of the slave population growth rate.

In the early years, there was virtually no resistance to the idea that the richest soils of the promised land would be watered with the sweat of black slave labor. The Virginians in particular were coming in, and it seemed unexceptional that they were bringing their Negro people with them. Some vigorous objections would be raised about the whole business from time to time, but as far as most settlers were concerned, it can best be described as an unthinking decision. Slavery in Kentucky has, in addition, traditionally been glossed over with a gauzy romanticism of the "happy darkies" and "kindly massa" school. From the outset, it was fashionable to argue that bondage rested lightly upon the shoulders of Kentucky Negroes. It followed that the masters were more refined and paternalistic than even those of Virginia itself. That mystique served to protect the institution against its critics in both the pioneer and antebellum periods. In fact, while the physical burdens of slavery were less harsh on the smaller plantations and farms here than was true in the Lower South ("down the River"), the notion of Kentucky as a sort of playground for slaves had always been oversold. That was especially true during the first decades of settlement, when frontier realities and the keen ambition of rising young squires often made conditions of life and work and the severity of punishment very hard. In any event, whether harsh or not, slavery was undeniably a crucial ingredient in the process of economic, geographic, and social-class sorting out that occurred in these years. As it provided economic advantage to the few, it offered white supremacy and race control to the masses.

With much land and enough slaves, the foundation existed for a new form of deferential democracy. Like their future cousins in the cotton and sugar regions of the South, the rising Kentucky gentry sought less to lord it over the less fortunate than to expropriate the richest soils and preserve the right of slaveholding. Outright domination was undesirable and, indeed, impossible in the coming age of Jeffersonian and Jacksonian democracy, but local and state politics could still be manipulated, in the Virginia manner. Meanwhile, the whole would soon come to be coated with a bright cultural garment that made it all seem natural and inevitable. In a remarkably brief time, rude log cabins were replaced by more impressive brick homes. The lovely Jessamine Creek mansion Chaumiere du Prairie, built by David Meade in 1796, was an imposing signpost on the road to benevolent plutocracy. Outside the slaveholding region, there was insufficient wealth to support a "broadcloth and crinoline aristocracy devoted to philosophy and the arts, horseracing, and

fox hunting.'' [6] Within the charmed circle, the emerging
squirearchy aped English-cum-Virginia manners, pursued neo-
classical studies and culture, and perfected the oratorical, military, and political skills appropriate to their rank. Beyond the
island of wealth and higher culture, the yeomanry on hillier terrain watched, for the most part complacently and admiringly.

   Not all families that attained high social and economic positions had their origins in the gentility, nor was the making of
wealth and status wholly confined to land and slaves. Opportunity was not boundless, but it was there. Among noteworthy examples is Green Clay, a poor Virginian who, despite his unlikely name, rose rapidly to become one of his adopted state's
foremost citizens. Characteristically, this future Kentucky squire
was a native of Powhatan County, which lies west of Richmond
in the rolling piedmont. After bearing arms for a time in the
Revolution, he followed the lead of many ambitious fellows and
journeyed into Kentucky. Arriving in 1780, at the age of
twenty-three, Clay soon parleyed his developing knowledge of
surveying into an extensive landed estate. A scant eight years
later, he had returned to Richmond as a prosperous gentleman,
representing his constituents at the convention held to ratify the
federal constitution.
   Perhaps Clay felt driven by his humble background to prove
himself, for his energy was remarkable. By the turn of the century, he possessed tens of thousands of acres of fine bluegrass
land and many slaves. While his consuming passion remained
business, he did not fail to acquire the other political, military,
and social virtues associated with ''making it'' in early Kentucky society. He was a leader in the Kentucky Constitutional
Convention of 1799 and, altogether, served for two decades as a
state legislator from Madison County. The sometime-patriot soldier also emerged in the War of 1812 as General Clay, when he
ably commanded the state militia sent northwest to reinforce
William Henry Harrison. Earlier, he had married a young lady
of more gentle upbringing and eventually built a fine home that

   6. Arthur K. Moore, *The Frontier Mind: A Cultural Analysis of the Kentucky Frontiersman* (Lexington: University of Kentucky Press, 1957), p. 152.

he named White Hall, in Madison County. Though Green Clay may chiefly be remembered today as the father of Kentucky's fiery emancipationist Cassius Marcellus Clay, he was himself an important figure in the early development of the state.

The diversity of Clay's business activities is also typical and instructive. His ambitions, like those of many rising Kentuckians, went beyond land and slaves. While those holdings were often considered the prerequisites for social acceptability, the opportunities for economic advancement were far broader during that period of the state's history than they would be in the future cotton states of the lower South. Indeed, Kentuckians demonstrated considerable interest in economic diversification in those formative years, perhaps more than they ever would again until the twentieth century. In part, that reflected the illusion that dependency on the East could be broken and that Kentucky verged on becoming the economic keystone for the rising western empire. Those hopes affected regional politics and were also manifested in such propaganda schemes as the Kentucky Society for the Encouragement of Manufactures, founded in 1789 to promote commercial and manufacturing investments. Doubtless it was this kind of invigorating spirit that helped shape the philosophy of one particular new arrival from Virginia. Young Henry Clay, who came to Lexington in 1797, would later have his name and policies intimately associated with the idea of economic diversification.

The important fact was that Kentucky witnessed a remarkable flowering of economic activities in the generation after the Revolution. Green Clay himself invested in toll roads, ferries, and distilleries, and even built a small resort, which became a local favorite, at Estill Springs. Most of the new small factories that sprang up involved the processing of raw materials produced in the region—hemp, tobacco, grain, paper, and powder mills. In the same manner, the development of merchandising in such bustling young towns as Lexington and Danville and, later, in the River City, Louisville, was even more obviously tied in with the agricultural base. Such businesses acted principally as conduits for northern and European goods and credit flowing back into the interior farming communities. Nevertheless, in these early decades, Kentucky did offer a great variety of opportu-

nities to its immigrants. Certainly, the state seemed on the verge
of a critically important breakthrough toward diversity, prosperity, and abundance.

Although nineteenth-century Kentuckians were not destined
fully to realize that economic promise, it was clear from the
start that they would avoid the curse of a one-crop economy.
The early decades saw the birth of those enterprises that were to
have an enduring effect upon the life and popular image of the
state. Long before Henry Clay crossed the mountains, Kentuckians had taken the first steps toward the production of
hemp, whiskey, and tobacco and had begun breeding fine horses
and other livestock. It is perhaps ironic that the only one of
those products that has disappeared from the modern scene—
hemp—was also the only one not deliberately produced by Kentucky farmers to meet human frailty or vice. Widely known
today as the source of marijuana, hemp then was grown for entirely utilitarian purposes. The hemp plant was brought to the
American colonies by the British. Its rough fiber was useful
around farm homesteads, and it became a valuable trade commodity when it was made into sturdy cordage and rough cloth.
Since strong rope and material for sails could be made of
hempen fibers, it had considerable potential during the era of
sailing ships. Kentucky hemp was first grown on a patch near
Danville in 1775, and its cultivation spread rapidly because the
fibers and seed were a valued medium of exchange for cash-
poor farmers.

American hempen products never matched the strength and
durability of European goods, but hemp was destined to become
a key element in the Kentucky economy because of the cotton
boom. Kentuckians were to gain an unfortunate and exaggerated
reputation as breeders and sellers of slaves to work the plantations of the lower South. A more important economic link to
slavery and the South was the hemp connection. For most of the
antebellum period, Kentuckians were the chief suppliers of the
hempen rope and coarse bagging used to pack huge bales of raw
cotton for the domestic and European market. In addition, slavery probably would not have developed as fully in Kentucky if
hemp had not been grown and manufactured, for those processes proved to be the largest and most reliable employers of

black labor. Low commodity prices would not support substantial use of slave labor on tobacco farms, so Bluegrass hemp production was largely responsible for preserving Negro bondage in Kentucky. In time, slaves constituted a large proportion of the population in such major fiber-producing counties as Fayette, Woodford, Bourbon, Franklin, and Jefferson, though individual hemp farms usually only approximated the size in land and slaves of the true plantations of cotton, sugar, and rice. Despite strong competition from Missouri, Kentucky remained a chief producer of hemp until the post-Civil War years marked the beginnings of a long and steady decline in demand for the fiber.

All that was quite unanticipated by the early settlers, most of whom probably assumed that Kentucky's agricultural future lay in the growing of tobacco. In the early years, however, sale of the "nasty weed" was hampered by severe transportation problems. It was difficult to move heavy hogsheads of cured leaf down rutted paths and snag-strewn rivers. The key was New Orleans, gateway to the western waters. Following the opening of the port of New Orleans in 1789, Kentucky tobacco began to find its way to eastern and European markets in increasing quantities. Cigars, pipe and chewing tobacco, and snuff began to be manufactured in small Louisville factories as early as the 1790s. Improved river transportation played an instrumental role in these developments, and for awhile, Kentuckians enjoyed a colorful, if mixed, reputation for their native hardwood flatboats and keelboats, and their "half-horse, half-alligator" riverboat men. However, fluctuating world prices and the European wars severely weakened the tobacco trade after 1800. For the next thirty years, Kentucky flour, pork, salt, whiskey, and even gunpowder greatly outstripped tobacco exports down the Mississippi. But tobacco, to borrow a recent cigarette commercial, would rather fight than switch. The leaf began a long comeback, thanks in part to the introduction of the spectacular new river steamboats and the completion of the first canal around the Falls of the Ohio at Louisville in 1829, both of which greatly reduced shipping costs. The production of improved strains of coveted burley tobacco surged, particularly in the northern counties along the Ohio River and in the newer western counties, which were conveniently crossed by the Tennessee, Green, and Cumberland rivers. By the end of the Civil War, the increasing world appetite for "smokes and chews" had pushed Kentucky into the forefront among tobacco-growing states, with most of the crop produced in the forty-two far-western counties. Tobacco represented half the state's agricultural cash income by 1860, and it grew in significance as a manufactured product. Until surpassed in 1929 by North Carolina, Kentucky remained the premier tobacco-growing state in the Union. Despite many disruptions and changes over the next century, including the advent of blended cigarettes, the expansion of Bluegrass and eastern-county production and the like, burley tobacco remains the central and characteristic Kentucky crop.

Quite as well received as Kentucky burley was the sea of alcohol produced by Kentucky distilleries. It was some time before that uniquely mellowed and delicious corn liquor called bourbon was created, and even then it was probably accidental. There never was any doubt, however, that powerful concoctions would be brewed from local grains and fruits. The pioneers brought along an impressive thirst, and almost as soon as the first crops were in, they were producing immense and various quantities of intoxicating beverages. Legend has it that Kentuckians turned to distilling their grains because the product was easier and less costly to transport in liquid form. The story also notes the influence of Pennsylvania whiskey-tax rebels migrating southwestward into these parts, along with Scotch-Irishmen with a fondness for corn brew. While there is some truth in these notions, the overriding fact was that Americans had a prodigious and unquenchable yen for all forms of hard drink, and Kentuckians were quick to cater to the local and national appetite. Average per capita consumption in those days might make our modern plague of alcoholism appear trivial. By the 1780s, Kentucky farmer-distillers were producing—and doing their best to help consume—large quantities of cider and peach brandy from their new orchards, as well as grain distillates.

Corn enjoyed advantages from the start. It was the ideal first crop on new lands; it provided food for man and beast; and the surplus, as mash, yielded excellent quantities of distilled spirits. Still, it is undeniable that modern bourbon was only approximated in the first half-century of Kentucky life. Rye was a very popular base and was widely grown, distilled, and relished, either by itself or mixed with corn in varying proportions. Federal law today decrees no less than 51 percent corn content in a true bourbon mash, with the spirits aged at least twenty-four months in new white oak barrels with charred interiors. The charred-oak barrels are crucial in creating the distinctive amber-red color of modern bourbon. There is no reliable evidence to indicate that anything like those standards were reached until the years just before the Civil War, if then, nor were the key elements of charred barrels and systematic aging adhered to during those early decades. Many a clear tumbler of "bourbon" was raised to toast whatever was convenient for toasting.

There are other unanswerable questions about this world-renowned American liquor. We know the word derives from the name of the French royal family of Revolutionary times and became associated with the Kentucky potion after Bourbon County (originally all of the northeastern part of Kentucky) was created in 1786. We cannot tell with certainty the name and location of the first distiller, as hundreds of farmers came west bearing both knowledge of the art and crude distilling equipment. Kentucky's first governor, Isaac Shelby, was such a distiller, as were Green Clay, Elijah Craig (often mistakenly identified without reservation as the state's first distiller), and many others. What we can say is that, thanks to the matchless limestone spring water and the improving skills of many small-scale distillers, Kentucky slowly gained a reputation throughout the nation for its distinctive brew. By the early nineteenth century, the country's favorite hard drink was being exported from Louisville in vast quantities. The age of the farmer-distiller had yielded to larger enterprises, which were producing a finer, more consistent beverage. Though under stiff competition in recent decades from "softer" intoxicants such as vodka, bourbon remains an integral part of Kentucky's economy. More than two-thirds of all American whiskey is manufactured in Kentucky, and bourbon has been recognized by the United States Congress as one of our distinctive national products.

The addition of horses to tobacco and bourbon completes Kentucky's economic and cultural trinity. And like the others, the beginnings of the livestock and sport-breeding industry stretch back across the nineteenth century into the pioneer phase. The lush grasses and limestone water of the bluegrass region were soon recognized for their potential as grazing land. Few migrants would have come without the essential family cow; and in the 1780s, Virginia cattle-breeder Matthew Patton and his sons moved their famous herd of purebred cattle to Nicholasville, just below Lexington, to give a significant start to that industry in the region. By the next decade, cattle were to be joined by increasing herds of sheep and hogs, foraging all across the verdant central-Kentucky meadows; such livestock proved the ideal accompaniment to Bluegrass hemp-farming. Superior English strains of sheep and cattle were being imported after the turn of the century, and, as roads improved, herdsmen inaugurated a profitable traffic each fall to eastern slaughter-houses. In 1812, for example, five hundred thousand hogs alone were driven to Pittsburgh and seaboard markets, many through fabled Cumberland Gap, styled by drovers the "Kaintuck Hog Road." Meanwhile, dozens of Louisville and Cincinnati firms were gearing up to do a flourishing antebellum business packing salted pork and beef for more distant sale. By the 1830s and 1840s, the livestock industry had expanded to the southern and eastern counties of the state, involving many persons of Scotch-Irish ancestry as herdsmen, an occupation traditionally connected with their historical experience. While the industry declined substantially after the dislocations of the Civil War and a major shift of the hog and cattle population to the trans-Mississippi West, Kentucky livestock has remained a valuable supplement to the farmer's income.

It was, however, the noble horse—and the less-than-noble mule—that really captured the hearts of Kentucky farmers and gave to this place its foremost symbol. Pioneer settlers brought thousands of these hardy beasts with them. They were no beauties, but tough, hardworking allies of farm hands, white and black. For much of the pre-Civil War era, Kentucky's reputation was associated with these very distant cousins of Man O' War and Secretariat, for Kentucky became the great supplier of work animals, particularly to the lower South. As surely as they loved their whiskey, Kentucky farmers were also fond of

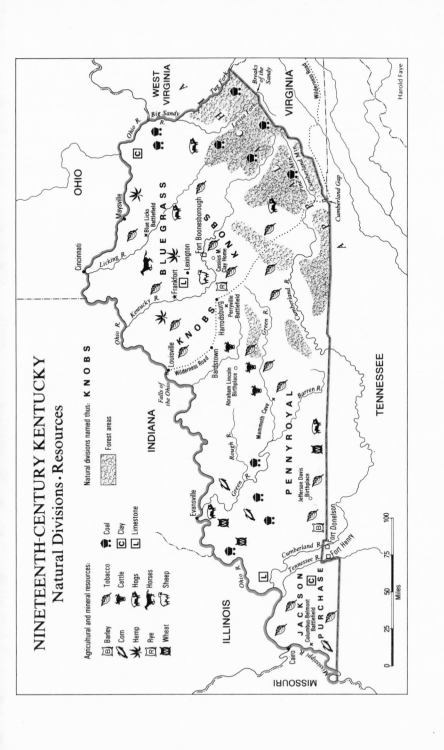

NINETEENTH-CENTURY KENTUCKY
Natural Divisions · Resources

Natural divisions named thus: **KNOBS**

Forest areas

Agricultural and mineral resources:

- Barley (B)
- Corn
- Hemp
- Rye (R)
- Wheat (W)
- Tobacco
- Cattle
- Hogs
- Horses
- Sheep
- Coal
- Clay (C)
- Limestone (L)

Harold Faye

Miles
0   25   50   75   100

MISSOURI
ILLINOIS
INDIANA
OHIO
WEST VIRGINIA
VIRGINIA
TENNESSEE

Cairo
Cincinnati
Maysville
Evansville
Louisville
Frankfort
Lexington
Harrodsburg
Bardstown
Fort Henry
Fort Donelson

Ohio R.
Licking R.
Kentucky R.
Green R.
Rough R.
Barren R.
Cumberland R.
Tennessee R.
Mississippi R.
Big Sandy
Tug Fork
Levisa Fork

BLUEGRASS
KNOBS
PENNYROYAL
JACKSON PURCHASE

Falls of the Ohio
Blue Licks Battlefield
Fort Boonesborough
Cassius M. Clay Home
Perryville Battlefield
Abraham Lincoln Birthplace
Mammoth Cave
Jefferson Davis Birthplace
Columbus-Belmont Battlefield
Wilderness Road
Cumberland Gap
Pine Mtn.
Breaks of the Sandy
Cumberland Mtn.

racing their swiftest horses, for the love of competition and wagering and the diversion of a race seemed an almost biological instinct to pioneers everywhere. The favorite places for these periodic tests were the most convenient straightaways—the town streets—which also offered taverns to celebrate the victory and drown the defeat. Things got so bad that the state legislature finally banned impromptu racing, after which race courses were rapidly established.

The breeding and racing of fine stallions had long been among the most attractive features of life in English and Virginia country society, so it was not long before the ambitious Kentucky squirearchy took up the same activities. By 1800, talk of bloodlines and newly arriving English stud horses were characteristic topics of Bluegrass conversation. Planters such as Henry Clay and wily merchants like John Wesley Hunt were among the many importers and syndicators of these handsome animals; Clay's beautiful estate, Ashland, just outside Lexington, gained wide fame as a breeding place for superior thoroughbred and trotting horses. In time, many central Bluegrass counties assumed a parklike quality as dozens of splendid farms arose, including the legendary Fayette plantation of Dr. Elisha Warfield—Meadows—and neighboring Woodford County's magnificent Woodburn, the estate of the famed horse-breeding family sired by Scotsman Robert Alexander. Following the wartime devastation of the 1860s, the industry began a long recovery, fueled by the investments of northern nouveaux riches capitalists eager to buy the same matchless equine symbolism that had inspired Kentucky's own newly rich earlier in the century.

Clearly, the important economic and social patterns that developed in these early decades proved to be remarkably persistent. The life-styles and attitudes laid down in those colorful, formative years strongly influenced the behavior of Kentuckians, not only throughout the nineteenth century, but well into the twentieth. What was true for social and economic ways was also true for the political life of the new country, particularly the issues of autonomy and statehood and the local political culture.

Unlike the beginnings of most other states, the origins of

Kentucky as a separate state were marked by bitter controversy and confusion. The thirteen colonies entered statehood naturally as part of the Revolution, while most future states were the foregone results of territorial planning. But not Kentucky! One is tempted to suggest that Kentuckians have always shown a skill at political invective and a fondness for brutal politics. Why should their origins have been any different? But we realize at once that the struggle for independence from Virginia occurred during the 1780s, when there was not a single white adult native to the region. It would appear, then, that the tumultuous statehood fight itself prepared the ground nicely for generations of vendetta-style politics. Those with a penchant for the supernatural might suggest that a spirit of discontent somehow emanates from the Kentucky hills—a sign of that "dark and bloody ground" warning, again.

While the real essence of the problem seemed to be the Virginia connection, the new Kentuckians contrived to add their own spice to the brew. Even before the close of the Revolutionary War, much unhappiness was being expressed against Virginia rule. One source of hostility was the 1779 land law, which left many feeling cheated. Of course, it was possible to leave and seek more secure titles elsewhere, and thousands did so; but for many who remained, whether they were landless tenants or aggrieved Pennsylvania speculators, Virginia was no friend. Nor was she a friend to those experiencing Indian depredations. While red-white violence in Kentucky was greatly reduced after Blue Licks, it did not entirely cease. As late as 1789, more than twenty whites were killed during a series of particularly bloody episodes. Angry settlers charged that Virginia was indifferent and had failed to provide adequate frontier defense.

The Virginia Assembly made honest efforts to alleviate some of these difficulties. Late in 1780, three counties were created to improve local government and militia: Fayette, north of the Kentucky River; Jefferson, west; and Lincoln, south. Then, in March 1783, the name *Kentucky* was officially revived when a new Judicial District and Court were established. These sensible steps did not, however, reduce anti-Virginia feeling among many Kentuckians. The new court acted principally to validate

Virginia land claims, while the many new offices created by court and counties chiefly went to the Virginia-born new Kentucky gentry. A core of advancing Virginia men had been emerging since the Revolution to claim control of county politics, just as they were extending their economic and social positions. Now many of these emigrés—who all along considered themselves the proper governing class—were taking political and legal power as county officeholders. A reaction was inevitable, if only because most Kentuckians, by that time, were not natives of the Old Dominion, and in that era of more intense localism and interstate squabbling, North Carolinians, Pennsylvanians, and Marylanders were not known for their affection toward their powerful and prideful sister state. Trouble was likely, as one Virginia-born Lincoln County magistrate warned the governor in 1784:

> Many of the natives of this place are not natives of Virginia, nor well affected to its government, and they are sowing sedition among its inhabitants. . . . I fear the faction will increase, and ere long we shall revolt from the government in order to try if we can govern ourselves, which, in my opinion will be jumping out of the frying pan into the fire.[7]

Although Kentuckians were unready to test the heat of independence in 1784, that year did mark a turning point. Public sentiment began to swing decisively in favor of some form of separation from Virginia. After all, separation was logical and necessary. Even with the best of intentions—and there was much wisdom and sympathy among Old Dominion statesmen— the Richmond government faced severe obstacles to the fair ruling of its western district. The distances were immense, not only in miles, but in the slow and uncertain communication around the rugged Appalachian Plateau. Unreliable delivery of mail and newspapers often caused lengthy delays in receiving official word of laws affecting Kentucky. The whole orientation of Virginia's economy and government, moreover, was east-

---

7. James Speed to Governor William Harrison, May 22, 1784, in *Calendar of Virginia State Papers and Other Manuscripts,* 11 vols., edited by William P. Palmer (Richmond: n.p., 1875–1893), 3:588–589.

ward: her rivers flowed that way, her planter-statesmen looked toward the seaboard and Europe, as they had for 180 years. Kentucky's rivers, meanwhile, flowed westward, and in that day, before the development of canals and railroads, that meant that her products would inevitably seek to move down the Mississippi to New Orleans. And that suggests the way economic and political developments were beginning to work together to accelerate the separation movement. American trans-Atlantic commerce was already suffering from the continuing trade dispute with England. The end of the Revolution brought worse news still for Kentuckians: the Spanish government had closed the port of New Orleans (and thus the lower Mississippi River) to American shipping.

At first, that was mainly a political grievance, for the district was not yet producing an exportable surplus; but the rate of economic and population growth in the 1780s was phenomenal, and quite soon there would be increasing quantities of Kentucky products available for the less-expensive national and international trade route down the great rivers to the sea. Kentucky farmers, whether or not they had slaves, were profit-minded. Like most enterprising American farmers, they were not satisfied with the idyllic little self-sufficient homesteads of agrarian myth. Soon there were surpluses of corn and rye, hogs and beef. Horses increased in number, as ambitious farmers shifted from hoe to plow. Good springs everywhere became sites for the ubiquitous distilleries, gristmills, sawmills, paper and hemp mills. The frontier was rapidly vanishing westward. People were moving out of garrison stations to join the horde flocking out from the seaboard states. Log, stone, and frame houses, unique and astonishing sights in 1784, were soon dotting the countryside and the muddy street fronts of a half-dozen fast-growing towns.

The political implications of all that seemed obvious. Kentuckians were gaining maturity and self-confidence, along with distinctive goals and policies divergent from those of Virginia. Contrary to popular mythology, western settlers were not anarchists, hostile to all authority. They had definite need for a government that actively protected their lives and property against frontier Indians and rascally land sharpers, while it promoted

economic development and trade. Agitation for autonomy or
statehood arose not from no-government utopianism, but from
the circumstances of Kentucky life and specific grievances
against the policies of Virginia and the United States government. How could this vast region remain under the rule of
another, eastern state? The answer was apparent; more ominously, how long would this flourishing new country remain
content as part of an American government that seemed to ask
much and give so little?

The tortuous route to statehood began in a meeting held at
Danville during the last days of 1784. Here, certainly, was an
unprepossessing start for a sequence that would become so
meaningful. On the surface, the meeting was a convention of
senior militia company officers who called themselves together
to consider alleged Cherokee unrest. Not too much earlier, such
a meeting would simply have initiated a military excursion ending in burned villages, drunken soldiers, and some pot shots at
the few braves unwitting enough to tarry behind. But now the
Cherokee were technically across a state line, in North Carolina,
beyond the jurisdiction of a Virginia county militia. In fact, it
appears safe to say that those attending this "First Convention"
all along had in mind a bigger mission. Separation from
Virginia was what these Lincoln County leaders were after, and
the unhappy Cherokee were mainly a convenient excuse to have
a meeting and mull over frustrations. In any event, a call was
soon issued for a second, larger convention, to be held in the
same place the following spring.

The May 1785 Convention was unabashedly political in
make-up and purpose, with elected delegates and counties represented according to population. Some later claimed that that was
because Lincoln, the most populous county, was hottest for action; still, the democratic precedent was a good one. Gentlemen
all, and uncommonly united in opinion, the Second Convention
attempted to make the strongest case yet for separation. Their
argument, in essence, blamed the distance and apathy of
Virginia for the ineffectual condition of district militia and administrative affairs and accused the United States government
likewise for the sorry state of frontier protection and the con-

tinued illegal presence of British forts on the Great Lakes. But what to do now? Most residents of Kentucky at that moment were virtual newcomers, small farmers mainly worried about getting in enough corn and building a proper cabin by wintertime. In fact, it is reasonable to say that, throughout the entire period of the statehood struggle, the majority of citizens, while vaguely favoring some form of separation, were hugely indifferent to the specific plotting and machinations going on. The gentry-leaders of the movement were operating in a unique political context. The Declaration of Independence was not yet ten years old. Freedom, independence, and self-government were the heady words of the triumphant Revolution itself, a rhetoric that was vital and full of meaning. The Kentucky independence movement sprang naturally out of the national struggle against Great Britain, just ended. Kentucky's self-proclaimed "Patriots" were only following the lead of the heroes of the Revolution. And who can deny the role of propaganda, committees of correspondence, conventions, and leadership itself in the coming of the American Revolution?

It was a time for words and symbolic action. The result was the calling of still a third convention, to meet that August, and to prepare and transmit a petition to Virginia. It was also a time for statesmanship, and here emerged another one of those marvelously colorful and contentious figures who dominate early Kentucky history. The man was James Wilkinson, a consummate self-seeker, unexcelled intriguer, and controversial leader in the separation movement. Wilkinson's astonishing career traversed the entire early national period from the Revolution to the 1820s, a time during which his reputation vacillated between the heights of wealth and honor and the depths of conspiracy in treason. If there were any constants in his life, they may have been his driving desire for position and admiration and his curiously consistent bad judgment about the ways to fulfill that ambition.

Wilkinson's Kentucky career illustrates his discordant talents. He came west in the winter of 1783–1784 and rapidly established himself as one of the foremost men of the Bluegrass. A native of rural Maryland and an experienced merchandiser, Wilkinson quickly built up an imposing landed estate and trading shop and debts equally as imposing. With his flowery style of speaking and writing, his imported brandies and silks, and his elegant Lexington home and carriage, as much as in his incandescent political energies, James Wilkinson shouted out his thirst for attentive friends and conspicuous power.

It was not long before he had both. He was said to be the author of the call for the August 1785 Third Convention, was elected to that body, and dominated its proceedings. A petition drafted by Wilkinson, spelling out the need for separation, was eagerly dispatched to Richmond. On the surface, at least, affairs seemed to be moving smoothly toward inevitable statehood. But evidently Wilkinson and his close friends were already contemplating grander visions. Kentucky boatmen had brought home the troubling news that the port of New Orleans had been closed to American river traffic. Subsequently, Kentuckians were told that Virginia had agreed to separation, but had imposed certain irksome conditions. Troubled by economic and political problems and divisions in the new nation, Virginians demanded that their western counties assume part of Virginia's state debt and pledge to enter the federal Union by June 1787. Had Old Dominion leaders begun to hear rumors about intrigue, across the mountains? Were they afraid that their surging western counties might prefer the power and prestige of independent nationhood to the frustrations of statehood under the Articles of Confederation? Perhaps, for the Richmond government also demanded that all Virginia claims on Kentucky land be guaranteed, along with the free navigation of the Ohio River, which lay entirely within the boundaries of Kentucky—a pact concluded in 1784 had resulted in Kentucky's border being drawn along the northern shore of the Ohio, instead of at mid-stream as was usual.

Separation had appeared to be a simple idea; Kentuckians were finding ways to make it complex. Over the next three years—1785 to 1788—additional conventions, official and unauthorized, met to draft more petitions, both to Virginia and to the federal Congress in Philadelphia. The level of debate in the district became increasingly rancorous. Duels were fought or threatened. Editorials and pamphlets blasted away at the imbecility of this or that opponent. In short, the squirearchy was having a grand time. By 1787, Wilkinson had emerged as the moving force in a clique that definitely favored some kind of radical political action. Indian troubles on the northwestern frontier were in the news again, and the British were still ensconced in their forts there. Not only did New Orleans remain closed, but Kentuckians were vexed by a report that Congress intended to trade away Mississippi River navigation rights for a commercial treaty with Spain. Here was proof that the eastern states were indifferent to the problems of westerners. In addition, Congress was nearly moribund, and a move was already launched to draft an entirely new federal constitution, one which, so rumor had it, would provide for a much stronger central government. Where would Kentucky fit in all of that? Men and events seemed precariously balanced, tilting first one way, then another. Here hindsight is our enemy, for knowing how things turn out steals the sense of uncertainty, of potentiality that permeated this moment.

James Wilkinson thought he knew or could control the direction in which Kentucky was headed. In the spring of 1787, he loaded a cargo of tobacco and other goods on flatboats bound for the forbidden city, New Orleans. Publicly proclaiming his determination to contest the ban on American trade, he himself climbed aboard and set out on the long voyage. During his year-long absence, Wilkinson's point of view was kept alive in the persons of such influential sympathizers as Harry Innes, Attorney-General of Kentucky District, and John Brown, Kentucky's lone congressman in the Virginia delegation. By the time Wilkinson returned, sentiment among the gentry had polarized to the extent that two political factions had emerged. One, calling itself the Court party, was associated with Wilkinson's point of view: more urban-minded, more concerned with economic diversification and the southwestern river trade. These men seemed willing to endorse and follow the example set by the neighboring State of Franklin—a section of the upper eastern tip of what would later be Tennessee—in which locals led by John Sevier set up an independent state whose fate in or out of the Union was still uncertain. Opposed to such revolution were members of the Country party, more plantation-oriented, favoring a peaceful, orderly separation from Virginia, and immediate statehood—all of which would assure absolute security for their own estates and position.

When Wilkinson returned in February, he was pitched into the first of the great contests for public support that mark 1788 as a decisive year in the history of Kentucky: the elections for delegates to the Richmond convention held to ratify or reject the proposed new federal constitution. It appeared at once that the Court party had won an important victory. Kentucky sent fourteen delegates to Richmond, and, when the dust had settled, only three of her representatives voted for ratification; one abstained; the remaining ten pro-Wilkinson men voted nay. The latter were suspicious of eastern influence in the new and stronger federal union, and saw the new Constitution as an instrument for limiting western economic development. And there was that persistent New Orleans question; there seemed to be little prospect that any brand-new government could budge the Spanish from their intransigent hold on that gateway to the Mississippi.

Indeed, Kentuckians had already learned that, where governments may fail, James Wilkinson could succeed—for when he had returned to Lexington, in a splendid new coach-and-four, it was to announce that New Orleans was now open to Kentucky products. At least, it was open to all willing to sell through the only American granted a trade permit—who was, of course, the same J. Wilkinson. In exchange for that trade monopoly, Wilkinson had secretly agreed to pay what to many might appear a substantial price: he was to continue his efforts to influence Kentuckians toward independence, and he had pledged to work for Kentucky's subsequent union with Spain as a colony, with Wilkinson as governor. Working toward that fine day, he had taken an oath of allegiance to Spain and agreed to act as its agent in Kentucky. Tingling with intrigue, Wilkinson confided the full plot to only a trusted few, while publicly he spoke cautiously of independence from the United States and commercial alliance with Spain. Just as dangerous was the fact that the district's congressman, John Brown, had begun informal secret conversations in New York City with the Spanish ambassador, Don Diego de Gardoqui. Like many Court party men, Brown was growing increasingly sure that a bright future lay ahead for

Kentucky as the dominant western power only if she struck out on her own now.

It was within that heady aura of conspiracy that the Sixth Convention met, late in July 1788. The men had come together in full expectation that Kentucky was about to be admitted to the Union as the fourteenth state. All that remained, they believed, was the task of drafting a state constitution. Instead, to their bitter annoyance, they learned that Congress had tabled their bid for admission. That meant further delay, perhaps years more delay. And for what? Heated words were exchanged as Wilkinson and his friends—the largest bloc in the convention—called outright for a declaration of independence. Kentucky's representatives had already declared against the new federal Constitution; now they were on the brink of a fateful decision against the Union itself. Finally, more moderate voices prevailed, at least to the point of calling for a seventh and perhaps final and decisive convention to meet the following November. The great questions would be taken to the people, and the new convention was given extraordinary power to determine the future of the district.

The battle for votes that followed was the most hotly contested political fight yet waged in Kentucky. Whatever happened, the people were fast maturing as a political body. While the Court party again gained only a strong plurality of delegates, one of its leaders, Samuel McDowell, was elected president of the convention, and Wilkinson occupied a dominant position in its proceedings. The great intriguer was in his most brilliant form, cajoling, insisting, holding out the most luminous prospects if only the convention had the wit and the will to endorse the independence movement. The play reached its dramatic climax when Wilkinson suddenly pointed to fellow delegate John Brown, recently returned from New York. Here was a man of consequence, a man privy to inside information, one who, Wilkinson confidently believed, would now tip the scales irreversibly toward immediate separation from Virginia and the United States.

All eyes turned toward Brown, expectantly. But Brown proved to be a weaker reed than the Court party men had expected. Perhaps he was still genuinely uncertain about the right path to follow, or he may just not have been cut out for a life of cunning and deceit. He had conversed with the Spanish minister, he admitted, but the most he would own to, guardedly, was that "provided we are unanimous, every thing we could wish for, is within our grasp." Indeed. The Greek oracles could not have said it better in their most inscrutable fashion.[8] Though the convention continued to discuss the Mississippi trade question and prospects for a Spanish connection, it was obvious to Wilkinson that the mood had definitely shifted against radical action. The moderates had won again.

In the end, the Seventh Convention contented itself with two more addresses—one to Virginia, the other to Congress—pleading once again for orderly separation, statehood, and the opening of the port of New Orleans to all. Kentucky's Spanish romance was rapidly falling into well-deserved pieces. During the next two years, key members of the Wilkinson clique were plucked out of that fold and fastened into loyalty to the new federal government through the time-honored device of being appointed or elected officeholders. Brown was elected to represent the district in the new federal Congress, and Innes, McDowell, and others were cleverly given federal positions in the district by wily officials in President Washington's administration. Moreover, in the spring of 1789, Wilkinson lost his short-lived trade monopoly, as the Spanish finally opened New Orleans to American commerce. Embarrassed by mounting debts, the irrepressibly high-living Wilkinson returned to a commission in the United States army and left the state forever. Although he served as the highest-ranking officer in the army for twelve years, Wilkinson's career was marred by many episodes, particularly his involvement in Aaron Burr's own alleged Spanish conspiracy. After an inglorious spell in the War of 1812, Wilkinson spent his remaining years on his Louisiana plantation. Ever the intriguer, he died in 1825 in Mexico City, where he was negotiating for Texas land.

Kentucky's tortuous road to statehood involved two more conventions, but there was no longer any doubt that the district would soon be granted statehood. By the spring of 1792, Ken-

8. Marshall, *History of Kentucky,* 1:359.

tuckians approached the last hurdle: the drafting of a state constitution.

A constitutional convention is one of the impressive creations of political man. Here, in theory at least, the elemental ingredients that have gone into the making of a community come to a focus. The convention at once reflects what has been, as it shapes what is to come. What does the 1792 convention tell us about the balance of power and interests in Kentucky? Many Americans looked to the emergent western regions as sanctuaries for true agrarian democracy. Would this first frontier giant strike out in novel directions or hew closer to traditional patterns of political organization?

These were not exclusively questions of local concern. The Convention of 1792 took place during the most energetic period of voluntary constitution-making in the nation's history. The thirteen colonies had begun the process, and some had already drafted revised documents. Then, of course, the new United States Constitution influenced everyone's thinking. As a result of the war against colonialism and monarchy, with the political creativity that followed, Americans had entered an era of more sophisticated political thinking. Significant new notions had come to be accepted as naturally desirable—among them the ideas of democracy, representative government, the need to write down and thus describe and legitimize a community's political arrangements. The issues concerned not only who ruled, but how—not just in the political sense, but in the social and economic sense, as well.

In that golden age of serious debate and law-making, the first frontier state assumed a rather ambiguous position. Innovative in some respects, the Kentucky constitution above all was to mirror the realities of that society. Kentuckians did have alternatives to traditionalism. As the time for the convention approached, a fierce debate raged between defenders of Virginia-style moderation and advocates of a more radical form of government. As proponents of change, the latter group took the offensive, holding many county meetings, forming committees—reminiscent of pre-Revolutionary activities—denouncing the status of affairs in the district, and publishing forthright calls for

reform. They were aided in that by the editor of the only newspaper in those parts, John Bradford of Lexington, who was sympathetic to reform and opened the pages of his *Kentucky Gazette*
to all. Although the radicals were led by "gentlemen of property and standing," as the saying went, their proposals aimed at
advancing the condition of ordinary citizens. Their suggestions
were a catalogue of the reform ideas of the day, which aimed
essentially at opening up the political and legal process through
such devices as universal white manhood suffrage, voting by
ballot instead of by voice vote in front of courthouses, popular
election of all state and local officials, a one-house legislature,
and a simplified code of law to reduce dependency upon the
despised lawyers. Some—Baptist and Presbyterian spokesmen,
especially—even proposed outright abolition of slavery.

The enthusiasm of the radicals, however, proved a flimsy
weapon against the determination of the better-financed moderates. Add to apathy and illiteracy the "treating" of voters with
profuse quantities of liquor, and public voice-voting for candidates, and the result was predictable. A third of the constitutional convention consisted of men who were political novices,
most of them probably reform-minded; but the convention was
dominated by propertied interests. These men had more than
numbers and tradition on their side; in the person of their leading figure, George Nicholas, they had a man of formidable skill
and experience. Nicholas already had a distinguished record as a
lawyer, a Revolutionary War colonel, aide of Madison in their
struggle to ratify the federal Constitution, and a leading Jefferson supporter in the Virginia Assembly. Though he had only
moved to Kentucky during 1789, he soon had a fine house in
Lexington and a substantial farm and mill near Danville; it was
short work for such a man to rise to pre-eminence in the little
world of the Kentucky squirearchy.

Elected to the 1792 Convention, George Nicholas quickly
moved to dominate its proceedings. He had prepared a series of
resolutions that he successfully introduced as the basis for dis-
cussion; within sixteen days, the moderates had drafted a state
constitution conforming in most respects to the Nicholas resolutions. The Nicholas men associated themselves with the Old
Dominion life-style and looked on their reformist opponents as

wild-eyed "mobocrats." Nevertheless, Nicholas and his friends were no enemies of representative government. They were, after all, Jefferson men who would go on to help form the Democratic-Republican party in Kentucky—the group opposed to the policies of Alexander Hamilton and, later, John Adams.

There was much, in other words, in the George Nicholas-inspired 1792 state Constitution that everyone could applaud. For the first time in any American state constitution, all religious and property qualifications for voting were abolished; all free white males who were Kentucky residents and over twenty-one could vote. The use of rum, whiskey, and similar emoluments to influence voters was restrained by the introduction of ballot voting. While the one-house legislature idea was rejected, representation in the new state house and senate would be proportionate by population. The new state constitution was also forward-looking in abolishing imprisonment for debt, provided the property was returned to the creditor. On the other hand, the 1792 constitution was something of a hollow victory. The convention rejected popular elections for governor, senators, and most other officials; the first two were to be selected by a college of electors; the rest were to be appointed by the governor. In addition, no commitment was made to inaugurate any institution of higher learning or any system of public education. The assumption that the sons of the gentry would receive their schooling at private academies and eastern universities explains, as much as anything else, that unfortunate lapse.

Most ominous, however, was the battle fought over slavery. Considering the over-representation of slaveholding planters in the convention, the warmth with which that issue was debated was remarkable. However, the philosophical dogmas of the Revolution, which included a spirit of egalitarianism and hostility to human bondage, were still much in the public mind. The minds of many slaveowners, especially among the Virginia gentry, were troubled by the paradox of slavery and freedom flourishing side by side in America. Some supported gradual emancipation; others acted privately to rid their consciences of the dilemma by manumitting their black property. Diminished agricultural profits during and after the war encouraged that action. Moreover, it was only five years earlier that the federal

Congress had adopted a Northwest Ordinance banning slavery
from territories *above* the Ohio River. Meanwhile, most of the
northeastern states had adopted or would shortly adopt gradual
emancipation schemes. Although the new United States Constitution contained a number of proslavery clauses, the fate of the
increasingly peculiar institution seemed delicately suspended between a troubled past and an uncertain future.

Its destiny appeared really to hinge on the question of westward expansion. If slavery remained hemmed in and confined to
the seaboard states, its elimination by some means seemed certain. As it happened, the coming flood tide of western slave
migration for the most part moved south of Kentucky, so that an
antislavery decision by her in 1792 might not have had great
practical significance. Yet, Kentucky *was* the premier frontier
state. Psychologically, politically, a judgment against African
bondage could have had real impact beyond its own borders,
particularly in Virginia, not to mention the consequences of
such a step for the history of Kentucky.

A full sense of the historical and moral issues involved played
upon the thoughts of the convention delegates in 1792. The antislavery position was vigorously advocated by a bloc of
clergymen-delegates led by Presbyterian minister David Rice.
The major Protestant denominations were still on record at that
time as witnesses against the peculiar institution. (The so-called
great apostasy, in which the southern churches vigorously
swung over into the proslavery camp, lay in the future.) The
targets of the antislavery attack were the proposed bill of rights,
with its guarantees for all property rights, and an article specifically protecting slaveholders against uncompensated, compulsory emancipation. But their adversary was George Nicholas,
slaveholder, along with the convention majority, dominated by
owners of large tracts of land and defenders of the right to hold
human chattels. Many, including Nicholas himself, admitted the
evil of African bondage and hoped for its eventual elimination,
but they were unwilling to act against it during the disturbing
days of the 1790s. Slavery, it seems, had also become a symbol
for the security of property rights in general. In the end, the
ministers could not muster a majority, and the slavery-
protection article was installed in the new constitution by a vote

of 26 to 16. In June 1792, with the constitution completed and
Isaac Shelby inaugurated as governor, Kentucky officially entered
the Union as the fifteenth state. Yet, even as flags were flown
and church bells rang out a celebration of the great day, there
seemed little doubt that Kentucky would be a divided land.

The state did not sink into a political or legal morass from
that point. On land questions, Kentucky did remain a pet-
tifogger's delight, but the choicer tracts beyond the Green River
were not always engrossed by speculators and the advance
agents of planters. Those first decades of the commonwealth
were a period of gratifying economic growth and diversification. In addition, the level and quality of politics were heightened and enriched by association with the great national issues
of controversy and by the rise of the anti-Federalist opposition
party that triumphed—with the aid of Kentucky votes—in the
election of Thomas Jefferson in 1800. Later, Kentuckians, from
classic warhawk Henry Clay to the commonwealth's eager militiamen, would play protagonists' roles in promoting and fighting the War of 1812, the so-called Second War of Independence
from Great Britain.

Geographic and class divisions, jealousies, and hostilities
would by no means disappear with the coming of statehood to
Kentucky. Early evidence of that appears in the agitation that
sprang up almost immediately after 1792, attempting to reform
alleged abuses of the first constitution. The roots of reformism
plainly lay in the anticipations and discontents of the mass of
less fortunate Kentuckians, the tenants, the debt-ridden and vulnerable smaller farmers, the more recent settlers of the eastern,
southern, and western counties. A chorus of protests began to
center on the ''aristocratic'' features of the government: the
selection of governor and senators by electors in a patronage-
rich closed circle of power and the positive protection accorded
to slavery were singled out for criticism.

Once again the state was showered with a torrent of hotly
worded pamphlets, letters, speeches, and editorials. And once
again the increasingly less charitable conservatives geared up
for the fray. Men of property asked what legitimate grievances
lay behind these prorevisionist fulminations; and, according to

their leaders the Virginians George Nicholas and John Breckinridge, there were none. According to them, it was only the ancient conflict between great landowners and the poor, between
slaveholders and the jealous masses denied that privilege. "This
is the Canker that preys upon you," Breckinridge admonished
his foes. "This is what produces all your bellowing about conventions, conventions. This is what stirs up your envy, wounds
your pride and makes you cry *aristocracy*." [9] The terrifying
lessons launched by the French Revolution, only ten years before, were not lost upon propertied Democrats of the Breckinridge school.

Realizing that the call for another convention was unavoidable, wealthy and skillful conservatives gained control of its
proceedings even more thoroughly than they had won control of
the first constitutional convention seven years earlier. The 1799
constitution, drafted in the new statehouse at Frankfort, largely
recopied the old, with some remarkable differences. Governors
and senators were to be elected by popular vote, but voice voting was now restored in place of ballots, with all of the potential
for mischief and abuse of local influence that implied. Appointment rather than election of all state and county officials, including all judges and sheriffs, was preserved or instituted, as
was the article protecting slavery. The entire package was
wrapped up within a binding new clause that made the new constitution, with its proslavery article and other features, exceedingly difficult to amend.

Kentucky was beginning a long and lamentable slide into political and cultural provincialism that was not to be arrested until
the twentieth century. And the forces of parochialism within the
state were given a major boost by provisions of the 1799 constitution regarding the county courts. Local government was an
important and healthy aspect of life in the agrarian America of
those times, and the county court was the body that wielded
local judicial and executive authority. Unfortunately, these
localist tendencies came to assume exaggerated and pernicious
proportions throughout nineteenth-century Kentucky. Beginning
with the revised 1799 constitution, the state increasingly dele-

9. Breckinridge Manuscripts, April 20, 1798, Library of Congress, Washington, D.C.

gated its primary responsibilities of taxation and the regulation of business activities to these local bodies. With their proximity, patronage, and power, they became the most significant agencies of government, touching the lives of everyone, from sellers of hogs on court day to sellers of grandiose railroad-bond schemes. Kentuckians were capable of creating—and did create—new counties at the least provocation, so that Kentucky soon had nearly the largest number of counties for its size and population of any state in the Union.

Problems arose, however, when the county courts came to represent more and more exclusively the interests and personnel of the local elite. Thanks to the constitution of 1799, the power of the courts was greatly enlarged. Membership, composed of the local justices of the peace, could now evolve into the self-appointing, self-perpetuating cliques exemplified by the expression "courthouse gang." And the courts did so, with a vengeance. It was perhaps unavoidable that men of property should dominate local government even more surely than they did state government. It was not inevitable for these agencies to become closed and frequently abusive machines engaged in influence-peddling, manipulation of their considerable authorities for private benefit, and the flagrantly illegal sale of county offices. Incredibly enough, these offices were occasionally even sold at public auctions in which the office was "hawked about the streets, and sold like a horse in the public market so that he who had the most money might get the office." [10]

By itself, such widespread corruption and fragmentation of power might not merit attention. Kentucky was hardly unique in that, except perhaps in the way that much of it was flaunted and accepted. Two points are worth noting, however. These unfortunate tendencies ultimately shaped the political culture of counties throughout the state; they became enduring attitudes and forms of behavior that intensified during the century until, by the post-Civil War years, they had become a poison infecting citizens at every level of government and contributing to a vir-

10. Remark of a Simpson County delegate to the 1849 Constitutional Convention, in *Report of the Debates and Proceedings of the Convention for the Revision of the State of Kentucky, 1849* (Frankfort: A. G. Hodges, 1849), p. 387.

tual paralysis of the political and economic will. Second, for all its close-to-home intimacy, the liabilities of Kentucky's emerging system of county government were only symptomatic of a slowly growing provincialism and of cultural divisions that were seeping into the very texture of life across the state.

Fortunately, the impact of most of that still lay in the future. For now, the epoch of frontier settlement was ended. The story of that era was a tale of regeneration, a renewal of personal fortunes and spirits, a reaffirmation of faith in republican government. In creating the first transmontane state, the founding generations had given tangible form and meaning to the promise of western freedom and economic opportunity. And the Kentuckian as folk hero was playing a gigantic role.

And who was the Kentuckian, this new man? Whether visualized as a woodsman, like Boone, loving and killing the Indian, or as an 1812 Long Rifleman fighting beside General Andrew Jackson at New Orleans; whether a rough keelboatman in the elemental world of the western rivers, or a sturdy pioneer loving and despoiling the land—the romanticized Kentuckian assumed epic stature in the American national imagination. Idealized, he was brave, stubborn, fierce, and belligerently hostile to authority. Bears "can't stand Kentucky play," the crusty pioneer James Finley told us, "biting and gouging are too hard for them." [11] In short, the Kentuckian of myth and fiction was an American original, an untutored hero who stood at the frontier edge of organized society, a mediator between civilization and the wilderness. These were potent images, and they were immensely useful to an American people seeking national unity on the corner of a vast continent.

Of course, one would search in vain for any such epic figure in the real world. Instead of *the* Kentuckian, we can see at least two, or three, or more. Like nearly all the states of the Union, Kentucky was a divided country, divided between the wealthy and the struggling, between the landed and the landless, between the farmer and the factory worker, between those who

11. James B. Finley, *Autobiography of Rev. James B. Finley or, Pioneer Life in the West*, edited by W. P. Strickland (Cincinnati: Cranston and Curts, 1853), pp. 83–84.

were slaves and those who were free. Two predominant cultures, at least, had arisen. The familiar one, centered around the hemp-growing and horse-breeding farms and towns of the Bluegrass, embraced more cosmopolitan, urbane values. The other, centerless and often locked into narrow valleys and the less fertile soils of the hills and hollows, struggled against a more demanding environment. Through a celebration of life in music and dance, through close family ties and ethnic bonding, and in such orgiastic devices as the 1801 Great Revival at Cane Ridge involving thousands of newcomers in a spasm of evangelism, these ordinary folk preserved a sense of pride and community. Yet, in a peculiar way, these cultures maintained a kind of symbiotic balance. For very different reasons, both rejected universal education as unnecessary. Both considered strong state government odious and prized the parochialism of the county court. Nearly all Kentuckians were essentially agrarian in sympathy, and every white man was an aristocrat, each in his own narrow fashion: Bluegrass gentry, eastern mountaineers, western tobacco farmers. The next half-century of Kentucky life, climaxed by the horror of the Civil War, would, however, shake those social bonds to their foundations.

3

Era of Bad Feelings:
Banks, Slaves, War

*Kentuckians may be called the Irish of America. They have
all the levity of character . . . that buoyancy of the spirit,
that jocular ferocity, that ardour, both of attachment and
of hatred, which distinguish the natives of the Emerald
Isle.*

Thomas Hamilton, Manners in America

$\mathcal{T}$HE "middle period" of Kentucky history, the time from
the 1820s to the 1860s, has long been portrayed as a golden age
in the life of the state. According to legend, those years were a
time of splendid peace and prosperity, shattered only by the
coming of the Civil War. Unquestionably, the era has been
shrouded in myth as strongly affective as any in the American
experience. The soft and timeless image of Kentucky and the
Old South was no modern contrivance of Hollywood
filmmakers in *Gone with the Wind*. Rather, it was largely the
creation of post-Civil War southern whites, such as Kentucky
novelists John Fox, Jr., and James Lane Allen, people who experienced an intense nostalgia about the lost world of the Old
Regime. And such a vision they had: "Perpetually suspended in
the great haze of memory, it hung, as it were, poised, somewhere between earth and sky, colossal, shining, and incompara-

bly lovely" [1]—a land of contented slaves, harmonious whites, and a genteel, self-satisfied culture.

While the power of that mystique may never be fully broken, most historians have seen enough through the shimmering veil of time and "the War" to notice some jagged features on the other shore. The half-century before the Civil War was, on balance, a time of growth and prosperity for most Kentuckians. Nevertheless, three of the gravest decisions ever faced by Kentuckians occurred in that eventful period. These crises were to have great consequences, not only for the state, but for the nation as well, for each involved, in one way or another, Kentucky's relation to the Union. Each generated acrimonious divisions and political controversy belying tales of unbroken harmony and quiet growth. The turmoil over banks and courts in the 1820s, a renewed slavery debate in the middle years, and, finally, the anguished verdict regarding southern secession were disturbing because all three concerned fundamental questions about the nature of Kentucky society, and each influenced the course of the state's history profoundly.

The roots of Kentucky's disruptive crisis involving the banks and courts of the 1820s lay in the nation's economic experiences during the first decades of the nineteenth century. From the outset, Kentuckians and their countrymen were no isolationists. They were an ambitious trading people, and the key to their good fortune was seen to lie in a healthy flow of trade and currency between Europe and the eastern and western states of the Union. While the Napoleonic Wars surged across the European continent and onto the high seas, Americans enjoyed a time of opportunity and danger. America's infant industries and early agriculture flourished, as war-torn Europe's production and exports diminished. By the time peace came to Old World and New, the population of the western states seemed especially gratified and prosperous. This region was fast becoming the breadbasket of the world. Immigration soared, and the prospects of such rising towns as Lexington and Pittsburgh, Louisville and

1. Wilbur J. Cash, *The Mind of the South* (New York: Vintage, 1960), p. 127.

Cincinnati, appeared boundless. By 1820, Kentucky's population approached 570,000, sixth largest in the nation.

Who could have realized that 1816—the first year of peace in a generation—would see the foundations of such unparalleled western good fortune begin to crumble? Yet the signs were there to be read, the troubles foretold. It did not take a greying prophet to predict that British industrialists would seek to reclaim lost markets, indeed, that they would also attempt "to stifle in the cradle those rising manufactures in the United States which the war has forced into existence contrary to the usual course of nature." [2] It did not take a genius to see that agricultural production would soon rebound in Europe as battlefields reverted to wheatfields. And it took no financial wizard to recognize that tens of thousands of Americans, unaware that they were approaching the crest of an economic roller coaster, were borrowing their way into chaos.

All prolonged international wars generate an after-shock of economic retrenchment. What made matters after 1815 slide from the merely uncomfortable to the disastrous was the orgy of speculative expansion that gripped Americans from the East Coast to the Mississippi Valley. The principal focus of that boom was an unprecedented inflation in land prices. Future prospects were sound, but farmers and other investors seemed caught up in a mad buying fever that far outstripped present realities. What could justify such behavior? The value of farm products was the usual explanation. For a time after 1815, crop prices continued to soar. Cotton in particular seemed a magic key to instant fortunes, and Kentuckians, as suppliers of hemp, foodstuffs, whiskey, and work animals to the South, shared in the glow of an extraordinary inflation. Credit was abundant. Debt increased everywhere, like mushrooms after a spring rain. Moreover, the money to repay loans was increasingly cheap and plentiful. The West had long suffered from a shortage of hard specie and reliable currency, but in their financial naiveté and intoxicating self-confidence, Americans had more and more taken to solving the problem via the printing press. Since the

2. George Dangerfield, *The Era of Good Feelings* (New York: Harcourt, Brace and World, 1952), p. 177.

turn of the century, hundreds of new state and local banks had been incorporated, principally to extend loans and churn out millions in bank notes, often backed by little more than the grand illusion of endless prosperity.

Kentuckians were not to be outdone at this feast. By the time of the War of 1812, the state had set up two banks to meet demands for loans and cheaper currency coming from the powerful Bluegrass farming and commercial interests and from the emerging "South Side" faction representing the Green River country. Yet even those banks failed to match the postwar frenzy. There were demands for freer credit and more plentiful currency, and the state legislators were not about to permit such unhappiness to go unnoticed. Two branches of the revived Bank of the United States had gone into business in Kentucky, but townsfolk and farmers wanted more. So, in 1818, forty new independent banks were chartered, with six more added soon thereafter. As in other western states, that reflected as much a political as a financial decision. What need did Barbourville or Greenville—quiet country villages of less than a hundred souls—have for their own banks? But banks they would have— or paper mills, really, spewing out credit and bank notes founded upon fantasy.[3]

"From 1815 to 1818 the bubble grew and grew; beautiful, iridescent, fraudulent, opaque," pumped up month after month by insubstantial currencies, loose loan policies, and rampant speculation.[4] But the piper had to be paid sometime. The paying commenced in the fall of 1818, as the ominous news began arriving from England that cotton prices—the keystone to the whole edifice—had begun to weaken. By 1819, they had plunged by two-thirds. Tobacco, wheat, hemp, slaves—all the rest followed, in a headlong tumble; most frightening of all, land prices as well fell precipitously. Hard times were by no means confined to the West, for, in the so-called Panic of 1819, the entire nation experienced one of the sharpest economic depressions in its history. The impact of eastern bank and business

3. Dale Maurice Royalty, "Banking, Politics, and the Commonwealth, Kentucky, 1800–1825" (Ph.D. diss., University of Kentucky, 1971), pp. 10–12, 36–38.

4. Dangerfield, *Era of Good Feelings,* p. 179.

failures spread across the mountains, ripplelike, to strike a severe blow to the rickety economic frame that had been hastily built up by western merchants, manufacturers, and farmers.

Led by the influential Bank of the United States, banks began calling for immediate repayment of loans in hard currency. The hopes of Kentucky farm families and other investors had proven to be constructed on sand, and their distress was genuine. Thousands were dispossessed as mortgages were foreclosed. Meanwhile, the state's banking system itself began rapidly to melt away under the cold rain of deflation. Within a short span of time, the original banks and the newer 1818 independent banks—now rightly dubbed by one wit the "Forty Thieves"—collapsed into bankruptcy. As one traveler of the day truly reported, "Nothing is to be seen but a boundless expanse of desolation! Wealth is impoverished, enterprise checked, commerce at a stand, the currency depreciated." [5]

The turmoil was only a prelude to the coming storm. Impassioned calls for relief soon arose, and they became the most insistent political outcry yet heard in the state. By the time of the critical state elections of 1820, Kentucky's citizens had fallen sharply into pro- and antirelief factions, generally divided between the more debt-ridden counties and the relatively less-hard-hit Bluegrass. Suggestions for relief measures boiled down to two related proposals: one sort, so-called stay laws, would postpone due dates on loans and mortgages; another relief proposal called for printing more currency, which might allow debts to be repaid with cheaper dollars.

Following the narrow victory of John Adair as governor, a multitude of bills, ill-conceived, for the most part, began to pour out of the relief-minded legislature. Sympathetic to the plight of the state's poor farmers and innocent of economic wisdom, Adair signed these bills into law; before long, the fat was in the fire. Conservatives found all of the proposals naive and dangerous, but the measure that drew the sharpest outrage was one that created a new bank, the Bank of the Commonwealth. The relief men had fastened on the remarkable notion that, if the villainous banks had inflicted such miserable debt-slavery upon

5. *Niles Weekly Register,* 17:19.

the common folk, a bank of their own would lead them out of bondage to the promised land of endless inflation, prosperity, and escape from the clutches of sheriffs and foreclosure.

As its advocates freely admitted, the Bank of the Commonwealth had been created chiefly for the purpose of printing currency to be used by debtors to cancel their obligations. It was, as one of its bitter enemies styled it, "an association of Bankrupts to *borrow* money." [6] Within two years, the bank proved as good as its promise: it had lent nearly two and a half million dollars and issued about the same amount in paper currency while possessing less than three thousand dollars in hard specie. If that were not awesome enough, any creditor refusing to accept its unpalatable bills was barred from pressing his claim in court for two years. These various devices may have afforded some temporary protection and relief for many citizens who were then able to borrow money and avoid massive dispossession during the depths of the depression. At the same time, these acts did, in effect, defraud creditors, if for no other reason than that, by 1822, each Bank-of-the-Commonwealth dollar was worth about fifty cents in specie.

Almost in spite of such relief measures, Kentucky began to experience a small restoration of business confidence by the summer of 1823. In fact, though times were still difficult, the national economy had been on the mend since it had hit bottom in 1820. Faith in the legal and fiscal integrity of private citizens, banks, and in the state government itself may have played some part in this disparity, for revival depended, in part, at least, on mutual trust and a willingness to invest capital and labor. But such was not the case in the commonwealth. For Kentuckians, the fierce "Irish of America," the curtain was about to go up on the last, most tumultuous act of the play.

The debates over the relief program had gone on long and loud, but rarely had anyone raised the question of whether they violated state or federal constitution. It was not long, however, before creditors were bringing suit contesting the relief laws,

6. Speech of Charles Wickliffe of Nelson County, reprinted in *Argus of Western America* (Frankfort, Ky.), November 23, 1820.

and, to the horror of the relief party, their legislation was almost uniformly overturned as violations of the Kentucky and federal constitutions. The bitter reaction across the state can scarcely be imagined. That relief measures were to be annihilated by un-elected, "aristocratic" defenders of the propertied classes was intolerable. Or so the rhetoric went. All of that was eagerly exploited by politicians; yet, it really did seem to be a con-troversy over principles, a split between the social and eco-nomic interests of the creditor, wealthier and more conservative groups and regions in the state versus all the rest.

Some forgotten wit once said that any stick is good enough to beat a dog with. While the hated judges of the state Court of Appeals appeared easy enough to hold, however, the angry legislators had trouble finding a weapon with which to pummel them. At first, the mood was for the direct action of removal from office, which could be accomplished by two-thirds majori-ties in both houses. Governor Adair was certainly ready to sign any such bill, but the action failed repeatedly for want of the necessary majority. The relief party then attempted to call a constitutional convention to "dethrone" the offending justices, but the idea was rejected in the antirelief-minded Senate.

Breathing fire, the frustrated relief majority then turned openly toward a political solution. In the state elections of 1824, relief men sought to muster overwhelming majorities in both houses of government. Popular feeling had never been more in-tensely aroused, and the enmity between supporters and oppo-nents of action against the courts sent many men home with gouged-out eyes and bloodied fists. Frontier democracy was not for the faint-hearted. The worst scenes naturally took place where both sides claimed support. "Hard-fought" barely de-scribes the animus in Lexington, for example, where at one point an open riot broke out. Partisans found the cobblestones of the city's streets handy weapons, but when word spread that rifles had been seen behind the barricades, the spirit of ordinary mayhem seemed about to degenerate into real civil war. Luck-ily, the two opposing legislative candidates appeared at that moment, walking arm in arm down the street between the mobs. If that crisis was averted, it was nevertheless true that that cam-paign and its inflammatory themes had increased disrespect for courts and law generally. Newspapers carried numerous distressing notices of lynch law and of families fleeing such an apparently violent state.

The landslide election of Joseph Desha as governor, together with an enlarged majority of fellow prorelief men in the legislature seemed a signal for momentous developments. The legislature convened in November 1824, and relief party leaders moved at once to intimidate or remove the three offending justices of the state's highest court, the Court of Appeals. In early December, the judges themselves were summoned to an inquisition in Frankfort. The three justices—John Boyle, William Owsley, and Benjamin Mills—pulled no punches, denouncing the war upon the court as an invitation to the chaos of "another Shays's rebellion." "No country was ever legislated out of debt," they lectured their furious audience, "nor ever will be." [7] The comparison to Shays's Rebellion was apt, for that brief insurrection of militant western Massachusetts debtors in 1786 had deeply frightened men of property everywhere. Perhaps it was the courage of the three justices, perhaps it was their logic, but whatever the reason, when the vote was put to remove them from office, it passed the house, but failed narrowly of achieving the necessary two-thirds majority in the state senate.

Now the rage of the relief men overflowed. Yet it is vital to remember that issues of great importance were being debated. Why should the judicial branch of government be superior to all others? In that age, when nearly every Kentuckian considered himself a true Jeffersonian, the elected legislature—not the "aristocratic," appointed judiciary—was considered sovereign by the people. Was Governor Desha wrong in asking whether elected government was to be powerless to alter laws or suspend contracts, regardless of the crisis vexing the people? In time of insurrection as well? In time of war? Famine? During the early years of the nation, all of the states were testing the nature and outer limits of their powers. Here was a constitutional crisis of the first order: who shall rule, laws or courts, majorities or con-

7. George Robertson, *Scrap Book on Law and Politics, Men and Times* (Lexington: A. W. Elder, 1855).

stitutions? The implications of Kentucky's imbroglio echo down the corridors of our history from the decisions of John Marshall to the proslavery Dred Scott case, from Franklin D. Roosevelt's "court-packing" scheme down to the civil rights and school busing decisions in our own time.

By late December 1824, the enraged relief party was ready to charge into this constitutional no man's land with all flags flying. A bill was drafted to abolish the Court of Appeals and create a brand-new court, one that would uphold relief legislation. For days, the debate surged back and forth. Finally, on the night of December 24, the issue was brought to a vote in the house. There had never been such a Christmas Eve as that in the commonwealth. For hours, the floor was a scene of heated speechmaking and disorder, punctuated by loud clapping and hissing from visitors in the gallery. An evangelical "camp night-meeting" would have barely matched the "confusion and clamor." [8] With Governor Desha himself unlawfully entering the chamber to rally his forces, bills were passed abolishing the "Old Court" and establishing a "New Court." Feeling ran so high that Ben Hardin, a principal "Old Court" defender, was bashed with a hickory stick while leaving the capitol.

The bashing and confusion had only just begun. The justices of the "Old Court" denied the legitimacy of the court bill and refused to vacate their positions. Officers of the "New Court" were sent to force their way into the rooms that held the Appellate Court records and to remove whatever furniture and papers they could lay hands on. Were there two state supreme courts, or one, or none? For a time, prorelief lawyers took their cases to the New, opponents to the Old. This mad *opera bouffe* continued throughout the spring and summer of 1825 and would have been comical if not for two glaring facts. The legal and financial condition of the state was being made a farce and a shambles; and, after all, serious issues were involved: the validity of the relief program, the political struggle between the two great factions, and the matter of constitutional powers in the state.

Leaders of the Old Court party wisely decided to take the

8. Robertson, *Scrap Book,* p. 127.

case to the people in the election of 1825. Conducting a calm and forceful campaign that emphasized the peril of having courts subjected to the whims of changing legislative majorities, the Old Court group won control of the house, though they fell short in the senate. Why had the people begun to turn against the New Court party? From the viewpoint of strict economic-class interest, the election results appear incongruous. But clearly, the New Court men did not command every vote from the "debtor class, the backwoodsmen, the poor generally." If they had, they would have won virtually every county outside the Bluegrass since, as one historian observes, "there can be no question about the poverty of the great majority of the state's people." [9] Many charges of voter intimidation and fraud crowded the pages of sympathetic newspapers. But the larger fact was that Kentuckians were beginning to weary of the endless turmoil; their innate conservatism dictated a return to traditional leaders and traditional *laissez-faire* policies. Following a year of tension between the two parties, the Old Court men won entire control of house and senate. The legislature eventually dissolved the abortive New Court and restored the Old to its privileges and back salaries. [10]

Was the controversy all sound and fury, signifying nothing more than the passing of an economic storm? The experience unquestionably retarded economic development in the commonwealth. The optimism of farmer and businessman was shaken, leaving in its wake a persistent wariness. Other western states moved more vigorously toward recovery, while Kentucky's internal, national, and foreign trade continued to suffer from a sluggish lack of confidence. Eastern newspapers as well as banks and mercantile houses had followed the curious wanderings of Kentuckians through their bank-and-court nightmare, which did little to inspire faith in future Kentucky investments.

Throughout all that, Lexington became an exaggerated symbol of the larger malady, for the town was stricken in a way that

9. Arndt M. Stickles, *The Critical Court Struggle in Kentucky, 1819–1829* (Bloomington: University of Indiana Press, 1929), p. 70.

10. All acts and decisions of the New Court were declared null and void in a case with the intriguing name of *Hildreth's Heirs* v. *McIntire's Devices* (1829).

left it economically moribund for much of the remainder of the century. Lexington had been the foremost trading place in Kentucky since the 1780s, and with the coming of European war and the credit bubble, industry had also flourished there. Postwar changes, punctuated by the Panic of 1819, destroyed the hothouse atmosphere in which the town had grown. Lacking a riverfront location, the city fathers worked desperately to promote construction of turnpike and railroad connections to break its isolation, but these were of little help. Economic dominance in the region passed relentlessly to Cincinnati and Louisville. In their anxiety, the town leaders even turned to the expansion of local Transylvania University in part as a device for economic relief. Though the success of the school arrested Lexington's decline only slightly, the unique educational experiment did prosper for a time. With mixed state and private support, the university grew wonderfully after 1818, adding schools of law and medicine and vastly expanding student enrollments and graduations.

As important as size was the heightened quality of education. Under the leadership of the nationally recognized liberal minister Horace Holley, who had been called to the presidency of Transylvania from Boston's Unitarian South End Church, the size and caliber of the university's faculty was much enhanced. During Holley's tenure in the 1820s, Lexington became the location of the pre-eminent university west of the mountains, truly the "Athens of the West." But soon both president and school fell victim to the relentless social and economic forces sweeping across the commonwealth. In a sense, the school and the Bluegrass culture that best supported it were anachronisms, an island of less dogmatic, more secular and liberal thinking. Transylvania had been founded by Presbyterians; but in the early 1820s, Holley and his faculty were coming under increasing pressure from conservative Presbyterian leaders in the state who were bitterly hostile to their alleged free-thinking infidelity. By the middle of the decade, these attacks on Transylvania were reinforced by the growing class opposition of the Relief and New Court parties, whose members despised and feared the "aristocratic" high tone, the probing scientific secularism, and "godless" teachings of the university. With state funds virtually cut off and orthodox religious hostility reaching a crescendo, Holley finally abandoned the place in 1827. His departure shattered the morale of liberal religious and educational opinion in antebellum Kentucky, as well as the possibilities for sustaining an open, nondenominational state university. Transylvania soon joined Lexington itself in a decline into prolonged somnolence and charming provinciality.

But the boom-and-bust relief era inflicted its sharpest blows upon the yeomanry. The whole process had proven to be a monstrous machine for the production of farm tenantry, with thousands of families dispossessed by mortage holders. From counties everywhere came ominous news of vacated property and wagons headed westward out of the state. The sturdy farm families that are the backbone of all developing regions were now leaving what they had believed to be the promised land in great numbers. Old and New Court men disputed the reasons for that troubling sign. The former blamed the inept ''mobocratic'' legislation of recent years; the latter saw it as proof that people were voting with their feet against the ''Lords of Kentucky'' and their blind determination to possess all the best land. Whatever the cause, the contrast with the bright hope and promise of the pioneer period could not have been greater.

Considering its many long-range consequences, the surface political passions of the court controversy subsided in a remarkably brief time, as political interest turned to the fascinating presidential contest shaping up for 1828. Broad national, or, at least, regional parties were coalescing around the incumbent John Quincy Adams; his opponent, Andrew Jackson; and Kentucky's perpetually favorite son, Henry Clay, Secretary of State under Adams. One could still see some of the outlines of the court struggle in the emerging political lineup, since the ''democratic'' Jackson's appeal to the common man over aristocratic privilege smacked of New Court rhetoric. More persuasive for many Kentuckians, however, was the fact that Clay was so widely admired and Jackson himself so suspect because of his earlier slanders about the performance of Kentucky riflemen at New Orleans.

Even as Kentucky domestic political alignments and issues were submerged under the title of national party organization, one incidental effect of the court fight should be noted. New Court leaders Francis Preston Blair, Amos Kendall, and William Barry all found comfortable situations in Washington in the new world of Jacksonian spoils. But they gained more than mere position. These three, who had cut their political teeth in Kentucky's banking and relief battles, certainly helped to influence Jackson toward his fateful decision to wage war on the "monster" Bank of the United States. Thanks in part to Blair, Kendall, and Barry, Kentucky's strife was re-enacted in transmuted and more enduring form on the national stage.

The thirty years preceding the Civil War were decades of enormous consequence to the American states and nation. Constitutional issues that were circled tentatively during Kentucky's bank and court controversy began to be met head-on. Considering the immense impact of the Civil War, it is no wonder that Americans have been fascinated by the story of its coming. Although Kentuckians were to play an important role in that drama, it is worth pausing to consider other aspects of life in the antebellum world. All was not sectionalism and states' rights, the anxious plotting of rebellion and coercion; few contemporaries had the sense that they were moving toward an unavoidable civil war. Indeed, the nation and its people were engaged in an era of tremendous growth and social vitality.

These currents did not leave agrarian Kentucky untouched. Economically, the state had slowly rebounded from its earlier troubles, only to be hit again by the century's second severe depression, which began in the late 1830s. Happily, many of the Relief era excesses were avoided this time, and Kentuckians began to share in the unprecedented national prosperity that characterized the remaining antebellum decades. Outside of Louisville, manufacturing occupations did continue to decline. But by 1860, the development of the River City placed it in a dominant financial position in the state, and it was home for a majority of Kentucky's urban population.

Meanwhile, the rest of the commonwealth was also making economic progress. Coal mining began in western fields near Owensboro in the 1820s, while the 1840s saw the beginnings of barge shipments down the Kentucky River from eastern coal fields. The hallmark of these years, however, was the boom in transportation itself, as countless private companies, virtually every county government, and the state as well went heavily into debt to finance a vast number of projects:·improved roads, river channels, canals, and, later, the great iron god of the age, railroads. The main object of most of it all was to serve farmers by facilitating the movement of bulky agricultural products. The years between 1820 and 1860 were the farmer's age in America and that was certainly true for Kentucky. More than that of any other southern or border state, the largely rural population of Kentucky lived on small farms. Indeed, 90 percent of her people resided in the country, and three-fourths of these farm families owned places with fewer than one hundred cleared acres. In an era that worshipped plain and simple democracy, many were the counties that practically borrowed themselves into bankruptcy attempting to enhance trading opportunities for gentry and yeomanry alike.

The apparent triumph of "small *d*" democracy was evident in other ways, as well. Politically, while all men claimed to have supped at the same Jeffersonian table, antebellum Kentucky enjoyed the most vigorous two-party competition in its history, dominated until the early 1850s by the towering figure of Henry Clay and his Whigs, and thereafter by the Democrats led by the more divisive John C. Breckinridge. The glaring evil of widespread corruption at the county level—sale of offices, sinecures, and election gambling and manipulation—grew more intense year after year. By the 1840s, the abuses had become so bipartisan and flagrant that a public outcry finally had effect. Thanks to constitutional changes made at the Convention of 1849, much local political venality was reduced—or at least forced to change its form. Biennial elections replaced the annual affairs, all votes were to be cast on a single day, and urban representation in the legislature was enhanced; in addition, all legislators now had to take an oath against the archaic mayhem of dueling. Most important, however, county judges and sheriffs and most other local officers were now elected for fixed terms, rather than appointed. As in the early twentieth century's Progressive Era, democracy was regarded overoptimistically as a curing balm for whatever ailed the political body.

A related panacea, universal public education, also began a belated advance during this period. For generations, Kentucky had declined to take that part of the Jeffersonian recipe seriously. Its eighteenth-century constitutions were unique in their silence on public education. Though the principal towns began to meet their responsibilities, the great rural districts slumbered in apathy, preferring to emulate the other southern states in hostility to public, so-called poor schools. As governor after governor protested in vain, scarce school funds were siphoned off into projects to build turnpikes and railroads between sleepy villages and empty crossroads. A half century after the birth of the commonwealth, three-fourths of the counties had no public schools. But the prolonged labors of many private and official citizens were finally rewarded during the tenure of the Reverend Robert J. Breckinridge, State School Superintendent. Successfully playing upon his prestigious name and his reputation as a nationally respected Presbyterian minister, Breckinridge launched a vigorous speaking and writing campaign in 1847 that brought to a focus the opinion of the gentry. It had been a long time developing. Funds quickly followed middle-class sentiment. The new 1850 Constitution incorporated solemn guarantees for the school fund, and, by 1853, all counties had public schools. Daily attendance, compared to national averages outside the South, remained low, perhaps reflecting the enduring hostility and suspicion felt by the mass of country folk to such a "needless" intrusion as book-learning. Still, the commitment had begun.

Though fledgling schools began to join the more customary jails and courthouses dotting countryside and villages, many antebellum Kentuckians continued to demonstrate a wonderful indifference to external forms of "modern civilization" or authority. Thanks in part to its exceptional proportion of small farms, Kentucky exhibited an intense localism combined with an unrestrained spread-eagle fondness for the federal Union, a government that had the wisdom to recognize that the Lord's finest creation—next to Kentucky itself—was the independent white farmer. Nowhere was that dimension of the state's mentality evident in so pure a form as in the eastern highland counties.

Here, according to northern abolitionists, was a spiritually broken population, men and women defeated by competition with slaves and aristocracy, while to the arch-southern writer they were a people forced back onto less desirable lands by their unambitious and idle manners. Neither of those images satisfactorily explained why and how the mountain people persisted and even took delight in their location and ways.

In fact, rather than being squeezed out of the low country, many highland settlers had deliberately chosen their environment, for they had come from similar country on the other side of the Appalachian Plateau; indeed, the Scotch-Irish and the English in particular retained fond recollections of beloved highlands across the seas. Traveling through such counties as Breathitt, Floyd, Harlan, and Pike, the critical outsider wept needless tears about the local state of things, for the homes of the South's leading herdsmen were in those areas. Their rough cabins had none of the cultural finery of the Bluegrass mansion, but in that they were typical of the average Kentucky farm family. More primitive ways of cooking and soap-making, along with the community joys of corn-shucking and cabin-raising, did persist much longer in the highland counties, but more from stubborn choice and absence of external stimulation than from poverty and apathy in the modern sense. The frontierlike economy of hunting, grazing, and subsistence farming was the logical response to geographic realities, while the cruder forms of cultural life were cherished by a people given to exuberant humor, self-confidence, and a love of nature. These ways would not become ''social problems'' until long after the Civil War. In time, peaceful valleys would come to be seen as unfertile land traps, and close family ties and intermarriage would be criticized as a breeding ground for isolation and unhealthy homogeneity. The railroads would begin to reach into the hills, less to bring people closer together than to carry out their timber and mineral resources. Hostile to change in a world that increasingly worshiped progress before all other gods, the Kentuckian of the hill country and the Knobs would begin a slide from boisterous self-assurance toward the downcast look of the hillbilly.

But the time for those troubles had not yet come. On the eve of Civil War, the vast majority of rural Kentuckians, wherever they lived, remained fervently attached to their traditional social values and organization. Family allegiance remained paramount in a way that was clearly diminishing in the northern states. There, a broader, more complex web of institutional loyalties was rapidly taking shape—concepts of urban community, morality and reform, of labor rights, economic progress, and nationalism that were absent or only vaguely recognized southward. In Kentucky and her sister states, the patriarchal family unit remained the principal instrument for managing the labor of kin and slave. Paternal authority determined what was acceptable and what was deviant behavior. Schooling and professionalism were less highly honored here than elsewhere, because the rural family exercised such sway over education—the passing on of traditional, not bookish knowledge—and because the career choices in an overwhelmingly agricultural economy were limited. Marriage ties were as extraordinarily important to the poor as to the wealthy. Both sought to preserve their family security, its property, and its prestige, for the integrity of the clan was the surest guarantee against personal failure and social chaos. That was the democracy of the breakfast table. All had rights, all spoke with self-assurance, but all knew their place within the hierarchy from head to foot, and were ready to fight to defend it.

In every Kentucky county, local family clusters linked by blood and marriage sorted out and organized society in the traditional, intimate, particularistic way. The few real cities were exceptions, especially Louisville, with its size and its growing foreign-born population; most Kentucky "communities were simply chance gatherings of these family units in a neighborhood." Church life occasionally transcended these family-local attachments; but even here the predominant sects among the yeomanry were the democratically individualistic, evangelical denominations, shaped and cast in the fiery crucibles of the Great Awakening and frontier revivals; they were churches in which congregations tended to be "collections of intimately familiar kinfolk," whose dogmas and imagery stressed an "elemental dualism" pitting a sinful Satan against the redemptive

Jehovah.[11] With each family, in a sense, a band of watchful Israelites, anything that threatened their clan, or clannishness in general, was to be resisted. Consequently, outside of the more cosmopolitan towns and planters' homes, the higher concepts of humanitarianism, religion, public education, civic-mindedness, and government had little influence in Kentucky.

To the outsider, antebellum Kentucky society appeared to be a disconcerting bundle of conflicting parts. One found "strange mixtures of statute law and Lynch law," one traveler recalled, "of heathen brutality and the most Christian excellence, of disregard for human life and self-forgetting philanthropy." [12] Yet those contradictions amused more than troubled the yeomen native to the area. Local humorists loved to spin extravagant tales teasing their fellows about their affection for fits of monumental drunkenness and holiness, for military titles and violent individualism, for their suspicion and renowned hospitality. In the end, Kentuckians recognized that such highly exaggerated attributes were merely excesses of style that masked an underlying cultural unity among the masses. The basic values of agrarianism, fundamentalism, and, above all, the ties of kinship made up a great closed circle within which the lives of most Kentuckians revolved.

These folkways also had considerable influence upon the two major crises that antebellum Kentuckians still had to face: the verdicts to be rendered on the fate of black bondage in Kentucky and the future of the commonwealth in relation to the Union. During the turmoil over slavery, the commonwealth seemed, in many ways, almost a replica of the entire nation. Kentuckians were vexed by tensions between opponents and defenders of slavery, between radical abolitionists and anxious proponents of Negro removal, between poverty and wealth, and, ultimately, by the conflict over freedom itself: a jealous

11. Bertram Wyatt-Brown, "Religion and the Formation of Folk Culture: Poor Whites of the Old South," in *The Americanization of the Gulf Coast, 1803–1850,* edited by Lucius F. Ellsworth, *Proceedings of the Gulf Coast History and Humanities Conference,* 5 vols. (Pensacola: Historic Pensacola Preservation Board, 1972–), 3:22–29.

12. Jacob Burnet, "Notes on the Early Settlement of the Northwestern Territory," *North American Review,* 65 (October 1847):335–348.

possession of whites only, or the birthright of all Americans? And when the moment of decision came to each voter, it may be that Kentucky's predominantly Southern pattern of folkways proved critical in resolving that internal dispute in favor of slavery.

It is a truism to say that, while there was some slavery in this state, it was an altogether unique variety of the institution. Lacking the vast and coldly repressive plantations devoted to cotton, sugar, or rice, which supposedly characterized slavery elsewhere to the south, it was said that bondage in the commonwealth became more a matter of personal service relationships than a capitalistic, profit-making institution: here were only sunny, cheerful places, immortalized by Stephen Collins Foster—and perhaps nowadays unconsciously celebrated on national television each year, in May, just before the running of the Kentucky Derby; here were the farms and meadows plaintively recalled by ''darkies'' sold down the river, longing for their ''Old Kentucky Home'' far away. Or, as a somewhat more recent historian tells us, it was in this land of ''ample hospitality and benevolent bondage that the folks in the big house lived and enjoyed life in those colorful and romantic days.'' [13] Given the choice, most black people would probably have preferred a Bluegrass farm to the steamy flats of coastal South Carolina or the Mississippi Delta. Few of the 225,483 slaves who called Kentucky home at the outbreak of the Civil War had a choice, however.

Contrary to prevailing belief, in some important respects slavery in the commonwealth was typical of the peculiar institution in the Deep South. Southwide, a majority of owners possessed only five or fewer slaves; two-thirds of the slaveholders in Kentucky held a similar small number. Indeed, as in the South generally, a large number of Kentuckians owned but a single bondman or bondwoman. Across Dixie, then, slavery was far from being altogether a system of massive plantations owned by a minute portion of the white population. Though the so-called true planter—owner of twenty or more chattels—unquestionably

13. J. Winston Coleman, *Slavery Times in Kentucky* (Chapel Hill: University of North Carolina Press, 1940), p. 47.

held a unique and dominant economic position in the cotton-, sugar-, and rice-growing states, ownership *per se* was not a "peculiar" status. Actually, in Kentucky, there were 38,645 slaveowners in 1860; only Virginia and Georgia had more, and their black populations were very much larger.

It would be misleading to overlook the feature that most distinguished Kentucky from the lower South, namely, the absence of a substantial number of very large plantations. In that frequently noted respect, the commonwealth was akin to the other border slave states. Kentucky's geography and agriculture were not conducive to many large-scale farming operations in the dimensions found farther south: long, wet winters limited the profitable employment of slave labor year-round, while the principal products grown—hemp, tobacco, grains, and livestock—offered no real economies if grown on a very large scale. Most Kentucky Negroes therefore lived on farms that were modest by comparison with black-belt plantations; indeed, even the terms *plantation* and *planter* had largely been abandoned by Kentuckians well before the Civil War. But it is possible to exaggerate the importance of that comparative difference. Apologists developed a powerful mystique around it, using that to argue that slavery was relatively inconsequential to whites, and that it lay upon the shoulders of its subjects like a feather.

The evidence speaks otherwise; for, while Kentucky had no system of vast plantations, and most of its owners held few slaves, the state's agricultural economy was undeniably dominated by farmers who were slaveholders. Not in numbers—Kentucky's slaveowning families made up only a quarter of the total population; the small, independent yeoman farmer was indeed king, and for years his numbers had been growing more rapidly than that of any other group. But ask how *wealth* was distributed, and the balance is jolted. The Federal Census of 1860 answers that key question: the average value of Kentucky slaveholders' farms was $8,387, that of nonslaveholders $1,452. In fact, the cash value of slave farms represented more than 70 percent of the total value of *all* Kentucky farms in 1860, and none of those figures includes the value of the slaves themselves.

The census suggests the answer to such a discrepancy. Farms

employing slave labor were more productive, earning substantially more income for their owners. The statistics are startling. Slave farms produced approximately two-thirds of the state's wheat and livestock, more than half of the corn and tobacco, and 95 percent of the hemp sold by Kentuckians in 1860. The explanation is simple: slaveholders' farms were larger and were generally located on better soil. Actually, nearly 60 percent of the cleared, arable land in Kentucky was farmed by slave labor or slaves working alongside whites. Taking statistical comparison one step further, the state's owners of ten or more slaves represented but 2 percent of the rural population; yet, they owned a majority of all slaves, possessed more improved acreage, and produced more of the farm products sold in 1860 than did *all* the small, nonslaveholding farmers put together. Clearly, if slavery was unprofitable in Kentucky, all agriculture was unprofitable.[14]

Slaves had also occupied a position of unique importance in the state's urban and industrial life. Factories processing hemp, cotton, and wool, which had flourished in Lexington for a time, were largely manned by slaves rented or purchased for those jobs. Though such occupations had declined over the years, those that continued to exist often fell by default to an unusual number of skilled blacks, because whites exhibited a decided preference for the agricultural life. It was, disproportionately, black people who labored on the docks and wagons of Louisville, and it was they who built many of the state's streets, bridges, and canals, and waited on tables in private homes and hotels. The arrival of increasing numbers of European immigrants in the last two decades before the war created competition and tension, and with many rural Kentuckians entrapped by land problems into becoming tenants or day laborers, slavery was under rising pressures on the farm as well as in the city. But so long as "the rich hold labor in contempt, and frequently make the possession of slaves a criterion of merit," as an early

14. This evaluation from the 1860 Census is taken from Richard L. Troutman's analysis of selected representative counties in his "The Social and Economic Structure of Kentucky Agriculture, 1850–1860" (Ph.D. diss., University of Kentucky, 1958), pp. 33, 38, 50, 70–76.

writer observed, the institution clung to a peculiar strength in the commonwealth.[15] Slavery, then, was no mere domestic convenience, for ownership was both widespread and a source of economic advantage.

Once that is recognized, the determination of Kentucky's antislavery movement is even more impressive. The motives of those involved, which frankly included racial hostility and economic jealousies, were not always laudable. Yet it must be said, to the everlasting honor of the state, that until 1850 Kentucky was the arena for the fullest and most prolonged public debate over slavery ever to occur in any of the slave states of the Union. Among the chief arguments against the institution was that of Christian piety. Ministers had led the effort to purge the commonwealth of slavery in the 1790s, and certain Baptist ministers kept the fight going against avarice and apathy in the early decades of the nineteenth century. The Kentucky Abolition Society was founded by such men in 1808, and although it sputtered to a close during the Relief wars of the 1820s, it was perhaps prophetic of the fate of the entire movement. A good deal of vague antislavery feeling existed, but with white and black immigration high and slave labor employed in diverse ways, the group made little headway.

The inevitable rejoinder to moralistic appeals was: What about the freedmen? Will they remain here, and with what rights? Antislavery folk seemed to have succeeded in preserving the Revolutionary era sense that slavery was somehow wrong; yet their efforts were daunted by these pragmatic concerns. Removed from those days by more than a century, one might reply that it was mere racism. But who then could point to any society in which the two races lived together as equals? Most of the northern states had undergone successful gradual emancipation programs, but that model was spurned. "With them the evil to be subdued was a pygmy," the Kentucky legislature officially lamented in 1828, "with us it is a monster." [16]

15. Samuel R. Brown, *The Western Gazeteer or Emigrant's Directory* (Auburn, N.Y.: H. C. Southwick, 1817).

16. William E. Connelley and E. Merton Coulter, *History of Kentucky,* 5 vols. (Chicago: The American Historical Society, 1922), 2:800.

A way of apparently subduing both hobgoblins and legitimate anxieties arose with the birth of the American Colonization Society in 1816. Founded at Washington, D.C., the society reflected both the heady spirit of national pride and confidence then current and the conservative antislavery mood of enlightened rationalism prevalent during the Revolutionary era. Its program seemed subtle and clever; the society proposed to establish a sanctuary in Africa to repatriate free Negroes and freed slaves—first by the hundreds and, ultimately, perhaps the entire Afro-American population. To those who wished the entire hateful institution put on a gradual road to extinction, to those pious and cautious slaveholders who only wished to rid their own consciences of their personal black burden, and to those who cared little about slavery (or even approved it) but desired to expunge their communities of free blacks, such a society seemed to meet all needs. For a time, the society grew prodigiously in Kentucky. Henry Clay was one of its founding fathers and served for a time as its president. By 1832, there were thirty-one local chapters in the state, and the legislature had given them its approbation—but no funds. The problem of money had already become a sore point, however, for even to colonize only Kentucky's small free-black population (which was about six thousand during the 1830s) would have cost upwards of $150,000. To colonize merely the increase in the slave population of seventeen thousand during that decade would bring the total to $600,000, leaving all those who were slaves in Kentucky as of 1830 unaffected.

Money was far from the only problem that had begun to chill the prospects of the society. More critical was the contest for public opinion in state and nation. Beginning with the publication of William Lloyd Garrison's newspaper *The Liberator* in January 1831, a far more militant abolitionist appeal began to be heard. Garrison, who had worked as an agent of the society during the 1820s, targeted its members for relentless attack as misguided or blatantly hypocritical apologists for the evil of slavery. As a propaganda ploy, his tactic was brilliant, for the national organization never recovered the prestige and financial support of northern antislavery men it had previously enjoyed. These problems, combined with the certain fact that most Afro-

Americans utterly rejected the colonization idea, served to drain life from the American Colonization Society. Although the society was able to establish the colony of Liberia, with the aid of the federal government, as its proposed sanctuary, only a few thousand black Americans—among them a relative handful of Kentuckians—ever retraced the ancient routes of the slave ships back to Africa.

Ironically, the society also suffered in states such as Kentucky by a kind of guilt by association with radical abolitionism. The period of Andrew Jackson's presidency was a time of intellectual and social ferment, and Kentucky emancipationists of every stripe were emboldened to declare themselves, including those who were nominally members of the Colonization Society. Even the more uncompromising message was disseminated in the commonwealth by visiting speakers and pamphleteers, though the experience of Danville native James G. Birney was a forbidding one. Birney's efforts to launch an antislavery newspaper were squelched in typical fashion when a "committee of gentlemen" bought out his printer, and the local postmaster refused to accept abolitionist materials. "The freedom of the press is one thing—" declared the Kentucky legislature on the whole phenomenon, "licentiousness another." [17] Kentucky demonstrated more restraint on these matters than most, for she experienced far less of the mob violence that brutalized many *bona fide* abolitionists in northern cities and suspected infiltrators in Southern rural districts during the 1830s. But Kentuckians certainly reacted against serious consideration of antislavery actions. In part, the reaction was against outside agitators and outside criticism. More to the point, however, was a revulsion against the antislavery idea itself. Black emancipation without black deportation seemed unthinkable.

The monster, however, would not lie still. For one thing, agitation not only did not cease, it escalated into the realm of national politics. Denounce it, ignore it, do what they would, the people of the slave states could not arrest the antipathy their northern countrymen were developing toward the peculiar institution. Kentuckians were made painfully aware of that when

17. Connelley and Coulter, *History of Kentucky,* 2:803.

Henry Clay was defeated by Tennessean James K. Polk in the presidential election of 1844. Because of votes cast for the small abolitionist Liberty party in New York, Clay lost that state and the national election. A haunting touch was that the founder and nominee of the third party was Kentuckian James G. Birney. All the great political issues of the 1840s—Texas annexation, California and western expansion, and the Mexican War, to name the largest—became inextricably involved with the question of the future security of slavery.

But more disturbing to Kentuckians were the immediate problems surrounding the present status of slavery. The issue of runaway slaves, for example, had long vexed owners in the state with a special intensity. No other slave state had so long a border as Kentucky had with free states. Despite the fact that the entire border was guarded by the broad Ohio River, which lay entirely within the commonwealth, thousands of desperate, determined runaways had escaped northward since the eighteenth century. Slavery apologists liked to believe that that costly migration could only have been caused by the meddling of white and black abolitionists, mostly Yankees, coming into Kentucky's peaceful and contented slave communities to disseminate false notions and generate discontent. In fact, the appealing drama of a so-called underground railroad channeling fugitives to freedom has always been grossly exaggerated. Most of the agents involved were black, not white, and most of the escapees made their way through less systematic routes. But after the rise of militant abolitionism, border-state Kentucky was unquestionably a vulnerable target of abolitionist intrigue.

As a result, the later antebellum years were alive with periodic rumors of slave insurrection plots and runaway schemes. Most such rumors were the product of the imagination of frightened whites. Still, the potential for violence was always high in slave communities. An overseer suddenly killed by an exasperated slave, a white mistress poisoned by a long-trusted "mammy," the cry of arson in a quiet countryside—these were ordinary events that now sparked extraordinary rumors. Kentucky slaveholders believed themselves to be more kindly and paternalistic than the average and believed their black people to be more genuinely contented than anywhere else in the nation.

They all claimed to know blacks perfectly. Yet few indeed truly recognized the strains and latent abuses in a system of "toil without recompense, life without liberty, law without justice, wrongs without redress . . . punishment without guilt, and families without marriage," as John Young, president of Danville's Centre College, described it in 1835.[18] Kentucky's slaves generally lived on farms that were comparatively modest; but while that offered certain benefits, it also meant that white surveillance and supervision—the master's presence—was unremitting. In a way, the field hands on a plantation in the Deep South at least had each other's company in greater numbers and perhaps were better able to work out a sense of separate black cultural life and identity. Even putting that aside, however, the reason for escape too often was no mystery at all. "To be compelled to stand by and see you whip and lash my wife without mercy when I could afford her no protection . . . was more than I felt it to be the duty of a slave husband to endure while the way was open to Canada." So wrote famed runaway Henry Bibb to his former Trimble County owner. "My infant child was also frequently flogged . . . until its skin was bruised and literally purple. This kind of treatment was what drove me from home and family to seek a better home for them." [19]

The potential anguish went far beyond such day-to-day indignities. The world view of most, white as well as black, was, after all, shaped by the fundamentalist's Christian fatalism, which held that man's lot was not supposed to be one of continuous happiness, but a time of trial and struggle. The tribulations of slave trading, however, exposed its victims to a dimension of powerlessness over their lives, to arbitrary and mortifying abuses, which strained even the most morbid philosophy about obedience and rendering unto Caesar. No matter how cheerful and compliant the slave, the fact was that the fear of the auction block was ever-present. White Kentuckians contributed fully in that, perhaps the most corrupt and corrupting aspect of the

18. Robert L. Stanton, *The Church and the Rebellion* (New York: n.p., 1864), pp. 438–439.

19. Henry Bibb, *Narrative of the Life and Adventures of Henry Bibb, an American Slave* (New York: n.p., 1849), pp. 177–178.

whole situation. The entire business was replete with hypocrisy and deliberate fraud. The idea that the trade involved few in number, that selling was never done for mere personal profit but for other compelling reasons, that no "good" Kentucky master would ever sell his people, that black families were commonly sold as units and rarely broken up—those dishonesties and more were built up as integral strands in the fabric of self-deception woven by antebellum whites and perpetuated thereafter.

Kentucky's black population had always been in a condition of dynamic change. By the 1830s, the earlier rapid rate of increase had slowed considerably. The fact that the best lands were largely taken, combined with the economic troubles of the Relief years and the dramatic expansion of the plantation system westward into Mississippi, Arkansas, and Texas induced many Kentucky families to move with their property to new homesteads on those more fertile cotton lands. Yet here and there were ominous signs of the slave-trading orgy to come. Coffles or caravans of slaves in irons could be seen being marched through Lexington or transported on river flatboats bound southward even before 1820. Ten years later, it was apparent that significant numbers of Negroes were being sold to buyers in the lower South. In 1833, responding to antislavery agitation, the Kentucky legislature adopted a law forbidding the importation of slaves destined for sale out of state. Clearly, slaves were being brought into the Kentucky "clearinghouse," probably down the Ohio River from eastern states, to be sold in one of the growing Bluegrass slave markets. Of course, native black men and women were unprotected by the legislation. Every slave was vulnerable to sale from a variety of domestic, intrastate causes. An owner might die intestate, leaving his property to be sold at auction by the county sheriff. Incorrigible troublemakers were commonly sold off. Farmers were inveterate traders, always looking for a sharp deal on a piece of land, a cow—or a slave. Priding themselves on having a higher sense of paternalism than most, many Kentuckians made it clear that they would resist separation of slave husbands from wives, children from mothers; but the threat of bankruptcy could easily make a mockery of such noble resolutions, no matter how sincere.

Such local dangers made the risk of sale enough of a worry for Kentucky blacks. An additional and far more sinister threat, however, lay in the renewed push to maximize cotton production in the lower South in the last two decades before secession. In addition to supplying other staple crops, the South provided most of the world's raw cotton, and production soared in response to the unusually high prices and demand of the 1840s and 1850s. With the foreign slave trade closed to them, planters had to obtain the laborers needed from within the slave states. As a result, during the single peak decade of the 1850s, more than 43,000 slaves were exported from Kentucky alone, representing nearly 16 percent of her entire slave population. Of course, many of these were predominantly younger men and women, who migrated as part of whole families, white and black, vacating less profitable soils for the deep and loamy plains of a new western estate. But the majority went by way of the auction block, to be degraded—grey hair darkened with boot-black, illness disguised as health, voyeurism gratified—and publicly sold at such market places as Cheapside, across the street from the county courthouse in Lexington.

The town experienced a minor revival feeding off that human traffic, and while a sensitive few wished the haggling would take place at some more discreet location, few failed to understand why the trade was flourishing: it was not because slavery was unprofitable in the commonwealth, though no expansion was likely, and not because slaveowners were eager to join the ranks of the nonslaveholder. Rather, it was because of the exceptional prices available. Farmers proved all too ready to respond to the hundreds of advertisements that flooded country and city newspapers announcing auctions or promising $1,000 or $1,200 for "No. 1 young men or women." Such prices could make the difference between financial success or just breaking even, since at least 10 percent of the average total income of slaveholders in the exporting states derived from interstate sales. What was profitable trade to the owners, however, created an intense drama of quiet anguish in the black community. Here was threatening motivation enough for desperate escape attempts across the Ohio.[20]

Slaveholding and landholding were growing more concentrated; posses were seen regularly riding off to subdue bands of runaways; slave-mongering was increasing; and all these things remained obnoxious to many Kentuckians. In 1838, emancipationists supported a proposed constitutional convention to consider the future of slavery, but the proposal was defeated by a decisive majority. By the late 1840s, sentiment strongly favored a convention to rewrite the aging and flawed state constitution; dedicated reformers saw that as perhaps their last opportunity to educate and persuade the people into supporting a gradual emancipation scheme. Many problems needed attention, but that was not evident from the campaign for delegates to the 1849 convention. It was slavery and antislavery, from the mountains to the Mississippi. And what a spectacle it became. That was no era of the cool approach or the sating of interest through the medium of television; it was a struggle for support from a people who adored the word, written and spoken. Every newspaper ranted on, virtually every town and village was the scene of a heated debate. Whatever the outcome, the people got their money's worth in oratory and spectacle.

The antislavery group was blessed with leadership from some of the most admirable men in Kentucky history. Although too ill to take an active role, Henry Clay contributed significantly as an organizer and as author of a widely read statement ridiculing the proslavery faction's lack of logic and favoring gradual, compensated emancipation and colonization. The towering figure in the fight, however, was Presbyterian minister Robert J. Breckinridge, then in the midst of his successful tenure as state school superintendent. An eloquent debater, Breckinridge skillfully combined moral objections with powerful economic arguments directed at the self-interest of Kentucky's nonslaveholding

20. Richard Sutch, "The Treatment Received by American Slaves: A Critical Review of the Evidence Presented in *Time on the Cross,*" *Explorations in Economic History,* 12 (October 1975):396–417; and "The Breeding of Slaves for Sale and the Westward Expansion of Slavery, 1850–1860," in *Race and Slavery in the Western Hemisphere: Quantitative Studies,* edited by Stanley L. Engerman and Eugene D. Genovese (Princeton: Princeton University Press, 1975), pp. 173–210.

farmers and laborers. It was wise strategy to play down the
moral appeal, for it smacked too strongly of Garrisonian militancy. As a result, nowhere did the economic argument flower
so luxuriantly as in Kentucky. Men whose credentials were im-
peccable came forward to deplore the painful cultural and physical impact of slavery. Among them was Judge Samuel Nicholas, son of the famed conservative George Nicholas. No one
could "cross the line from a slave state into a free state," wrote
Nicholas, "without being struck with the contrast in all the elements of visible prosperity." [21] But when jobs and economic
opportunity for whites is mentioned, attention is inevitably
drawn to the greatest spokesman for the white yeomanry in the
entire pre-Civil War South.

Fiery is the word commonly used to characterize Cassius
Marcellus Clay, and that barely captures his ardent spirit. Clay
spent a lifetime raging at a multitude of public and private
enemies. Tilting at windmills, some said; out for personal
power and reputation, declared others. All of that was true; yet
we cannot help marveling at his energy. Son of the slaveholder
Green Clay, young Cassius had always gone his own way. That
path led to study at Yale College, which helped to nourish his
budding antislavery sensitivities. Why were the yeomen of Kentucky apparently less prosperous than those living in the harsher
climate and thinner soils of Connecticut? Slavery was one reason; the absence of public education, another; and related to
these was the lack of industrial diversification. Get rid of slaves
and slavery, Clay believed, and Kentucky would move into the
mainstream of nineteenth-century economic change and progressive values. Clay was to be scurrilously and unfairly attacked as
a "nigger-lover," in the ungentle parlance of the day. Actually,
he was no advocate of freedom and equal rights for blacks; he
did not appear to share his cousin Henry's confidence in the innate competence of blacks, perhaps realizing, as an ambitious
would-be political leader, that such a stance was anathema to
most whites.

Still, no one doubted his courage to speak out against the
slave-power interests in Kentucky. He fought too many battles

21. *Louisville Daily Journal*, March 7, 1849.

for that. Unquestionably, Clay frightened proslavery folk for a time. When his short-lived Lexington newspaper *The True American* was finally shut down, in the summer of 1845, and the press shipped off to Cincinnati, bands of masked "black Indians" roamed the streets, exultantly beating, tarring, and feathering every poor Negro they could catch. But such intimidation only inspired Clay. He continued to speak, in churches and assembly halls when permitted, or under the sky when he could not. Clay gladly denounced the racist slurs of the opposition, but he was unable to develop the anticipated base of political support among either the mountain people or those living in other largely nonslaveholding regions of the commonwealth.

Undaunted, Clay and his polemical skills were of great value in the great 1849 campaign. As always, he believed he knew better than his milder-mannered colleagues of the obligation to carry the message directly to the people. "How can we get at the non-slaveholders but by agitation?" he asked. "The newspapers, as a general thing, do not reach [them]. We must seek them out at the crossroads and places of public resort in their neighborhoods. . . . We want men on the stump." [22] And men they did have, faced by a proslavery host of equally resolute speakers. All spring long and into the hot summer the debates raged. A cholera epidemic scourged the land, but the controversy was not to be stilled. Following a mid-July debate at the Paducah courthouse between James Campbell and Benedict Austin, two candidates for the convention, tempers became so aroused that the angry Campbell pulled out his pistol and killed his opponent. More horrible still was the brutal altercation in Madison County a month earlier in which Clay was attacked, stabbed in the chest, and beaten over the head before he finally threw off his assailants, recovered his bowie knife, and stabbed his principal antagonist, a man named Cyrus Turner, to death. Cassius was carried away, seriously but not mortally wounded, yet lost to the campaign.

In the end, neither the carrot nor the stick proved of much use in swaying the mood of the electorate. Not one candidate who

22. Asa E. Martin, *The Anti-Slavery Movement in Kentucky Prior to 1850*, Filson Club *Publications*, no. 29 (Louisville: The Filson Club, 1918), p. 35.

favored even the most prolonged and carefully hedged emancipation proposal was elected. Even the Reverend Mr. Breckinridge himself was narrowly defeated. As usual, the slavery
men had proved equal to the challenge. They controlled most of
the newspapers. They took the offensive on the speaker's platforms, pandering to the racial phobias of their audiences. They
showed themselves to be more politically astute than their opponents, as well. Not only did they control the party machines in
all the slave counties—they also cleverly conspired between
parties to field the strongest tickets to oppose emancipationist
candidates. Their whole strategy became intertwined with the
larger Democratic-Whig contest for state control. And the Democrats ultimately emerged on top as the party more closely identified with slavery, white supremacy, and the democratization of
the state constitution. The history of Kentucky approached a
great watershed. Within a relatively short time, death would
claim Henry Clay; Kentucky's first Democratic governor in a
generation would sit in Frankfort; and from Clay's own Ashland
district, proslavery Democrat John C. Breckinridge would be
elected to Congress.

The 1849 Convention that helped precipitate these changes
was itself something of a curiosity, with many of the state's
foremost citizens absent. Slavery was much discussed, but
mainly from the perspective of how best to preserve and protect
it against its enemies. Clauses were adopted making it practically impossible ever to adopt any general emancipation
scheme. Earlier in the year, the legislature had repealed the
1833 law against importation of slaves intended for sale. The
proslavery spirit was on the ascendancy. Emancipationists were
stunned by the events of the year, but harder times lay ahead.
Flushed with their sense of advantage, slavery forces moved to
destroy all vestiges of their opponents. Mobs attacked "radical"
newspapers in Louisville and elsewhere, forcing them to close.
Individuals noted for outspoken views against slavery were visited by county committees and invited to make tracks out of the
state. The night air glowed with periodic book-burnings, and in
1860 a new law legitimized these rituals by making it illegal to
print or circulate any "incendiary" document.

An unpleasant illustration of the hypersensitivity of Kentuckians during those years took place in Cassius Clay's home county of Madison. There, in the beautiful rolling foothills of the eastern mountains, had come an intense young abolitionist minister named John G. Fee. Son of a slaveholder on a small northern Kentucky farm, Fee had studied with the radicals of Lane Seminary across the river in Cincinnati. At first, Clay supported Fee's work, even giving him land on which to build a home and bringing armed friends to defend his right to preach the Christian antislavery doctrine. In 1856, however, the two men had a public falling-out, not only because Fee was advocating civil disobedience to slave laws, but because he had revealed his belief in the fundamental equality of all races. Fee and his supporters had founded Berea, a small college for the children of eastern Kentucky, white and—he hoped and planned—black. Tolerance for his activities had always skirted the thin edge of violence; Fee was mobbed more than twenty times in those years. But when word reached his neighbors late in 1859 that Fee had preached in the church of famed New York abolitionist Henry Ward Beecher and had overenthusiastically used that occasion to praise John Brown's recent raid on the U.S. arsenal at Harpers Ferry, their patience was exhausted. Before New Year's Day, Berea College was shut down and its teachers dispatched to Ohio.

Why had Kentucky, with its vast nonslaveholding majority and its lack of great plantations, chosen to emulate Mississippi in this respect, rather than strike out on a new path leading toward the eventual end of slavery? The impact on the nation would have been incalculable. Cassius Clay was an incorrigible dreamer, but was his vision of a free and progressive Kentucky such a poor one? After the 1849 debacle, emancipationists had bitterly chided the slave-power clique for its control over newspapers and county political machines and for its unflinching exploitation of racial scare tactics. Their opponents, on the other hand, ridiculed the naiveté of the reformers and stressed the native conservatism of Kentuckians. A number of proslavery men had revealed their true colors in the convention, when they admitted to feelings of dislike for slavery and pity for the bondsmen. Like most Kentucky whites, they believed the institution could be ameliorated but not eliminated. And like most, they were captives of their own racially stereotyped ideas about the Negro, convinced that his traits guaranteed economic and social chaos if freedom came in the foreseeable future.

Threatened property rights, states' rights, prideful resentment of northern interferences—these fears and more proved too great a hurdle for mere dreamers to leap. It is also true that slavery was not exclusively the economic burden sustained by kindly and long-suffering masters that its apologists liked to portray. And finally, what of the yeomanry, the tens of thousands with no personal economic stake in the institution? Were ingrained habits of deference, private ambitions for upward mobility, fear of competition, mere racism and the desire to keep all black men below themselves their reasons for standing with the pro-slavery faction? Each of these were motives of great inner force. Yet, in the end, the essential nature of cultural life in the state was also a consideration. The attachment to traditional folkways meant not only resistance to change *per se* or to the "modern" values tied up with the notion of abolition and free labor. They were part of it, but more fundamentally there was the sense that Negroes—slaves—were outsiders, beyond the circles of kinship that defined the status of all whites. Slavery and racial stereotypes had always worked to set the alien clearly apart. What would fill the vacuum created by emancipation? What would separate and define one's fellows from aliens and make order and sense in a free biracial society? [23]

Kentucky's role in the secession winter of 1860–1861 reflected the same imperatives. In many respects, the ultimate crisis came down to being a struggle over personal identity, a choice between conflicting self-images, conflicting loyalties. The contest over Southern secession and Northern resistance to it may be portrayed on a vast canvas, a cyclorama of great social and economic forces; but to grasp its full meaning, one must comprehend that the anguish was experienced in an intensely intimate, personal way. Great decisions occupied presidents and Congress, governors, legislatures, and constitutional

23. Bertram Wyatt-Brown, "The Ideal Typology and Antebellum Southern History" (unpublished essay, in the author's files), p. 24.

conventions. But in the last analysis, they were questions visited upon every citizen sitting on his cabin porch or in a city parlor: who am I, Southerner or Yankee? What do those concepts mean? Can they not still be embraced within the good old Union of our fathers, or must there be a political separation to preserve the abstract rights and the tangibly imperiled security of those living in slave regions?

Restlessly, most Americans turned away from the terrible idea of disunion, just as they had continuously turned away from the need finally to come to grips with the immense problem posed by four million slaves living in a democratic republic. Few citizens seemed as relentless in their desire to avoid those trials as did the centrally located Kentuckians. They had ardently supported the election of the politically innocent General Zachary Taylor in 1848, believing that a nationalist slaveholder reflected their own views. They had applauded the short-lived Compromise of 1850, and when their beloved Whig party disintegrated in the sectional division over slavery expansion, a majority of Kentuckians eagerly flocked to the banner of the American (Know-Nothing) party and supported its platform of unquestioning allegiance to the Union and hatred for Catholics and foreigners. When that, too, collapsed, the state moved at last into the Democratic column, less out of affection for the party of Old Hickory than out of dismay over the rapid rise of a new Northern party dedicated to free soil in the West and industrial expansion in the cities. Here in the Republican party was the organization so long predicted and feared by John C. Calhoun and his fellow slave-South defenders. Here, at last, was a formidable and exclusively Northern party founded upon undisguised hostility to the economic and cultural values of the South and the political intentions of her ruling class.

The Republicans were an unprecedented phenomenon. Born in 1854 out of disaffected elements of northern Democrats, Whigs, and Free-Soilers, they had captured two-thirds of the free states in the presidential election only two years later. As 1860 approached, a sense of imminent party victory and national catastrophe grew. Their nominee, Abraham Lincoln, was a disciple of Henry Clay, a Kentucky native, a moderate man, sensitive to the tragic dilemma of slavery; but the anxious

KENTUCKY

A photographer's essay by Joe Clark, H.B.S.S.

Photographs in sequence

Inside covered bridge, Walcott.
Cattle in pond near Franklin.
Horse near Lexington.
Men in town square, Franklin.
Farmer near Lebanon.
Road in Greenup County.
Rock wall near Boonesboro.
Harvesting tobacco near Germantown.
Berea College, Berea.
City Hall, Louisville.
Downtown Lexington.
House in Covington.
Frankfort.
Frankfort at night.
Louisville riverfront.

Southerner saw him differently and perhaps more accurately. Instinctively, the Southerner saw Lincoln and his party as wolves in sheep's clothing. Both nominee and platform denied any intention of striking against slavery where it already existed, and no doubt they meant it; but since John Brown had tarred all Republicans with the abolitionist brush, could their word be trusted? Was not Lincoln the same man who had described slavery and freedom as unable to endure together, locked in a relentless struggle for control of the nation, a contest in which freedom must prevail? Could the fate of the institution be confided to such uncertain hands? *Now* was the time to act, secessionists cried. The break-up of the Democratic party at its tumultuous Charleston convention in April 1860 meant not only the disintegration of the last remaining truly national organization; it also assured the election of Lincoln. Now was the time to act, before any overt act against Southern interests was inflicted, before a core of treacherous Republican support could be built up in the South itself, before slavery was diminished in the border states and cribbed and confined to the lower South, and most important, before the will to preserve the Southern way of life was sapped by time and patronage.

Southern fire-eaters had never before been capable of controlling regional opinion. On the contrary, moderate Southerners had directed national affairs since the birth of the republic, dominating the presidency, the Supreme Court, and Congress, and articulating a distinctive tradition of loyalty to nation and attachment to the culture of Dixie. No conflict was seen between these two loyalties because for decades there was none; slavery and the Union grew up together, thriving together symbiotically. But economic changes, North and South, over the past generation had raised grave questions about the future of that relationship. Many more Northerners now believed human bondage to be incompatible with the idea of America and held that a "slave-power conspiracy" was prostituting the national interest for regional gain and self-preservation.

Kentucky lay at the center of that uneasy balance, and her people were perhaps more alive than those of any other state to the perplexing nuances of the sectional controversy. Geographic location on the frontier of the two cultures was only part of the problem. Southern in folkways and economic values, Kentucky was also partly western in its frontier experience, partly northern in its diversity of products, typified by Louisville's lively town and factory life and Yankee and foreign immigration. Sensitive to the peculiar imperatives of black bondage, Kentucky was also the only slave state to have wrestled over the past seventy years with a native-born antislavery movement. Dominated for half a century by one of the towering nationalists in American history, Henry Clay, Kentuckians were almost as testy as South Carolinians in denouncing the undiluted and divisive sectional appeal of the Republicans.

The fact was that Kentucky lay at the heart of a web of interrelationships weaving in and out of the state in every direction. Elaborate accounting sheets have been constructed by scholars yearning to understand the diverse forces at work in the minds and souls of Kentuckians as they approached the hour of decision. Yet any such tabulation of self-interest and association is bound to end in frustration. Slaves, hemp, corn, mules, and whiskey moved along time-honored routes to Southern buyers, among whom were countless thousands of Kentucky emigrants. Yet the advent of the railroad had already begun to redirect much of the state's economic exchanges toward the free states, where a similar mass of former Kentuckians had migrated. Do such pocketbook or kinship connections determine the way a man votes on the issue of revolution? The cooling mineral springs that dot the commonwealth had long provided popular vacation places for Southern gentlemen and their ladies; but Northern visitors also joined the cotton planters at Crab Orchard in Lincoln County or Olympian Springs in Bath to play cards and watch the horses run. Whose votes were influenced here? As for slaveholders, Kentucky had more than any other state save two, but the evidence suggests that they were predominantly Whiggish and Unionist by tradition; they joined a majority of fellow citizens in denouncing the disloyalty and fanaticism of the secessionists. More strikingly than citizens of any other state, Kentuckians appeared politically enigmatic, Southern in culture, militantly hostile to the death of the Union. Both sides appealed to them, both sides desperately needed them, but

Kentuckians, seeking their own way, held back. Lacking the black majorities that excited deep racial fears farther south, lacking a militant band of younger slaveholders determined on expanding their fortunes, unwilling to abandon a tradition of devotion to the Union, realistic about the certainty of armed conflict, Kentucky held back.

So long as the crucial decision over personal identity and loyalty did not clearly touch the race question, a majority of Kentuckians would consistently uphold the Stars and Stripes. And in the election of 1860, few politicians dared do much except to affirm white supremacy. None of the four presidential candidates directly confronted the question of race relations and the destiny of Afro-Americans. All of them in effect endorsed continued life for slavery into the indefinite future. It seems appropriate not only that two of the presidential candidates were Kentucky's native sons, but that each represented opposite ends of the political spectrum. Yet even that is misleading, for Lincoln's Southern counterpart, John C. Breckinridge, candidate of the breakaway Dixie faction, spurned the secessionist, rabid-slavery-expansionist label. Therefore, when Kentuckians finally rejected both "extremists" and Stephen A. Douglas, regular Democratic nominee, to cast a plurality of their votes for John Bell, centrist candidate of the innocuous Constitutional Union party, they had yet to face either the dilemma of Southern nationality or the larger problem of race relations.

With Lincoln's election, lower South radicals seized the moment to inaugurate their long-awaited secession movement. Yet, on the very day that South Carolina led off the crusade, Kentuckians stepped briefly into the limelight to hold out the hope of achieving still another great sectional compromise. On December 20, 1860, a United States Senate Committee of Thirteen took up a series of resolutions proposed by Kentucky's senior Senator John J. Crittenden. With fifty years of service to state and nation, the silver-haired Crittenden seemed to have come forward at a propitious moment. He sought to place slavery utterly beyond the bounds of further controversy, beyond the reach of any national majority by proposing a series of constitutional amendments. Slavery, the interstate trade, and return of fugitives would all be guaranteed and the entire west divided to the Pacific Coast, slavery south, free soil north along the old central thirty-six-degrees-thirty-minutes line.

For a brief instant, the secession momentum appeared to stop, as Southern spokesmen Jefferson Davis of Mississippi and Robert A. Toombs of Georgia waited hopefully for endorsement by the incoming Republicans. At last, however, President-elect Lincoln signaled his opposition and the illusion was shattered. Crittenden's plan was oblivious to moral feelings about slavery, was antidemocratic in its perpetual guarantees, and it pushed slavery westward into places where it was either unlikely to spread or had already been spurned, as in California. Most dangerous of all, however, so Lincoln believed, was that the plan would provide neither peace nor stability, but merely postponement of the inevitable confinement of slavery. "The tug has to come, & better now than later," he wrote.[24] While hindsight cries out in favor of postponement, all such peace plans ultimately proved abortive, despite ardent support from Kentucky. And the war came.

Kentuckians had experienced a history of stress and challenge before 1861, but the furious struggle for the hearts and minds of her people during that year made all that had gone before seem tame by comparison. By the time the new president took the oath of office on March 4, the seven cotton- and sugar-growing states of the lower South had seceded and united themselves to form the new Confederate States of America, dedicated to the preservation of slavery and the Southern culture. The question of Kentucky now verged on becoming synonymous with the very fate of the Union. "I hope to have God on my side, but I must have Kentucky," Lincoln declared, and the question of which way the state would jump did appear to be the early turning point in the whole conflict. The entire upper South had held back from the first wave of secession, but by June, four more slave states—Virginia, North Carolina, Tennessee, and Arkansas—would add their strength to the burgeoning Confederacy. Kentucky was by far the most significant of the remain-

---

24. Abraham Lincoln, *The Collected Works of Abraham Lincoln,* edited by Roy P. Basler, 9 vols. (New Brunswick, N.J.: Rutgers University Press, 1953), 4:150.

ing four border slave states and the one whose future was most uncertain. If these border states added their three million people and rich resources to the Confederacy, victory for the Southern cause was virtually assured. Tiny Delaware, Maryland with its strongly Unionist governor, and Missouri, surrounded on three sides by free states—these could be held if Kentucky remained steadfast to the Union. But Kentucky secession would stretch the border of the Confederacy to the north bank of the vastly important Ohio River, imperiling the adjacent states and extending a potentially powerful bridge to Southern sympathizers from Ohio to Illinois. Lincoln did not exaggerate when he warned that "to lose Kentucky is nearly the same as to lose the whole game." [25]

The contest for Kentucky in 1861 became a nerve-racking affair, for while few shots were fired, the possibilities for great violence always lurked just below the surface. The stakes were high, but both sides feared antagonizing public opinion and losing all. Ironically, the principal movers of the chess pieces had been born barely a hundred miles apart, Lincoln at Hodgenville in Hardin (now Larue) County, and his Confederate rival, Davis, at Fairview, near the border of Christian and Todd counties. Crucially, the one had migrated north, finally to Illinois, the other at last to Mississippi, both as boys following their families, who fled Kentucky's land-title uncertainties. Both were inherently Kentuckians in their basic moderation and their love of the Union. Neither were war-lovers, and each craved peace on his own terms: reunion or Southern independence. A nation's trauma was symbolized by the chasm that now divided the two men.

The political situation in the commonwealth was like a microcosm of that distracting the nation. Governor Beriah Magoffin, the legislature, and United States Senator John C. Breckinridge had all been elected in 1859—a time of intense anti-Northern feeling. Magoffin and Breckinridge were overtly proslavery men who acknowledged the right of secession, while a dangerous

---

25. James A. Rawley, *Turning Points of the Civil War* (Lincoln: University of Nebraska Press, 1968), chap. 2, "Kentucky and the Borderland"; Lincoln, *Collected Works,* 4:532.

equilibrium prevailed in state house and senate. During the first months of 1861, the state seemed paralyzed by its inner division. Popular sentiment was antagonistic to both secession and coercion—use of arms to destroy the rebellion. Magoffin evidently hoped that Kentucky would join the new slave nation but was held back by majority opinion and by the certainty that an attempt to carry Kentucky out of the Union would invite a rush of federal troops into the commonwealth. By the time spring warmed the land, opinion still swayed perilously on the fence. The Governor's Neutrality Proclamation of May 20 probably expressed the true sense most Kentuckians had of themselves as mediators—spokesmen for peace in a land noisy with the din of plowshares being beaten into swords. Nevertheless, the proclamation proved to be a critically important move. Thousands of frustrated Kentuckians favorable to the Confederacy began to leave the state for the South; and the move also helped save the place—temporarily, at least—from the sort of guerrilla warfare going on in neighboring Missouri. Both Lincoln and Davis accepted the peculiar circumstance for the time being, afraid to push too hard and lose the prize.

But how long could the shadowboxing continue? As historian Lowell Harrison notes, "A bewildered observer from abroad might well have concluded that the United States had become three countries: the Union, the Confederacy, and Kentucky." [26] A photographic blow-up of that strange picture, however, would have revealed a thousand small violations of neutrality, especially in the tier of counties below Cincinnati and in the strongly pro-Confederate counties in the southwest, where troops were being illegally recruited and outfitted by one side or the other. Events were finally set in motion toward the denouement, after the crucial congressional election of June 20, 1861. With nine of Kentucky's ten seats won by Unionist candidates, Lincoln would no longer be silent, and two weeks later he openly denounced neutrality as *de facto* disunionism. All not openly defending the republic in this extreme hour must soon be consid-

26. Lowell H. Harrison, *The Civil War in Kentucky* (Lexington: The University Press of Kentucky, 1975), p. 9.

ered her enemies. A new age of loyalty oaths was fast approaching.

The overwhelming nature of the Unionist victory in June exaggerates the imbalance, for many voters had boycotted the elections; but a similar result in state elections in early August is strong evidence that public opinion was moving vigorously toward open support for the war effort. The trade embargo imposed on the Mississippi River and the Louisville and Nashville Railroad by Confederate and United States authorities also played a part in strengthening Kentucky Unionism, for trade to the South was now impossible, and the only markets for Kentucky goods now lay to the North. Emboldened by all this, Lincoln authorized the creation of the first camp for open enlistment of Kentuckians. The camp was located on the farm of Dick Robinson in centrally located Garrard County. The governor rightly denounced the move as a technical violation of neutrality, but that pretense was fast disintegrating. Open Confederate recruitment of men from Kentucky was going on, just across the state line, in Tennessee; and on August 30, the Richmond government appropriated a million dollars for the taking of the commonwealth. The last vestiges of neutrality were obliterated a few days later, when a Confederate force moved northward out of Tennessee to occupy the Mississippi River town of Columbus, Kentucky; the next day, September 5, Federal troops under the command of General Ulysses S. Grant crossed the river to occupy Paducah. Kentuckians had yet to join the war, but the war had come to Kentucky.

Paducah had acquired the nickname "Little Charleston," so distinctively Southern was the character of the Ohio River trading center. Confederate officers were therefore deflated by the absence of a popular reaction against Grant's occupation. Their chagrin was even greater, however, at the subsequent news from Frankfort, for the militantly Unionist legislature now wrested direction of the state away from the hands of their reluctant governor. Resolutions were passed over his vetoes by overwhelming majorities, calling for withdrawal of Confederate forces, making renegade Senator Breckinridge an outlaw (he had abandoned his seat in Washington to accept appointment in the Confederate army), and, at last, calling for federal aid and proclaiming outright support for the war to subdue the rebellion. During the fall, thousands of Kentuckians fled the state, many to return in time as part of a would-be conquering army. In mid-November, a convention held at Russellville in Logan County created a rival pro-Southern state government and, in effect, opened the way to the admission of Kentucky into the Confederacy the following month. Time would tell whether the commonwealth would ever be much more than a ghost haunting the chambers of Congress in Richmond.

The people of Kentucky were no timid ostriches, furiously digging heads into sand to avoid danger. Eventually, they sent tens of thousands of their best and brightest to fight and die on both sides of a hundred battlefields. The secession crisis proved to be a cauldron testing the self-images and loyalties of each and every citizen. For now, a diverse majority proved loyal to a war aimed at preserving the Union and restoring the status quo. But a short war became an endless, unruly agony, disruptive beyond anyone's imagination. And the ancient divisions that ran like a thousand tiny fractures through society began to widen.

4

The Age of Feudalism

*So, on a gentle April day, when the great news came, it
came like a sword that, with one stroke, slashed the State
in twain, shearing through the strongest bonds that link
one man to another, whether of blood, business, politics,
or religion. . . . Nowhere in the Union was the National
drama so played to the bitter end in the confines of a
single State. As the nation was rent apart, so was the
commonwealth; as the state, so was the county; as the
county, the neighborhood; as the neighborhood, the
family; and as the family, so brother and brother, father
and son.*
    John Fox, Jr., The Little Shepherd of Kingdom Come

ERHAPS old John Crittenden was right, after all. Perhaps any peace, any delay, any compromise was preferable to the war that came. More than half a million men,
white and black, Yank and Reb, were killed. Countless more
were injured in mind and body, doomed to carry the marks of
their sacrifice all the rest of their lives. A harvest of sectional
bitterness resulted, watered by southern poverty, defeat, and
alienation. Americans had been the self-appointed political ge-
niuses of the western world, vaunted creators of a new and superior form of representative government. What a cruel mockery
they now made of their political heritage. Slavery was destroyed, the "mystic chords" of Union preserved, not by the
wiser arts of negotiation and gradualism, but by the sword, in a

new and terrible sort of people's war. Few were permitted to stand idly by, for the enormous physical and emotional energies unleashed by a democratic war touched everyone, affected all institutions. As much as the Revolution of '76 itself, the Civil War became a maker and shaper of modern America, influencing for good and ill the nature of the presidency, the structure of political parties, economic and race relations. As we continue to honor the idea of the war as a new birth of freedom, therefore, we ought to remember that it also marked the tragic failure of our political system.

The currents of Kentucky's history were certainly profoundly altered by the war. In a way, that is surprising, since the state that had attempted to "secede" from both North and South during her neutrality phase continued to occupy an anomalous position in the struggles that followed. Believed by many on both sides to be inherently sympathetic to the Confederacy, Kentucky was subjected to federal military occupation and repeated loyalty tests. Yet was Kentucky's adherence to the Union truly in doubt? Confederate leaders dwelled confidently on schemes to "redeem" the commonwealth from the alleged yoke of federal oppression. But Kentuckians failed to demonstrate popular support when invasions were actually launched by the Southern army. At the same time, who could have predicted that border-state Kentucky, untouched by the Emancipation Proclamation or Congressional Reconstruction Acts, would have experienced the proslavery reaction and ugly postwar racial violence that did occur?

The decades that followed may fairly be described as the nadir of Kentucky history. The antebellum image of a democratic, prosperous, and progressing community was largely obliterated in the orgy of misuse and abuse of power that characterized the postwar years. The age of "Grantism" found countless Kentuckians eager to cheat the state and one another. The age of industry found too many railroad companies and other corporations exploiting and extorting the material and human resources of the commonwealth. The age of laissez-faire found public education and other services lagging badly behind real needs; beyond the few urban perimeters, provincialism intensified. This age of feudalism found the spirit of too many

Kentuckians numbed by spasms of lawlessness, vigilantism, and unprecedented personal violence. Beneath the surface, some quiet economic and social progress was definitely taking place, but the approach of a new century still found the people of Kentucky distracted and divided by a confusion of voices.

Kentucky never occupied so critical a position in American history as during the Civil War. Not before nor since were her people's attitudes and actions so consequential to the nation. Lincoln knew better than anyone that Union victory was far from inevitable. Arms and men, territory and strategy were crucial elements, but as the war became a desperate test of endurance, it was clear that these were of no value unless the will of Northerners—and Kentuckians—to continue the war was sustained. So Kentucky's posture remained a controlling factor, endlessly vexing both Lincoln and Davis. And this despite the fact that, militarily, the fate of the commonwealth was determined in the initial stages of the conflict.

By mid-October 1862, the last full-scale attempt to "recover" the state for the Confederacy had collapsed. Few Yankee generals would have believed it possible to secure Kentucky from invasion so early in the game, for the ambiguities of war in this theater aroused paranoia in the most bullish of soldiers. So it was with William Tecumseh Sherman, future nemesis of the Deep South. In the fall of 1861, Sherman was a nervous commander of the Military District of Kentucky, and all he and his suspicious fellow officers could see around them were active young "traitors" fleeing to join the Confederate cause at Bowling Green, while passive sunshine patriots awaited salvation from the armies of the northwestern states. Before him, Sherman believed he saw a formidable line of Southern troops stretching from Cumberland Gap in the mountains through powerfully defended Bowling Green to the Mississippi. And within the state, the Union high command saw intriguers and outright enemy agents circulating everywhere, in army camps and towns, threatening destruction of the Union army's fragile hold on the state.

The Confederate commander, General Albert Sidney Johnston, might have been amused to read Sherman's anxious correspondence, for Johnston's problems were to prove infinitely greater. At first, it did appear that Johnston's forces had the upper hand. The decision of the legislature to support the federal cause was a bitter disappointment; still, true Southern men honestly believed that that was an act of treachery, violating the real convictions of Kentuckians. The Southern troops appear to have mobilized more quickly, and high-spirited soldiers poised along a four-hundred-mile front, eager to push the boundary of the new Confederate nation to the Ohio River. Among native Kentuckians Jefferson Davis, General Johnston, and the pro-Confederate "state government" now seated at Bowling Green, there was little doubt that Kentucky would be "recovered," and no doubt that it must be taken if the Confederate cause in the West were to triumph.

Most of these plans soon proved to be riddled with flaws. By late December 1861, nearly thirty thousand Kentucky Union men had volunteered for federal service, and thousands more had poured in to the defense of the state from Ohio and the Northwest. For now, at least, Sherman was wrong, and those who had predicted a great local reaction against the mobilization of bluecoats in Kentucky were wrong. A majority of Kentuckians opposed national disintegration, and as the winter passed into 1862, a force exceeding one hundred thousand was gathering in the commonwealth, determined to begin turning the tide in the Mississippi Valley theater.

Johnston's difficulties involved more than numbers, though those were daunting enough: a force amounting to less than half that of their Union foe spread thinly across the length of southern Kentucky; supplies were inadequate; there were monumental problems of transportation and communication; and on top of all that, he worked with a staff of almost uniformly inexperienced and incompetent general officers, many of them erstwhile politicians. It would have taken surpassing military genius to maintain this western front, let alone capture all of Kentucky for the South. Yet many believed that Albert Sidney Johnston was just that sort of man. It seems safe to say that, next to the apotheosis rendered the Virginians Robert E. Lee and Thomas J. ("Stonewall") Jackson, no military figure in the Confederacy was as esteemed in life and revered in death as this Washington, Kentucky, native. Johnston had a richly varied martial career, and, like Lee and many another, had been offered and had painfully declined high appointment in the Union army at the outbreak of the war. A striking, large, and handsome fellow, Johnston was born to command, the very model of an officer defending Southern chivalry.

Though undeniably brave, however, Johnston was in fact unequal to the task before him. The perspective of a century suggests that task may have involved nothing less than the success or failure of the Confederacy itself. Among other things, Kentucky was a gateway to the Southern heartland. In her eastern mountains and down the Appalachian Chain lay the great strongholds of Southern Unionism whose manpower might determine the very issue of Southern national survival; more than anyone else, Lincoln was keen on tapping that region for the federal cause. More immediately, in the western counties lay the major conduits of rail and water, the Louisville and Nashville Railroad and the Tennessee and the Cumberland rivers. Under Johnston, time and resources were expended to prepare the city defenses of Columbus and Bowling Green, and fine fortresses they became. Yet the real keys, the two river garrisons, Fort Henry and Fort Donelson, were poorly selected, badly commanded, and inadequately prepared for the inevitable assaults. Barely six weeks into 1862, both forts had been compelled to surrender their positions, guns, and men to General Ulysses S. Grant. Meanwhile, both Columbus and Bowling Green became untenable and were abandoned; the river highways were open to Union gunboats and supply trains, and, indeed, the Southern nation itself was in danger of being split in half by a thrust down the valley.

Badly outnumbered and outmaneuvered, the Confederate armies were forced to retreat out of Kentucky, out of prized Nashville, Tennessee, down to northern Mississippi, dogged all the way by Grant. Determined to regain the advantage, Johnston recrossed the Tennessee line, and on the sixth of April 1862, hurled his force across the plains near Shiloh Church in a bold and ultimately futile effort to dislodge and destroy the Union army perched on the banks of the Tennessee River. Mismanaged and horribly bloody on both sides, the Battle of Shiloh was classic in posing Kentucky men and officers against one another. Here George W. Johnson, Scott County planter and governor of Kentucky's shadow-Confederate government, fought and died as a private. And here Albert Sidney Johnston, doing his duty as he saw it, as always, was killed rallying troops in the heat of battle.

These setbacks did not erase a yearning for the recapture of Kentucky; if anything, the idea now gained a compulsive quality shared especially by her sons who had come south to fight for the Confederacy. The passivity of Union forces after Shiloh provided a respite for concocting invasion plans, and by summer the Confederate desire for another Kentucky venture was irresistible. Davis and the Confederate Congress were sympathetic to the idea; it would take pressure off the embattled eastern theater in Virginia, regain the offensive, and restore hopes for controlling the critical Mississippi Valley. Many naysayers held back, however, fearing destruction of the western army and expressing doubt about how eagerly Kentuckians awaited rescue from Lincoln's "dictatorship." The prize was great; so were the risks. Then, in July 1862, one of those astonishing figures in Kentucky history burst upon the scene to help erase all hesitation.

Though John Hunt Morgan did not invent the behind-the-lines cavalry attack, he did raise it to a fine art. From the moment he crossed the state line out of Tennessee and rode brazenly toward the Bluegrass, there was little doubt that he was also riding into Confederate mythology. In the days that followed, he captured and paroled twelve hundred bluecoat soldiers; did battle when and where he chose, slipping away when the odds rose too high; cut telegraph lines and threw the Union command in central Kentucky into confusion with expertly dispatched false messages. And all with barely eight hundred men! Southern sympathizers delighted in these forays and liked to speak of the dashing and gallant behavior of Morgan's men, perfect subjects for Southern idolizing. Those not so well disposed recalled depredations by shoeless privates. But reality was inconsequential when measured against the morale-boosting image of Morgan's Raiders. What did it matter that the man himself was neither a native Kentuckian nor a planter aristocrat, but an emigré from

Alabama who ran a hemp factory and general store in Lexington? And in all the excitement, who noticed the meager handfuls of recruits who joined, despite his romantic appeals for a great pro-Confederate uprising? The stage was set for the "redemption" of Kentucky.

Sadly, after all the expectancy, the affair was a failure, bedeviled by the same problems that had afflicted Albert Sidney Johnston earlier that year. Rich stores of food, clothing, and munitions were captured, but the key ingredient, volunteers, simply did not materialize in the hoped-for numbers; altogether, about twenty-five hundred joined, where ten times that amount were expected and needed to sustain a serious bid to take and hold Kentucky even into the winter. In addition, Confederate commanders Braxton Bragg and Edmund Kirby Smith exhibited to an even greater degree the incompetence in planning, lack of communication, and failure to consolidate forces and concert action that had hurried Johnston out of the state six months before. After early advances, including a brilliant Confederate victory in the Battle of Richmond, the initiative returned to the gathering Federal host, and by mid-October the Confederates were marching southward again, with an enormous train of captured supplies—but bitter disappointment over the collapse of their real hopes. It may have been more than symbolic that the most significant battle fought during the entire campaign—indeed, of the entire war in Kentucky—occurred almost by accident. The battle that surged over the dusty pastures near Perryville, though unanticipated and badly led, killed or wounded nearly nine thousand men, all told, only to end in virtual stalemate. Bragg subsequently had to withdraw or risk sacrificing all, and with that enigmatic warrior went the last effort to compel Kentuckians to see the wisdom of disunion.

The easing of the invasion threat by no means brought tranquillity to the commonwealth. Earlier and more intensely than any other wartime state, Kentucky entered a ferocious contest with itself over loyalism. The air was quickly filled with charges and countercharges of treason. In fact, most Kentuckians were not happy with the idea of a prolonged and unimaginably deadly war. They yearned for its end, hated the corrosive effects they believed the war was having on the institutions of the Republic, on the courts, the press, Congress, and the presidency. Most of them remained Henry Clay Whigs in their hearts, and they shuddered at the notion of a country bound together by blood and iron. Increasingly, the mood was: save the nation, but not this Lincoln administration; but that hair was too fine for others to split. The ultimate testing time had come.

The result was an orgy of recriminations. At first, no group exceeded the state legislature itself in energetic pursuit of treason. Anyone participating in "seditious" meetings, displaying the Confederate flag, uttering disloyal sentiments, or counseling hostile behavior in others was subject to harsh penalties. Test oaths were administered to teachers and ministers, while hundreds of citizens, caught up in this broad, fine net, had their property seized and were stripped of their citizenship. Polling places became uncertain indexes of opinion as troops and stringent oaths were more and more frequently employed by state and federal authorities to assure desirable results. Unquestionably, there were Southern sympathizers and spies present. After all, thirty thousand Kentucky men were known to have volunteered for Confederate service during the war; back home, their families would be subjected to a virtual inquisition. The problem was where to draw the line between the loyal man unhappy with the conduct of the war and the *bona fide* enemy of the Republic. Considering the perilous times, an atmosphere of suspicion was inevitable, but when military and civilian officials—virtually all of them native Kentucky Unionists—attempted the hopeless task of really purging all forms of antigovernment sentiment, abuse and backlash feelings were also unavoidable.

That only scratches the surface of the problem of law and order in Civil War Kentucky. A multitude of factors combined to create a state of virtual anarchy that laid the groundwork for generations of violence. The effort to destroy local enemies of the war effort too often led to outrageous harm inflicted on private citizens. The worst offenders here were probably units of the Home Guard, created in 1861 to suppress Confederate organizing in the counties. Composed of unpaid volunteers, the Home Guard operated without proper leadership and restraint, degenerating in some instances into mere armed bands of regulators wreaking harm on real or alleged pro-Southern families under the guise of legality. Officially, their mission was to suppress treason and protect local Unionists; too frequently the effect was to provide an opportunity to annihilate ancient enemies openly or by bushwhacking. The memory of Kentucky clansmen was elephantine, however, and the seeds of future family and county vendettas were being carefully stored away.

As time passed, many of these county bands became disorganized, beyond the control of the governor. To counter their Unionist influence and depredations, Confederates authorized local sympathizers, especially in the southern and eastern counties, to form companies of so-called Partisans. By the end of 1862, it would have been difficult to distinguish between the contending forces, except that the one murdered and plundered under the Stars and Stripes, and the other under the Stars and Bars. Still worse were outright guerrilla bands that began to multiply like a pestilence across the commonwealth. Some were composed of deserters or draft evaders—from which army, it hardly mattered—and all were fugitives from the law. Kentucky had become a refuge for a mass of vicious bandits and cutthroats, among them William Quantrill, the infamous Missourian, who was fatally wounded in Spencer County in May 1865. Long before that, however, innumerable counties had become possessed by a condition of neither peace nor customary war, but an aimless violence and anarchy. Under these circumstances, how could loyalty be proven beyond a reasonable doubt? For as Sherman wrote, "It does appear that in Kentucky you are such a bundle of inexplicable family and State factions, that the veriest murderer, and horsethief, and dirty dog, if arrested can forthwith present credentials of respectability that I could not establish or you either." [1]

Ironically, the state that had held back from conflict and counseled compromise more urgently than any other now found itself suspended across an agonizing void between peace and

1. Sherman to Leslie Combs, August 11, 1864, in *The War of the Rebellion: A Compilation of the Official Records of the Union and Confederate Armies,* 129 vols. (Washington: Government Printing Office, 1880–1901), series 1, 39, pt. 2:241.

war. In no area was the situation more distressing to the Kentucky gentry than in regard to slavery. The wisest Southern statesmen had known since the American Revolution just how devastating an effect war could have on the delicate psychology of slave subordination. Yet here was the Confederate South, at war to preserve its independence, its Negroes, and the politics and culture built upon slavery. And the war would destroy those very goals. In slaveholding, Unionist Kentucky, the counterpoint was even more startling. For a long twilight period during the first year of fighting, Kentuckians failed (or refused) to see that the federal side they supported must finally embrace antislavery war aims. Nevertheless, despite public pledges and honest intentions by the Whiggish Lincoln and others, war was becoming revolutionary in its impact and direction, impelled by a momentum beyond the dictation of those who had set it in motion. What would that do to the loyalty of Kentuckians? What would happen to Kentucky slavery itself, untouched by the Emancipation Proclamation but undermined in a thousand potent ways?

The war fulfilled the gravest apprehensions of Southern society: loss of control over the labor and lives of all black people. From its very outset, the Civil War intruded into that peculiar relationship. In the summer of 1861, the signs were there to be read. Newspaper columns carried more and more notices of runaways. Instances of insubordination, always sharply noted, appeared to increase; these included work slowdowns, unruliness, and arson. By fall, commanders of military posts were being vexed with the problem of escaped slaves coming into their camps, seeking protection. At first the runaways were ordered returned to lawful owners. But the problem was also political: what if the owner proved to be disloyal or had actually gone to fight for the Confederacy? Within a year, Congress decided to hold the slaves of disloyal men to labor for the army, along with thousands more forcibly conscripted from loyal owners to work on fortifications, bridges, railroads, and other military projects. Union men howled, but the army would have healthy workers, one way or another. By these subtle and not-so-subtle means, slavery was being assaulted in wartime Kentucky.

The close of the first war year, however, still found Kentucky politicians willing to claim Lincoln as a native son. When abolitionist General John Frémont took it upon himself to abolish slavery in the Missouri District, the president squelched both proclamation and general; a similar fate was met by War Department Secretary Simon Cameron, when he startled the public with a suggestion that blacks be freed and armed to fight for the Union. Although Lincoln's private feelings may already have been pointing toward the certainty of abolition, he was not yet ready to antagonize border-state sensibilities. In December 1861, the Kentucky legislature reaffirmed that slavery was guaranteed by the constitution and beyond the reach of federal authority. The president had no public comment.

The revolutionary implications of the war were nonetheless impossible to check. In March 1862, with Kentucky apparently secure, Lincoln called on all the border states to adopt schemes of gradual emancipation. Owners would be compensated, and the freedmen presumably colonized beyond American borders. Obliterate slavery in Kentucky and the upper South, Lincoln reasoned, and the Confederacy would lose all hope of capturing those critical states. Instead of sparking a serious debate, however, Lincoln's appeal was promptly denounced by leaders in Kentucky and the other border slave states. Their intransigence accelerated the momentum building toward more radical solutions to the race question. Why this obstinacy? Democrats ruled these states, and their motives reflected partisan hatred of the Republicans; but more was involved. These men were, overwhelmingly, conservative whites of the rural-gentry class; they mirrored the racial stereotypes of their constituency. Probably few even noticed that Lincoln's proposal was also hotly attacked by free black leaders who opposed forced removal from their American homeland.

Increasing wariness about Lincoln's intentions climaxed later in 1862 with the Emancipation Proclamation. While the document did not threaten the status of slaves in Kentucky and other Union territory, the implications for the state could hardly be avoided. And the reaction was swift and hostile. Some Kentucky soldiers were reported throwing down their weapons and vowing never to fight for emancipation. A great many saw the proclamation as weak and unlawful, an appeal to Africa, to servile insurrection and racial chaos in order to salvage a foundering war. More astonishing was that most slaveholders were still determined to retain their "people." Paternalists such as George Robertson clung to their fading sense of duty. "I was never proslavery," the aged jurist reminded Lincoln, "but living in a slave state I have been necessitated to own a few slaves who are happier with me than they could be if free and of a degraded caste [as free Negroes]." [2]

Different in spirit were the incorrigible "Negrophilists," men, according to John Anderson of Side View, Kentucky, who "would sooner own $1000 in the nigger than $10,000 in a good Bourbon farm." Abetting that "strange infatuation" was a militant core of folk nervous about the future, angry about the disintegration of the race controls and etiquette they had all known since childhood. They included the Lexington neighbors of Sarah Shelby, who tried to have her arrested "for reading the *Bible* to my *servants* saying I was teaching them of Lincoln and Freedom!" They were the ones who would remain loyal to the Union "so long as thereby they can keep their 'niggers' & prevent your proclamation from reaching us." [3]

Fending off the proclamation seemed a major triumph, considering the *de facto* erosion of slavery, but all that was only a prelude to the political explosion that erupted over the recruitment of black soldiers. Back in December 1861, Secretary of War Simon Cameron was rebuked for suggesting such a thing, but rising white casualty figures and waning ardor for more of the same had broken down antipathy to the idea. By the summer of 1863, free blacks and even willing slaves were being received not merely to carry shovels but as arms-bearing soldiers. Responding to the storm of protest in the commonwealth, Lincoln chose to postpone compulsory Negro enlistments that year; the suspension was like a bomb ticking away, however, for how long would the state enjoy such special status? Finally, in

2. George Robertson to Lincoln, November 26, 1862, Abraham Lincoln Manuscripts, Library of Congress, Washington, D.C.

3. John Anderson to Green Adams, January 24, 1864, and Mrs. Sarah Shelby to Lincoln, October 30, 1862, in Abraham Lincoln Manuscripts.

March 1864, the urgent need for men broke down the last barrier. Blacks were to be enrolled, Kentucky slaves would be recruited, and all those entering service would be freed. Another crisis in Kentucky's inner civil war had come.

The issue was tailor-made for political exploitation, for it evoked deep and undeniable fears in the white community. Negroes with guns—here was dramatic affirmation of a manhood systematically denied for more than two centuries. Here was a powerful affront to notions of white supremacy, to white social control over blacks. From respected army officers to leaders in Frankfort, men of hitherto unquestioned loyalty now openly denounced Lincoln and the Republican Congress and went about the state giving speeches threatening armed resistance to the new enlistment policy. Ultimately the focus shifted to Governor Thomas Bramlette, a man of sound Unionist credentials. Rumors flew wildly about the state: Bramlette had ordered defiance of the policy! Bramlette was going to pull Kentucky out of the war! The governor's own correspondence indicates that he was indeed close to sedition. He denied that blacks could or should be citizens. "If you require a soldier we offer you a Kentuckian," he had implored Lincoln on February 1. "Will nothing but a negro satisfy"? As public feeling was fanned hotter and hotter, the two men drifted toward an ominous confrontation. That moment appeared to have been reached on March 12, 1864, when Bramlette telegraphed the provost marshall of Boyle County: "If the President does not upon my demand stop the Negroe [*sic*] Enrollment I will." [4] At the same time, word spread that Bramlette was preparing to issue a proclamation of resistance. Kentucky, already badly war-torn, seemed on the verge of complete anarchy.

On the night of March 15, motivated by wisdom or moving as part of a ploy to force the president to back down, Bramlette held a private meeting with some of the arch defenders of the enlistment policy. On into the early morning hours they met and argued, read and rewrote the much-awaited proclamation. It is

4. Bramlette to Lincoln, February 1, 1864, Abraham Lincoln Manuscripts; Bramlette to William Goodloe, March 12, 1864, Breckinridge Family Manuscripts, Library of Congress, Washington, D.C.

certain that his guests prevailed upon Bramlette to retreat from his perilous course, for the proclamation as finally issued called not for resistance, but calm. The governor was never reconciled to black enlistments, but Lincoln subsequently wielded both the carrot and the stick to get the program underway. Certain face-saving adjustments were agreed to in its implementation, while some of those counseling violent resistance were temporarily arrested as seditionists. After an initial outburst of anti-Negro violence, black enlistments continued without major incident. In all, 23,703 Kentucky Negroes saw military service, a total exceeded only by the uniformed blacks of Louisiana among all the states.

The enlistment policy was only one among many forces demoralizing slaveholders, weakening the bonds of control, and eroding the economic base of the institution. Traditional attitudes and institutions had been subjected to tremendous strain, partly because of the need to choose between slavery and the Union. One of Lincoln's warmest supporters, James Speed, had predicted that, in 1861. Hostility toward the Southern rebellion and support for Northern loyalty would control the behavior of the state, he told the president. "This hatred and affection must soon embrace the institutions of the one and the other." More cynically, Speed also saw that slave prices would begin to fall, "and the emancipation feeling in Kentucky rises and falls with the rise and fall in the price of slaves." The experiences of the next two years appeared to bear out Speed's prophetic words. With Sam Lusk of Lancaster, more and more Kentuckians seemed to believe that slavery must be blotted out, for "there is something about the damned thing that deprives men of all reason." [5]

The critical year 1864, marked by excitement over black enlistments and the presidential election, helped raise political consciousness still further. Carrie Purnell of Caldwell County was aware of it. Her husband was serving as an officer commanding black soldiers there in western Kentucky—not an easy thing, for most of the Purnells' relatives were slaveholders. Yet

5. James Speed to Lincoln, December 22, 1861, and Samuel Lusk to Green Adams, February 4, 1863, in Abraham Lincoln Manuscripts.

she was glad to tell Lincoln that the day was past when it was courting death "to say a black man had a soul." And from the other end of the state, Leonidas Metcalfe was ready to predict that the years of "cringing and backing down from the unreasonable demands of this slave oligarchy" were ending. In 1862, he was hooted down and threatened when he tried to speak on the steps of the Nicholas County courthouse. "Now what a change in public sentiment." He gave a similar speech on those steps in April 1864, and men came up "to say they endorse every word." That fall Kentucky joined Delaware as the only states casting majorities for the Democratic presidential candidate George McClellan, a good indicator of the unhappiness felt over Lincoln's war policies. Yet it is also worth noting that nearly 28,000 Lincoln votes were cast in this state (30 percent of the total). A Republican majority in Kentucky seemed a distant prospect, but the foundations of the party were being laid, especially in many eastern counties.[6]

As the war entered its final days, one did not have to be a "born-again" Republican to recognize the disorganized, fluid condition of things. The state was about to enter a new era of growth and change. Could her leaders disenthrall themselves from the clichés and issues of the old regime? The war had elevated new groups, new values, most noticeable in the accelerated development of Louisville. Elsewhere in the commonwealth, labor and agricultural conditions were disturbed. Slavery was demoralized, while it was estimated that more than twenty thousand adult white men had been lost to the state by death and other causes. But Louisville's population had soared; her commerce and industry prospered from government contracts, reopened river traffic, and the aggressive pursuit of new business. Political implications were inevitable. For a moment, there briefly glimmered the idea of realizing Cassius Clay's old vision: a Kentucky that encouraged industry, urban development, modernized agricultural and labor practices, along with revitalized public education.

The really fundamental question before the people was

6. Carrie H. Purnell to Lincoln, January 20, 1864, and Leonidas Metcalfe to Col. Jesse E. Peyton, April 20, 1864, in Abraham Lincoln Manuscripts.

whether the traditional leadership, the traditionally dominant interests and viewpoints, would continue unaltered by the impact of the Civil War. When the fighting had begun, back in 1861, Confederate leaders had been confident that Kentucky would soon join them, for they believed the Bluegrass gentry in "the richest sections," the men of "superior intelligence, influence and wealth" favored the South.[7] Worse than that miscalculation was the corrosive effect of the war upon the wealth and prestige of that class. In that respect, the situation in Kentucky differed only in degree from the situation in the lower South. Everywhere it appeared that the crucial postwar struggle was not going to be over "the attempt of northern radicals to impose their system but the sustained effort of the southern upper class to maintain their position." Every gentleman and would-be gentleman knew that those who had the power to deprive him of office and influence were not so much Northerners as the mass of folk all around him.[8] Had the war undermined the structure of politics in Kentucky enough to inaugurate a grim struggle between old leaders and newer contestants?

An atmosphere of potentiality hung heavily over Frankfort in February 1865, as the legislature received a message from the governor that seemed to point toward new directions. Here was Bramlette, erstwhile defender of the faith, telling them they must accept "as an existing fact, that rebellion had destroyed property in slaves," urging them to erase its "effete" remnants in Kentucky.[9] Instead, the house and senate angrily refused to ratify the proposed Thirteenth Amendment. Astonished and distressed, Bramlette implored reconsideration, for its eventual rat-

7. Jeremy F. Gilmer to Adam L. Alexander, September 28, 1862, Adam L. Alexander Manuscripts, Alexander Series No. 11, Alexander and Hillhouse Family Papers, Southern Historical Collection, University of North Carolina, Chapel Hill. Gilmer, a North Carolinian, had served as General Johnston's chief engineer in Kentucky and Tennessee.

8. William R. Brock, "Reconstruction and the American Party System," in *A Nation Divided: Problems and Issues of the Civil War and Reconstruction,* edited by George M. Frederickson (Minneapolis, Minn.: Burgess Publishing Co., 1975), p. 108.

9. *Message of Thomas E. Bramlette to the General Assembly of Kentucky, at Their Adjourned Session of 1863–1864* (Frankfort: George D. Prentice, 1865), pp. 16–17.

ification was certain. Yet so strongly ran antigovernment feelings that the legislators again withheld approval. Just a symbolic act, perhaps, but a powerful one, nonetheless, the raging of conservative men against the disintegration of their familiar world. It was also good politics, the opening gun in what became a successful reactionary movement.

By the summer and fall of 1865, it had become clear that the ostrichlike vote against emancipation revealed significant new directions. Kentuckians entered the throes of a remarkable political reversal. It is difficult to say how whites, divided as they were over secession and the conduct of the war, should have reacted to the peace news. One thing became certain: returning Confederate soldiers were being welcomed with an unanticipated wave of public sympathy. In part, the mood was concocted by political and commercial propagandists. Mainly, however, it was a spontaneous reaction, rooted in the desire for reconciliation and in undiminished hatred for the military occupation and the social changes imposed by the Congressional Republicans. Here was a situation rich with political possibilities for those Kentucky leaders identified as conservative opponents of the war. Peace Democrats who had fought a blind and self-defeating struggle for slavery and against the war began to re-emerge from the shadow of disunionism.

Cleverly, these antebellum leaders saw at once that they could best articulate the popular yearning for the restoration of old-time rights and traditional authority. And their ranks would be swelled with soldiers and officers returning from the Southern armies—for, unlike any other state, Kentucky moved rapidly to erase political and legal disabilities against Confederate military and civil figures. Before long, men who had recently been dedicated to the destruction of the Union would be clamoring for office. Elections in August 1865 provided an early test of the approaching shift. Republicans and "War" Democrats must have shuddered, for the emerging conservative majority captured five of nine congressional seats and narrowly won control of the state legislature.

Many Kentucky historians have referred to that conservative renascence as a belated triumph of disunionism, a case of Kentucky joining the Confederacy *after* the Civil War. Certainly the many War Democrats who found themselves pushed out of office and influence made that charge loudly and often. To some extent, it was a case of antebellum leaders returning to positions vacated voluntarily or involuntarily during the conflict. But a better understanding occurs when Kentucky's political experience is compared with that of the lower South. Thanks to President Andrew Johnson's hands-off policies and generous pardons for Confederate officials, the seceded states held elections in the fall of 1865 and restored to accustomed places of authority the very leaders who had raised and led the rebellion. Men who might logically have been rejected as intellectually bankrupt and morally discredited were asked to lead their states again.

Why? An absence of organized and attractive opposition candidates and philosophies? A mood of confusion, apathy, resentment? A failure to recognize the need for at least symbolic leadership changes to satisfy Northern opinion? Or simply a natural turning to well-known and still admired leaders in a moment of crisis? Surely all of these were at work in the South. Variations on these themes existed in Kentucky, as well. Long-time conservative leaders, recognizing the strong mood of hostility to the plans of Republican radicals, were ready and able to capitalize on the situation following Appomattox. Their victory in 1865 and ascendancy thereafter was largely a sign that many Kentucky whites were apprehensive over the future, felt antipathy to imposed social change, and craved a return to a world that was in fact gone beyond recovery.

But like it or not, a new postwar world was going to be born. And it appeared that black Kentuckians were going to play a prominent role in that world. Kentucky became a scene of bitter turmoil during the Reconstruction era, as her citizens wrestled with the Gordian knot of race relations. Although a Union state and technically unaffected by congressional Reconstruction Acts, the commonwealth experienced in diluted form some of the same troubles visited upon whites and blacks in the lower South. Human bondage lasted lawfully until December 18, 1865, the day United States Secretary of State William Seward certified ratification of the Thirteenth Amendment. Well before that, however, Kentucky landowners had begun to work out a new structure of labor arrangements. Left to themselves, whites could easily figure out ways to guarantee the reliable, immobile labor they desired. Whether mutually agreeable terms could be reached between black men, formerly slaves, and whites, recently masters, remained to be seen.

It soon became clear that the gap between white and black expectations was going to be difficult to bridge. Attitudes and habits formed over a lifetime were not easily shucked off. Whites, for example, were convinced that free blacks would be lazy, untrustworthy workers, and so they sought to bind them within a sort of grey zone, neither slave nor yet completely free. Annual labor contracts were a common answer, contracts that few freedmen could decipher; these provided assurances of work and compensation to the propertyless, impoverished Negro, but at the same time wove a web of restrictions around his personal freedoms. Apprenticeships were another instrument that, in effect, gave a farmer or craftsman the equivalent of a slave's labor until the young man or woman apprenticed reached maturity. Of course, the most important form of labor relation in the cash-poor South was sharecropping, whereby seed, tools, and land were contracted to landless black (and white) farmers in exchange for a substantial portion of the crop. In Kentucky, sharecropping was especially common in hemp farming and in the expanding central and western tobacco belts. The system, combined with the high credit interest of country stores that sprang up to replace the defunct plantation stores, locked more and more families of both races into a morbid cycle of increasing dependency and poverty.

In the jubilant days of 1865, the freedmen had looked forward to better days. They desired physical mobility, land, fair labor arrangements, and the ability to withdraw their women and children from heavy field labor. They sought legal security for marriage and the right to establish independent churches. A thirst for education was clearly evident. Emancipation also signaled a drawing apart of the two peoples, much of it initiated by blacks eager to be free of white overlordship. In 1866 the state legislature enacted a code of basic civil rights for the freedman and adopted the first black public education bill. Thousands of marriages were performed, many legalizing relationships that dated back for years. Freedom also set blacks on the move, some migrating out of state, most looking for lost relatives or better jobs. Almost overnight, such Negro communities as Pralltown and Brucetown on the perimeter of Lexington sprang up, as the population of the state's towns and cities swelled with the influx of rural blacks.

Not all was progress. In January 1866, for example, the authority of the federal Freedmen's Bureau was extended across Kentucky. The agency had been created by Congress primarily to aid former slaves in the states that had made up the Confederacy, but offices were now set up in the commonwealth in response to reports of racial abuse and coercion. For the next three years, the bureau remained a constant thorn in the sides of conservative whites, intensifying feelings of antagonism toward the Republican Congress and blacks.

Yet the beneficial work it accomplished was also undeniable. The state legislature had authorized Negro public schools, to be sure, but the meager funding provided merely the illusion of progress. Under the Freedmen's Bureau, hundreds of day and evening schools were set up; and, by 1869, more than fifteen thousand pupils were enrolled in classes. In the face of bitter hostility from landowners, bureau officers attempted to establish satisfactory labor contracts and wages for blacks. The Kentucky legislature had indeed adopted a basic civil-rights bill, but at the same time had denied to Negroes the right to testify or sit on juries in all cases involving whites and had also withheld the right to vote. In partial response, Freedmen's Bureau courts arrested many men charged with violating the civil rights of blacks and whites and handed such people over for trial in federal court. Similar efforts were made to enforce the new federal Civil Rights Act and the subsequent Fourteenth Amendment. Kentucky's legal system was severely strained, as cases involving blacks around the state were conveyed into the federal district court in Louisville on the grounds of blatant race prejudice and denial of Negro testimony.

More persistent and distressing than any of that, however, was the expansion of interracial violence. Of course, one of the distinguishing features of the entire Southern region has been its extraordinary propensity to physical aggression, especially homicide. Characterized by one scholar as "that part of the United

States lying below the Smith and Wesson line,'' [10] Dixie has been endlessly examined in an effort to explain and expunge the alleged hair-trigger tendencies of its white and black natives. The persistence of the frontier heritage of rough-and-ready justice, the influence of its Negro-rapist fantasies, the hypersensitivity of the *code duello,* a romantic fascination with martial skills and values—these elements and more have been brought forth. The fact remained that whether white or black, urban or rural, the southerner of the post-Civil War era was even more violent than other Americans.

The chaos created by the war played a role in this unhappy drama, and the formal end of battlefield hostilities did not end the hatreds disturbing the hearts and minds of the people. For the preceding four years, there had been a blurring of war and peace in the state, and 1865 brought no sharp, clear sense of the end of fighting. No major armies ceased operations and surrendered. Slavery did not end in any precise way until late December. The state had been under martial law from the summer of 1864 and remained so until October 1865, while federal troops continued on duty in Kentucky through 1866. One knew, in an intellectual sense, that the war was ended, the South defeated; but the evidence of one's eyes denied the truth of that idea.

The result was that dozens of Kentucky counties continued to be infested with marauding gangs. Some of the evil was plain and simple banditry. A whole generation had been taught the arts of terror and robbery, and some were unwilling—or unable—to abandon the excitement of that life in favor of dirt farming. In addition, partisan feelings were overflooding the bounds of normal politics. In those intensely clannish eastern and southern counties, where dominance swayed between the two parties, bloodshed was almost certain to follow every election. Deeper than these party loyalties were the old wartime divisions between Union and Confederate sympathizers. Union men were content with the verdict symbolized by Appomattox, but some former Rebels continued to burn with frustration over real and imagined injuries. Clearly, they were ''more aggressive

10. H. C. Brearley, ''The Pattern of Violence,'' in *Culture in the South,* edited by W. T. Couch (Chapel Hill, N.C.: University of North Carolina Press, 1934), pp. 678–692.

and were responsible for much the greater share of postwar violence." Large numbers of local Ku Klux Klans and Klan-like
bands sprang up here as they did nowhere else outside of the
former Confederacy, and these regulators "were active sporadi-
cally in various parts of the state well into the 1870's, longer
than any other state." [11]

How to explain that curious affinity for mob action? Part of
the motivation was undoubtedly race-related, for most activities
of the Klan type occurred in counties with substantial black populations. Slavery was gone. What would replace it as a system
of race control? The Negro had always been economically and
socially subordinate, outwardly servile, and beyond the pale of
the kinship circles that gave order to Kentucky society. Now, as
a free man, he was perceived in a more threatening light. Blacks
were withdrawing from white surveillance, attempting to build
up their own identities and institutions. They were preparing to
compete for rural and urban jobs, even using the Freedmen's
Bureau and other agencies to assert their independence. They
were "uppity," pushing with intolerable haste for all the rights
of citizenship previously regarded as the special preserve of
white masculinity. Combine these apprehensions with the general collapse of law, order, and public morality, and the results
were predictable.

Outrages occurred throughout the state and became more flagrant as federal troops were withdrawn late in 1866. A dismay-
ing picture of beatings, lynchings, shootings, rape, and arson
emerged, a violence inflicted not only on blacks but on the families of well-known Union men and federal army officers.
Former Christian County slave Mary Wright recalled the terrifying sight of disembodied Negro heads mounted on stakes along
the Cadiz road, with signs that read "Look out Nigger you are
next." [12] The main arena for violence, however, was the broad
swath of central counties running from the Ohio River between
Cincinnati and Louisville down to the Tennessee line—in short,
the heart of the state's population, wealth, and culture.

11. Allen W. Trelease, *White Terror: The Ku Klux Klan Conspiracy and Southern Reconstruction* (New York: Harper & Row, 1971), p. 89.

12. Gladys-Marie Fry, *Night Riders in Black Folk History* (Knoxville: University of Tennessee Press, 1975), p. 159.

The situation in Marion County was typical. In October 1866, blacks in Lebanon, the county seat, were terrorized by a large gang of regulators who destroyed homes and mobbed the residents. County officials had advance knowledge and did nothing to resist or arrest the perpetrators. The next month, the Lebanon jail was stormed, and three prisoners were removed and promptly lynched. Federal troops still quartered nearby were never summoned, and local authorities calmly announced their approval of the hangings. Protests from the governor were contemptuously spurned in public print, while citizens denouncing the lawlessness became themselves the targets of death threats and harassment. The reign of terror in Marion and adjoining counties was only temporarily restrained when state militia were finally sent in, late in 1867.

The circumstances in Marion and elsewhere suggest that much more than racism was involved; many of the victims were not blacks, but whites who were openly unsympathetic to the rule of conservative Democrats. A complex form of vigilantism had arisen, a virus of "official lawlessness" which proved exceedingly difficult to erase. Vigilantism is an old phenomenon in American social and legal history, with roots that include our most revered rebellion against lawful authority, the American Revolution. In the nineteenth century, vigilantism frequently arose in frontier settlements attempting to punish outlawry and create stable, traditional communities in a hostile environment. The Marion "Regulators" typified that pattern. They were not bandits or impoverished farmers, but well-known citizens of the gentry and yeomanry. They were men who saw in the postwar confusion profound threats to their accustomed status and power, men of property who saw all around them threats to their modest affluence, ordinary conservative men driven to violence as a way of restoring the traditional shape and behavior of their communities. Terrorism was a cheap, quick, dramatic way to achieve those goals. "A vigilante hanging was a graphic warning to all potentially disruptive elements that community values and structure were to be upheld." [13]

13. Richard M. Brown, "The American Vigilante Tradition," in *Violence in America,* edited by Hugh Davis Graham and Ted R. Gurr (New York: New American Library, 1969), p. 176.

Moreover, vigilantism worked. Unwelcome, "radical" notions could be crushed, outside agitators (and local Republicans) silenced or ostracized. Where black labor and social behavior could not be controlled, it became "official" policy to intimidate or expel troublemakers. The result was a gradual exodus of substantial numbers of blacks out of the middle tier of counties into the larger cities and ultimately out of the state. Two generations before the so-called Great Migration of lower-South blacks to the cities of the North, Kentucky was experiencing a tidal shift of its Negro population into the larger towns and, ultimately, across the Ohio River. Again, Marion County was typical. Its black population steadily diminished in proportion to whites throughout the postbellum period until it was actually smaller in 1900 than it had been at the close of the war. Replacing these "unreliable" Negroes was an influx of landless poor whites—an ideal social element, for their political apathy and conservative attitudes would not disrupt established control over local and state government.[14]

These social "benefits" help to explain why vigilantism flourished. There were other reasons. Vigilantism offered fraternalism, drama, and an outlet for frustration. Regulator bands in Kentucky embraced the techniques of the Ku Klux Klan: secret handshakes and greetings, torch-lit mass meetings, "supernatural" invocations, burning crosses, and the inevitable resort to vicious beatings and lynchings inflicted by hooded nightriders. Once the cycle of retribution and vigilantism was set in motion, it was difficult to stop. Each act of mob justice made it easier for the next. Even those who wished to break the circle or withdraw from their blood pledges found such apostasy a dangerous game. A Shelby County klansman who turned state's evidence, for example, was promptly lynched by his former comrades.

The most insidious fuel for vigilantism was the fact that it was countenanced and even encouraged by officials of the Dem-

14. Ross A. Webb, "Kentucky, 'Pariah Among the Elect,' " in *Radicalism, Racism, and Party Realignment: The Border States during Reconstruction* (Baltimore and London: Johns Hopkins Press, 1969), p. 32. Marion County had 9,004 whites and 3,589 blacks in 1860. By 1900, the number of whites had risen to 13,479, while the black population had fallen to 2,811.

ocratic party. How could it have been otherwise? The party's conservative leaders counseled resistance to lawful change, while their enemies were the very same men being attacked by "regulators." State officials were not openly in league with the Klan, and the governors of the period most certainly opposed terrorism. Yet the outrages continued, applauded by many Democratic legislators, accepted by county magistrates, and celebrated by local newspapers as the best antidote to "immorality."

The wanton murders, the frightening din of horsemen clattering through a darkened town, the conniving and cowardice of sheriffs and judges—all have the surrealistic quality of bad melodrama. Perhaps it has all been dismissed too often as merely the passing phenomenon of an unsettled age. But vigilantism was more than that. It was one of many danger signs signaling social unrest in postwar Kentucky. The fact was that all Americans were passing through the most trying period of social change in their history. The trauma of war and reconstruction had shaken the confidence of men and women nurtured in the comparative tranquillity of the antebellum era. Now an explosion of industrial and urban growth was altering the traditional economic landscape, creating new palaces of wealth and corruption, power and impotence. America was being forcibly remodeled by conglomerates of railroads, banking, coal, oil, and steel industries. It was the birth of a new nation, and the experience involved more pain than pleasure. Kentucky vigilantism would end, but the trials of the industrial revolution were only beginning.

While this commonwealth remained predominantly a small-farm, small-town society, it was inevitably touched by these new economic forces. The state's features that strongly attracted outside interest included the city of Louisville and the massive timber and coal reserves in the eastern and western counties. In short order, the real power to shape the economic life of Kentuckians began to pass into the hands of corporate directors in New York, Pittsburgh, and Chicago. Triggered by that penetration, new power blocs began forming within Kentucky to do battle for control of state government and the largest share of the economic pie. The basis for the new power struggle was commercial rivalry, a rivalry involving cities, railroads, crops, coal regions, and leaders. Quickly, a new version of state sectionalism emerged, embraced by the image of the Bluegrass and the East versus Louisville and the West. Though not altogether accurate, there was enough truth and historic tradition in that idea to reshape the very structure of politics in Kentucky.

At the heart of the question lay the continuing role of Louisville as Kentucky's only substantial city. Antipathy to that fact, particularly from Bluegrass residents, dated back to the 1820s, when the River City first vaulted into prominence. The estrangement increased thereafter, cultivated by the urban-rural jealousies and suspicions typical of the era. Louisville's economic status, however, began to be undermined in the 1850s as rail lines joined the seaboard East with the Northwest, a reorientation of trade that, coincidentally, favored Louisville's arch-rival Cincinnati. The Civil War brought lucrative contracts, but also new concerns about the future. The age of the majestic commercial riverboats was declining, as was Louisville's earlier role as supplier to the slave plantations of the upper Mississippi Valley.[15]

Alert to these changes, the city's aggressive merchant class launched a counteroffensive. Vigorous efforts were made to develop packet and barge traffic on the state's smaller rivers, in order to tap the trade of western and eastern counties, but that was hardly enough. In 1851 a million dollars was raised to help construct a rail connection with Nashville. On the eve of war, the road had been extended to the major cotton-outlet city of Memphis. Thanks to its importance to the federal army, that route, the Louisville and Nashville Railroad, emerged in excellent condition in 1865; and within three years, feeder lines extended as far eastward as Lebanon and Richmond, Kentucky. The L & N and its emerging monopoly of the Southern market—supported by municipal bonds and direct subsidies paid by the city—were Louisville's principal weapons in the ap-

15. This account is drawn from the work of Thomas L. Connelly, "Neo-Confederatism or Power Vacuum: Post-War Kentucky Politics Reappraised," *Kentucky Historical Society Register* 64 (October 1966), 257–269, and Leonard P. Curry, *Rail Routes South: Louisville's Fight for the Southern Market, 1865–1872* (Lexington: University of Kentucky Press, 1969).

proaching battle for commerce in the Ohio and upper Mississippi River valley.

Aside from its position at the head of the major rail route south, Louisville enjoyed another obvious advantage at the close of the war—its location in a "Southern" state. Brandishing trade conventions and expositions, special hotel rates for Dixie customers, and an army of former Confederate traveling sales representatives, or drummers, the city's mercantile houses, tobacco exchanges, and growing industries reached across Kentucky and Tennessee deep into Alabama, to garner a major share of the market. There was rich irony in all that. Louisville, a bastion of Unionist support during the late war, had long been pleased to think of itself as a cosmopolitan, western town. Now, however, her planners saw the wisdom of erecting numerous statues honoring Confederate soldiers and in other ways embellishing her freshly minted pro-Southern image. These expedients were child's play, however, when compared to brass-knuckled business tactics. Propaganda, spies, sabotoge, blackmail, and political bribery on a dazzling scale were the rule. The conflict between Louisville, Cincinnati, and, later, Evansville, Indiana, had all the trappings of international imperialism—and with similar motives: the attaining of wealth, power, bigness, and the exhilaration of war by other means.

The efforts of Louisville's commercial, political, and railroad leaders—the three were often indistinguishable—to maintain supremacy naturally aroused enmity upstream in Cincinnati. More intriguing were anti-Louisville animosities generated within Kentucky. Many real and imagined grievances were leveled against the city and its railroad: the L & N was inadequately taxed, engaged in blatant rate discrimination, served the Bluegrass and the eastern counties poorly, was deliberately hampering their economic development. These charges meshed perfectly with traditional suspicions about Louisville. The Bluegrass region, moreover, was in a period of difficult postwar adjustment. Its industry was declining, and the impact of the new and increasingly popular bright-leaf tobacco was only beginning to be felt. Meanwhile, western dark-leaf tobacco farmers appeared prosperous. Labor problems, worsened by organized racial strife, contributed to a loss of population, a decline counterbalanced by very substantial gains in Louisville and Jefferson County. Coal production had begun to have a profound effect on the state's economy, but most of it still came out of the western fields, thanks to their superior rail connections to northern markets, leaving would-be eastern coal exploiters frustrated. In short, the makings of a first-class political donnybrook were all there.

Traditionally, the struggles of the postwar era have been pictured as a classic contest pitting Neo-Confederatism, represented by the conservative, rural-minded Bluegrass Brahmins, against forces favoring social pluralism and economic change. In fact, such an interpretation is more poetry than truth. There *was* much unhappiness with the stunning changes wrought by the war; many conservatives even countenanced vigilantism to restore fading standards of social order. And Neo-Confederate invocations of Republican radicalism and lost-cause imagery often *did* win votes—and help sell Louisville buttons and whiskey. But the real contest was between the commercial ambitions of the central and eastern counties, on one hand, and the rising Lousville/western axis, on the other. The tug was less over philosophy than over spoils and influence.

That becomes clear when the principal squabble of the era, involving the proposed Cincinnati and Southern Railroad, is considered. Jealous, disgruntled Bluegrass and eastern leaders had gained a powerful ally in the campaign to build a rail connection from the Queen City—Cincinnati—directly through the Bluegrass into East Tennessee. The benefits for Ohioans would be numerous. No longer would goods southbound from Cincinnati have to pass slowly through Louisville, and the L & N's domination of Kentucky, Tennessee, and Alabama trade would be broken. Kentucky supporters were excited by these advantages, as well as the prospect of cheaper goods, faster exploitation of regional timber and coal resources, and renewed prosperity for Lexington and neighboring towns. Neither were the political implications ignored, as was obvious when the measure authorizing construction came before the state legislature.

The "Great Barbecue" of vote-buying and corruption in

Grant's Washington was being duplicated by lesser feasts in most of the state capitals, and Frankfort was no exception. The L & N lobby already held much of the region served by its lines in virtual political and economic fiefdom. Privately, it feared a loss of its preponderant position in Kentucky and the South. Publicly, orators were trotted out to denounce the Cincinnati railroad proposal as just another Yankee scheme to plunder Dixie. Leading the assault for Louisville was, appropriately enough, John Hunt Morgan's brilliant subordinate, General Basil Duke. Not to be outdone, the Cincinnatians cleverly hired John C. Breckinridge himself, former United States senator, vice-president, and (more to the point) venerated general and secretary of war in the Confederacy. Unencumbered by laws curbing campaign contributions and lobbying excesses and the other impedimenta of our present distrustful age, the two cities and their agents rained favors and threats upon the heads of the legislators. The entire house and senate, for example, was taken on a gala trip to see the new iron railroad bridge across the Ohio River at Louisville. Unfortunately, the locomotive hauling the lawmakers derailed halfway across; it was nightfall before serious eating and drinking could commence at Louisville's Galt House.

But if the path to "aye" votes was through the stomach, Cincinnati again proved equal to the task. The next day, her city fathers escorted the legislators on a splendid river cruise to Cincinnati. The Queen City assumed "that the Legislature may be bought," the *Louisville Courier-Journal's* ascerbic editor Henry Watterson wrote, "and she makes haste . . . to beckon the Legislature hence that she may have the last bid for it." [16] When all such "bidding" was done, however, L & N lobbyists had the last laugh, for the Cincinnati and Southern bill was defeated, not only in 1870, but again the following spring. Central Kentucky promoters were bitter, and there was considerable talk of pushing for enabling legislation to be imposed by the federal government. Strange talk from Democrats supposedly guided by militant states'-rights agrarianism!

16. *Louisville Courier-Journal*, February 22, 1870.

The situation seems mystifying until we recognize that Kentucky's Democratic party was evolving along new lines, in directions identical to the Southern democracy throughout the former slave states. Everywhere, Congressional Reconstruction was creating unanticipated "mongrel coalitions" calling themselves the Democratic party: "old Whigs, Know-Nothings, Unionists, secessionists, businessmen, small farmers, hillbillies, planters"—men who before the war had naturally aligned themselves on opposite sides of the fence but who were now joined in opposition to the "menace" of race and Republicanism.[17] The Kentucky Democracy had also begun to move away from the pure Neo-Confederatism of 1865 toward a more pluralistic base. Of course, Kentucky did not have a black majority to frighten whites into unaccustomed unity; but it did have a significant bloc of Republican voters, a party whose strength was destined to increase, once blacks gained the Fifteenth Amendment.

The emerging coalition party in Kentucky and the South was dubbed the Bourbon Democracy by its enemies, signifying its supposed similarity to the French royal family that had forgotten nothing and learned nothing despite its experience in the crucible of revolutionary civil war. There was some truth in that, for many mossbacked reactionaries longed for nothing more than restoration of the "good old days" of plantation slavery. Yet the greatest achievement of the Bourbons was not obstructionism, but their success in reconciling tradition with innovation. They *were* defensive-minded, they *did* see their communities embattled by change, with traditional codes of class rule and deference eroded. But while venerating the myth of the Old South, the best of them saw the need for social adaptation and economic development. Individually, their motives may have been personal power and personal wealth, but as a new political force, their contribution was inestimable. It was the Bourbons who propounded a new and equally powerful New South myth: the image of an orderly and progressive South that adopted the best of Yankee capitalism, success and wealth, while retaining

17. George B. Tindall, *The Persistent Tradition in New South Politics* (Baton Rouge: Louisiana State University Press, 1975), p. 13.

the southern values of time, place, community, class distinctions, and deference to a transformed "squirearchy." [18]

The foremost advocate of this "New Departure" was *Courier-Journal* editor Henry Watterson. While a natural defender of the prerogatives of the L & N, Watterson was far more than a mere tool of that interest. His vision was broad, his grasp of changing realities unsurpassed. And his solutions came out of the notebook of Cassius Clay. Like Clay, he saw the wealth of the North as a judgment on southern backwardness. Let us have industry, railroads, foreign immigration, and improved public education, he wrote; let us stop waving the bloody shirt of Confederate defeat and put down rural lawlessness as bad for business and worse for morality; finally, and most critically for now, let us ratify the real outcome of the war by accepting the Fourteenth and Fifteenth Amendments and developing the Negro's full potential as a laborer.

Relatively young men such as Watterson and Lexington's William C. P. Breckinridge had fought for the Confederacy but now represented a new generation, a new vision of southern development. The Wattersons and Breckinridges were helping to define the emerging Bourbon platform. The question remained whether Kentucky Democrats were ready to walk upon it.

The climax occurred in 1871. State elections that year are among the most significant in the history of Kentucky, because they marked a watershed confirming the evolution of the new political coalition. Only rarely do elections provide a focus for crucial social and economic decisions. That one did, and the issues involved formed the essence of southern Bourbonism. Would Kentucky whites accept the idea of equal protection of the law for all citizens? If so, their law forbidding blacks from testifying against whites in state courts had to go. Would they acquiesce in Negro suffrage, though that might overturn Democratic control in some counties? Would Democrats accept the existence of a legitimate Republican opposition and find the

18. Tindall, *Tradition in New South Politics,* pp. 17–22. *Bourbonism* is used to characterize this coalition of diverse and often antagonistic elements. Many Kentuckians at the time used the term as a label for the powerful Neo-Confederate, Bluegrass-centered wing of the Democratic party.

sources of continued control of the state in unity and new approaches, rather than race-baiting and intimidation? If so, specific steps had to be taken against the Klan and similar forms of vigilantism. Lastly, would some accommodations be reached regarding the great economic and regional commercial rivalries, the strong claims of agriculture balanced against the need for industrial diversification? If so, the symbolic issue of the twice-defeated Cincinnati and Southern Railway bill had to be resolved.

Never before had Kentucky Republicans run such an effective campaign, keyed by their gubernatorial nominee, a thirty-eight-year-old Louisville lawyer named John Marshall Harlan. Although he was a Boyle County native and had been a Whig and a slaveholder before the war, Harlan had fought for the Union and become a dedicated Lincoln man. In 1871 he represented all that was progressive in the state, denouncing the racist and reactionary politics of the Democratic conservatives and the corrupt monopoly of the L & N interests. His opposition aptly reflected the inner tensions at work in the Democratic party. Preston Leslie, the nominee for governor, was a sort of coalition by himself. Though conservative, rural-oriented, and a former Confederate sympathizer, his home county of Barren was part of the L & N orbit, and Leslie had voted accordingly, as state senator. Moreover, he was no Bluegrass aristocrat, but a self-educated lawyer, an orphan accustomed to years of poverty and hardship. Leslie's running mate, John G. Carlisle, of Covington, added regional and philosophical balance, for Carlisle ably represented Watterson's "New Departure" brand of Democratic politics.

The election would have stirred Kentuckians regardless of the issues, for Harlan proved a marvelous campaigner. He was big and attractive physically, and he projected a sense of progressive vision. Not only did some prominent Democrats come out for him, but even Leslie was persuaded to incorporate more enlightened ingredients into his appeal. Cincinnati and Louisville lobbyists were exceptionally active in organizing meetings and debates and engaging in less savory efforts to aid their candidates. Harlan and the Republicans declared for the Cincinnati and Southern bill at the outset, and under the pressure of the

contest, Leslie felt compelled to declare only a few weeks before election day that, if the new legislature passed such a bill,
he would not veto it. In the end, Harlan's defeat was predictable, for it was impossible to dissociate his candidacy from the
deep revulsion felt toward the national Republican administration. The results were nevertheless startling. Harlan polled more
than 89,000 votes to Leslie's 126,455; he carried 25 of the
state's 116 counties, especially in the eastern mountains, along
with many of the major towns (except for Louisville), aided by
black suffrage.[19]

Although the issues and personalities in the election were too
contradictory to constitute a true referendum, Governor Leslie
and the noticeably more youthful legislature proved responsive
to the mood for change—encouraged, no doubt, by their fear of
the growing Republican minority. Thanks in part to Leslie's
surprising leadership, a bill was soon adopted removing the
odious ban on Negro testimony. Partisan vigilantism had flared
up seriously during and after the elections, but the governor and
the legislature at long last succeeded in passing a law aimed at
curbing organized violence, especially by those who conspired
to "go forth armed and disguised." [20] Activities of the Klan
type declined thereafter, owing perhaps mainly to the sense that
the race issue was being resolved under the Bourbon formula of
acknowledging the Constitutional Amendments while co-opting
a significant proportion of black votes at election time. The
highlight of the session was the resumed battle over the Cincinnati railway bill. The fight for the bill was close and bitter, passing the house but ending in a deadlocked tie vote in the senate.
When Lieutenant-Governor Carlisle stepped forward to cast the
deciding ballot in favor of the new line, he must have done it
with a sense of helping to close an era in Kentucky history.

The Bourbon coalition sought to deliver the New South promise to Kentucky, and in some ways the pledge began to be ful-

19. Harlan's reputation as one of Kentucky's most distinguished sons is, of course,
largely related to his thirty-three-year service as associate justice of the United States
Supreme Court.

20. E. Merton Coulter, *The Civil War and Readjustment in Kentucky* (Chapel Hill:
University of North Carolina Press, 1926), p. 365.

filled. During the last third of the century, the state hummed
with many new enterprises. The key remained railroad construction that ribbed the commonwealth in 1900 with three times the
track mileage it had in 1870. Who could deny the benefits?
Markets were closer, goods cheaper; new industries sprang up
to poke life and wealth into sleepy country towns. Coal, oil, and
timber production now leaped forward in response to demands
from neighboring states. Standard indexes tell an important
story. From the end of the Civil War to 1900, the number of industries in Kentucky, the dollars and workers involved in them,
and their productivity all increased three to five times. Kentucky's per capita income remained far below the national
average, but was still the highest of all the southern states.
Signs of change were especially evident in urban areas, where
such modern paraphernalia as electric streetcars and lights, telephones, and suburban residences were attracting white and
black rural immigrants. Though Louisville retained the lion's
share of this increased population, diversification, and wealth,
other towns—Lexington, Covington, and Ashland, particularly—were feeling some growing pains, as well.

But there were costs to be paid for even modest development.
The Wattersons, Breckinridges, Carlisles, and other ardent industrial propagandists never admitted it, but these changes were
bought at a high social price. Diversification was a necessary
and desirable goal, yet many Kentuckians came to feel that the
trade-off involved a sacrifice of their economic and political security and autonomy, not to mention the desecration of the
physical environment. In popular histories, it was the age of the
robber baron, and this commonwealth did prove an easy subject
for exploitation. The L & N and its principal competitor in the
east, the Chesapeake and Ohio, continued to own or control the
vast majority of track, and their powers of political corruption
remained breathtaking.

In addition, the railroads, like the major coal and timber companies, were the property of absentee owners. The unregulated
competition in which they engaged saw useless parallel rail lines
built, virgin hardwood forests destroyed, and the mineral rights
of innumerable mountain folk virtually stolen for future exploitation. Unfortunately, this was no economic rape, for the "vic-

tim" was altogether willing. Communities everywhere vied to have new access lines laid so that they could break cycles of subsistence farming and provinciality and become the principal town or county in their region. But Kentuckians did more than just advertise for outside industries. Louisville's success with the L & N proved an unfortunate model, in that respect. An enthusiastic and uncritical legislature granted hundreds of charters bestowing on proposed corporations special privileges not enjoyed by natives of the state, such as exemption from taxation. In a short while, citizens of many counties were protesting high rates imposed by railroads that they themselves had helped build with local bond subsidies!

The Bourbon formula of an open door for northern capital and a closed one to improved public services often contributed to other forms of social unrest, as well. Rural violence, that ugly legacy bred of war and fed by disdain for state and local authority, continued to infest areas of Kentucky, particularly the east. It was in the last third of the nineteenth century that Kentuckians gained national notoriety for their homicidal passions. A new coast-to-coast audience created by popular muckraking magazines and newspapers was eager to read about colorful murderers and backwoods vigilantism, and Kentucky proved all too obliging. Readers gasped when they were told that this state reported more homicides in 1890 than any other state in the Union, saving only much larger New York, and they chuckled over tales of moonshiners waging furious shotgun battles with "feds" along some remote and quaintly named mountain hollow. Best of all were the stories of great family wars, highlighted by the celebrated Hatfield and McCoy feud, for these had all the trappings of a sentimental romance: family honor, undying Union and Confederate loyalty, star-crossed lovers, and old-fashioned patrician guardians of the clan such as the infamous "Devil Anse" Hatfield.

These popular accounts from the pens of journalists and native story tellers such as John Fox, Jr., created romantic images and illusions that persist to this day. Less well recorded and largely unremembered were the conditions that spawned mountain violence that left its imprint upon the lives of eastern Kentuckians. The dreadful suffering aroused when thousands of men, women, and children were killed or maimed by assassins, open warfare, and arson—that was neglected by commercial exploiters. The cowardice of bushwhackers, the ignorance and moral depravity of vendetta leaders—these are inadequately remembered. The sources of such grief were no mystery. Take intense kinship feelings strengthened by isolation and intermarriage, mix with partisan hatreds, vivid memories of wartime injustices, weak systems of public education, and a heritage of vigilantism—and the results are not difficult to imagine.

An essential ingredient was the structure of law, or the pathetic imitation of it that existed in too many counties. Like the story of the chicken and the egg, it is impossible to say which came first, incompetent authority or disrespect for the concepts of law, order, and legal process. The anarchy that overswept Rowan County for two decades is a good example. Few places were as evenly divided as Rowan County between Democrats and Republicans, whose contest for power and patronage was symbolized in the struggle for community dominance between the leading Martin and Tolliver families. For years, not an election occurred without violent brawls, fraud, vote-buying, and loathsome assassinations. These culminated in a fantastic meleé in the county seat on June 22, 1887—the "Battle of Morehead"—in which many of the Tollivers and their allies were finally surrounded by state militia and either killed or arrested following a wild shoot-out.

A state investigative report about Rowan makes dismal reading today. During the three years prior to the battle, twenty men had been murdered and another sixteen wounded by bushwhackers and lynch parties in a county possessing barely eleven hundred adult men. And in all that time, not a single perpetrator had ever been convicted. Grand juries operated chiefly to persecute factional enemies, while criminal trials were frauds, for jurors were either openly approving of defendants or afraid of reprisals by the accused and his friends. Worst of all was the condition of local authority. Not only did officials clearly "sympathize with crime and criminals," but they were "totally corrupt and depraved," the deputy sheriff "almost daily drunk" and given to collapsing in court, the county judge virtually illiterate. It was perhaps half humorously that the Rowan investigat-

ing committee appointed by the state legislature recommended
that the only solution was abolition of the county! [21]

Such were the fruits not only of a generation of anarchy
sparked by the Civil War, but of a political structure that sapped
strength from Frankfort to benefit the local elite who controlled
county government more tightly than ever. Regrettably, many
of these "Little Kingdoms" had become financially bankrupt by
the latter part of the century, along with being bereft of moral
authority.[22] Most of the governors of the state in that difficult
era were men of ability and integrity; yet they were without real
power, except for the veto. The legislatures experienced periodic spasms of agrarian reformism that led to some positive
housecleaning, fairer taxation, and regulation of corporations;
but on the whole, there was little intelligent planning of legislation and much inaction in the name of fiscal economy. Fully 90
percent or more of legislative business at most sessions was
taken up with so-called private bills, bills usually sponsored by
sheriffs seeking to avoid payment of uncollected taxes and the
like.

Nowhere was the abdication of responsible government more
apparent than in regard to the schools. Despite the extraordinary
labors of a series of capable state school superintendents, public
education lagged far behind public need. This woeful condition
offers an unfortunately accurate indicator of social and political
conditions generally. A new Common School Law in 1884
brought improvement, but that was achieved principally in local
communities willing and able to raise and spend public dollars
for schooling. Disparities already vast worsened. Louisville, for
example, with a tenth of Kentucky's population, spent nearly a
third of the total amount allocated for education in the entire
state. Hundreds of individual schoolteachers, officials, and
parents labored to improve conditions, but at the time these efforts were drops in a sea of lassitude, poverty, and a persistent

21. Kentucky General Assembly, *Majority and Minority Reports and Testimony
Taken by the Rowan County Investigating Committee . . . March 16th, 1888* (Frankfort: John D. Woods, 1888), pp. 6–8, 228, 427.

22. Robert M. Ireland, *Little Kingdoms: The Counties of Kentucky, 1850–1891* (Lexington: The University Press of Kentucky, 1976).

class elitism that continued to sneer at public schools as fit only for the poor.

These education problems suggest that at a deeper level there were three "cultures" now vying for control of the Kentucky mind: the numerically dominant small farm/country village mentality; the wealthier, traditional squirearchy that still considered "the highest mark of the gentleman [to be] not cultivating the mind, not intellect, not knowledge, but elegant living"; [23] and lastly, the proschool ethic of the small but growing urban middle class. While the distant future belonged to the bourgeoisie, the present, as of 1900, remained a time of generally low school attendance, low teacher salaries, inadequate facilities, and high rates of illiteracy.

Such realities comported badly with the Bourbons' "New South Creed," but rural provincialism and conservatism were not to be wiped away by mere rhetoric. Though the national stereotype of rural Kentuckians grew sharper and more querulous, in fact they were becoming more alike, their lives marked by greater conformity and similarity. For one thing, the state was practically untouched by the waves of European immigrants who were reshaping societies elsewhere. For another, the increase in industrial and mining enterprises had yet to alter the circumstances of the great mass of folk whose world remained circumscribed by the familiar parameters of kin, farm, and church. The novel ways and ideas of the outside did not penetrate this tradition-minded setting very easily. One conservative reform that found favor among these largely fundamentalist Baptist, Methodist, and Church of Christ flocks was temperance. By 1900 more than fifty counties were dry by local option, though these very places quickly became centers of moonshining. On the other hand, the women's rights movement met great public resistance, though the redoubtable leadership of Cassius Clay's remarkable daughter Laura (along with other early feminists) brought about some definite progress by the 1890s in according basic property and coeducational rights to Kentucky women.

23. James Lane Allen, *The Blue Grass Region of Kentucky* (New York: Macmillan, 1892), p. 37.

These progressive laws were of undeniable value, particularly to women of the gentility. But they hardly altered the realities of life for the average Kentucky woman who, like her husband and children, was locked into a world of narrow prospects and burdensome obligations. It was too often a world of poor medical care and high birth and death rates, a world of primitive tools and agricultural practices, of relentlessly long work days for everyone, and monotonous diets of hog meat and cornmeal for poorer white and black families. Of course, there were social occasions to break the drudgery, the same communal pleasures that had delighted children and grownups since colonial times—corn-shuckings and weddings, quilting bees and barn-raisings, visits from the circuit rider, all-day preaching with covered-dish dinner, or an infrequent camp meeting. More reliable and important was court day, which transformed the county seats into colorful circuses of livestock crowding in to market, knives and hunting dogs being swapped and sold, patent medicine wagons, and drunken street brawls. Only dusk brought an end to the socializing and a return to the quiet routine of the close-knit household.

If the vast majority of later-nineteenth-century Kentuckians seemed to be living a farm life not greatly different in character from that of their grandparents, they were neither unique nor especially discontented with that condition. What did begin to rankle more and more of them, however, was the sense that they were declining economically, politically, and socially. And that was no illusion. In broad terms, the farmer's age had passed with the Civil War. No longer did he dictate currency, trade, and tariff policies to compliant national parties. Increasingly, farmers exhibited a feeling of being isolated, powerless to control the forces shaping their circumstances, even victimized by those forces, whether they arose from the railroads, banks, corporate monopolies, or the lobbyists swarming out of each of these interests.

The situation was complicated in Kentucky by the deterioration of the farmer's economic foundation during the last third of the century. Kentuckians were spared the full effects of a one-crop economy such as afflicted the cotton-growing South.

But their expanding reliance on tobacco (production multiplied 300 percent between 1870 and 1900) threatened to create that sort of dependency. Every downward variation in the price of tobacco sent shock waves through the commonwealth. Unfortunately, the era was one of extreme boom and bust, and each depression forced growing numbers of farmers into more costly mortgages, foreclosure, and ultimately tenantry. By the turn of the century, a *third* of all Kentucky farmers were tenants, working an average of fifty acres of someone else's land. Conditions were not much better for the typical landowner. The number of farm families increased three times in that period, but the average size of their farms fell precipitously to barely ninety-four acres. More farmers, working smaller, less secure holdings: an explosion of agrarian discontent was in the making.

The first effects of rural discontent swept over the state following the ruinous Panic of 1873. The collapse of tobacco prices and land values was bad enough, but news that the federal government was adopting a hard-money, gold-standard currency policy bewildered and angered farmers who were already having difficulty paying off mortgages and high taxes on shrinking farms. The area hardest hit throughout the era was the western tobacco-growing belt. That was the traditional heart of tobacco culture in Kentucky, producing a dark, heavy-bodied, strongly flavored leaf commonly cured with heat and smoke in closed barns. This fire-cured tobacco had long found its chief markets in Europe. The deterioration of prices led farmers to increase production, which in turn naturally led to oversupply and further price reductions. At the same time, the Bluegrass region was moving rapidly into the production of the newly discovered white burley, which, when air-cured in the fall, yielded a mild smoke that found favor in an expanding and more easily reached domestic market.

From out of the western counties there arose a chorus of complaints that inevitably sought new political vehicles. They had old villains aplenty: hard money, foreclosures, rising taxes and public debt; railroads and other corporations virtually untaxed; discriminatory transportation rates; the old suspicion and distrust of the Bluegrass. Added to these were newer enemies in the·form of centralized tobacco warehouse markets, culminating in 1890 with the birth of the American Tobacco Company, a collusion between manufacturers, led by James B. Duke, and warehousemen to set low prices and eliminate all vestiges of free-market competition. Agrarian discontent in the 1870s had led to the election of dozens of reform-minded legislators representing the Grangers and the Greenback party. Though they accomplished little, their success at the polls had frightened Democratic head-counters. Democrats nervously waved the now much-tattered bloody shirt of race and Republicanism as a warning against the dangers of third-partyism. But another severe depression might set the countryside aflame.

The return of better commodity prices in the early 1880s quieted rural discontent briefly, and the Democratic state government, reading the danger signals on the horizon, showed itself a bit more responsive to reform demands. A tax bill in 1886 imposed taxes for the first time on utilities, stocks, and railroads, though private citizens continued to be taxed at a much higher rate than corporations. A new Railroad Commission was at last created to introduce some restraints on the abuses of that industry. These events culminated in a tremendous struggle in the 1887 legislature, when the house, under heavy pressure from the L & N, narrowly adopted a bill abolishing the Railroad Commission. Determined to save the commission, foes of the L & N in the senate, led by Bourbon County's Cassius M. Clay (nephew of his famous namesake) and a young Kenton County lawyer named William Goebel, launched an investigation of the legislature that revealed lavish bribery and other corrupt lobbying practices. The commission was saved, and anticorporate feeling was heightened.

But the fight had barely begun. Farm prices had begun to fall again, and a new and more muscular national farmers' association called the Farmers' Alliance was busily organizing local societies in Kentucky, especially in the depressed and resentful western counties. The alliance was enormously influential in its campaign to politicize the farmer's plight, and, before long, dozens of candidates, especially in the Democratic ranks, were taking the alliance pledge to make war on "plutocracy."

The mood of desperate determination bore early fruit in a successful drive to call a new state constitutional convention. The new 1890 Constitution consequently bristled with alliance rhetoric and notions about the evils of special privilege and the need to curb the powers of government and corporate monopoly. Even as it was being drafted, the new constitution was being hailed by a sympathetic Lexington editor as a "bodyblow to those corrupt interests who have for so long bled the people of this Commonwealth." [24] Generations of political and judicial leaders have despaired over the weaknesses of the excessively detailed and rigid 1890 Constitution. But the people heartily approved it when it was submitted to them, for it expressed their distrust of industry, of their own government, and of power itself.

Any hopes that the new constitution would inaugurate a new age of sectional and class peace in Kentucky were quickly dashed by grim economic realities. The state was in fact powerless to bring much relief to the depressed circumstances faced by so many farmers in the commonwealth. No Kentucky governor could lower the high national tariff, inflate the currency, or break up the railroad, coal, or tobacco conglomerates. Further political and social unrest and frustration were inevitable. In 1892 the new Populist party won substantial support, especially among the more distressed and radical farmers of the dark-leaf tobacco belt. Political rhetoric grew increasingly shrill and paranoid on all sides. Still commodity prices continued to fall. Kentucky had a Democratic state government, and a Democratic president, Grover Cleveland, sat in the White House. But what good did that do? The party was rent from end to end between feuding "Silverite" reformers and "Goldbug" hard-money conservatives frightened by the specter of class revolution. The mood of impending catastrophe seemed almost palpable.

Kentuckians were not movers and shakers in that moment of national crisis, though its events deeply affected them. A state that was both southern agrarian and increasingly urban could hardly avoid the winds of change. Indeed, Kentucky seemed on the edge of a momentous political realignment. The twenty-five-year-old Bourbon coalition was breaking up. New issues, new alliances were arising that could no longer be held together

24. *Lexington Transcript,* March 26, 1891.

under the old Bourbon umbrella. The East-versus-West factional split was being supplanted by more significant interest groups. Small commercial farmers shared grievances over railroads, tariffs, and low prices. Tobacco farmers shared grievances against the American Tobacco monopoly. Coal miners and industrial workers were groping toward a sense of labor consciousness. Urban folk, especially in Louisville, were up in arms over the arrogance and corruption of their city government. These issues were rooted in fundamental social and economic developments and were not going to vanish by waving the Confederate flag. The shadowy form of the twentieth century may be seen in the emerging alignments. Where was the leadership to give voice and power to these new concerns?

Kentucky Republicans thought they had a better idea. The most distinctive and important feature of state politics since the Civil War had been the survival and steady growth of the Republican party. Expanding outward from its pillars of support among eastern whites and black Kentuckians, the party had garnered more and more votes in recent elections, reflecting both an increasing urban electorate and, more importantly, disenchantment with the tiresome familiarity and noxious corruption of the old Democratic "State House Ring" in Frankfort. The crux of this sequence came in the 1895 elections for governor and the state legislature. Any Kentuckian who reads about it will have a shock of recognition, for it began a pattern that persists to the present day: Democratic factionalism inviting Republican victory.

On the Republican side, a hungry and well-disciplined minority party put forth an attractive gubernatorial candidate, in this instance, Lancaster attorney and party leader William O'Connell Bradley. The times were ripe for change. Depression, unrest, and violence were overturning worn-out Democratic machines in other states. This hour of danger found Kentucky Democrats embroiled in angry feuding, while the new Populists ran a hard campaign in the traditional Democratic stronghold of western counties. At the same time, in Louisville and in the Ohio River counties, a vicious anti-Catholic organization called the American Protective Association busily garnered Republican votes in a scurrilous war against Romanism and immigration. The highest turnout of eligible voters ever recorded in Kentucky state elections—more than 85 percent—largely benefited the Republicans, who not only won their first Kentucky governorship but gained control of the state house, as well. Bradley received 172,436 votes; the Democrat "Wat" Hardin, 163,524; Thomas S. Pettit (the Populist candidate), 16,911; and T. B. Demaree (Prohibition party), 4,186. The Populist vote was significant, but most striking was the increase in Republican polling—56,000 over the state election held four years earlier.[25]

To the political observer, a vigorous two-party system might seem the perfect antidote to the state's troubles. But to Democrats who had dominated the patronage and power structure of Kentucky since before the Civil War, it looked calamitous. Amidst bitter factional infighting and charges of corruption at the polling places, Democrats set forth to ruin Bradley's administration. Republicans would soon discover the taste of victory to be like gall on their lips. Even before Bradley's inauguration, a battle erupted in the legislature over selection of a United States senator. Frankfort was soon crammed with angry supporters of one or another candidate, waving weapons and hurling curses and threats. "Turbulence, ruffianism, madness, anarchy reigned," Henry Watterson lamented, "a prostitution of political methods to the ends of insane partisanship and brutish barbarism." [26] The incumbent Senator Joseph Blackburn was the state's foremost supporter of the Populist-Alliance program and was therefore anathema to Democratic "Goldbugs"; the session finally ended in deadlock.

Immediately thereafter, the furies of the presidential election of 1896 were visited upon the state—William Jennings Bryan, "Cross of Gold," and all. Again, the results of this superheated contest served not to calm but to inflame public feeling even more, for the conservative Republican nominee, William McKinley, was declared the winner in Kentucky by a scant 281 of the total 436,000 votes cast. Silverite Democrats were livid, consumed with the belief that "corruptionist" money and in-

25. John Edward Wiltz, "The Gubernatorial Election of 1895 in Kentucky" (M.A. thesis, University of Kentucky, 1955), pp. 165–166.

26. *Louisville Courier-Journal*, March 12–14, 1896.

fluence—from the L & N, the American Protective Association, and similar reactionary interests—had literally stolen the election from their beloved Bryan. The legislature subsequently returned to the unfinished business of electing a senator, and, after fifty-nine ballots proved the inability of Democrats to unite behind any candidate, a Republican was chosen.

Kentucky now had its first Republican governor, speaker of the house, United States senator, and presidential electors. What a strange wilderness Democrats now found themselves wandering. "Kentucky is a Republican state!" Governor Bradley trumpeted, and who could prove him wrong? Kentucky's political world seemed to have been turned upside down. Since 1865 Democrats had become a divided collection of power blocs and conflicting philosophies, apparently exhausted by thirty years of internecine conflict. As the party in power, they were accused of intellectual bankruptcy, moral insensitivity, and corruption in high places and low, and many of those arrows hit their marks. In many respects, a Republican victory was a welcome change, for among other things it promised to clarify the muddied political waters. Governor Bradley seized the Bourbon "New South" banner and claimed it for his party. It was to be business expansion, and to the devil with Bryanite restraints on corporations. For their part, most Democrats had come to embrace Populist and Progressive reform goals, and so the gauntlet seemed to have been thrown down. Which way would Kentucky go? Only one problem remained. Who could unite these fractious Democrats for this new crusade? Many of the old leaders had passed from the scene, or continued to mouth the sterile clichés of a fading tradition. Again the question posed itself: as Kentucky rushed toward the twentieth century, who was ready for its challenges?

5

"As Ye Sow . . ."

*Kentucky political activities had about them an external
atmosphere of folksiness which made the democratic
process in the state seem almost an act of neighborliness
but underneath the surface there was always the iron hand
of control and power-snatching.*

Thomas D. Clark, Kentucky: Land of Contrast

*N*EVER was a decade so inaptly named as was the Gay
Nineties. The most severe depression in the nation's history to
that time had aroused social and political turmoil. Its rhetoric
was apocalyptic, suggesting a sharp cleavage of sections,
classes, and interests. Distress and corporate arrogance were
real, but so was political hysteria, the inevitable search for
scapegoats. Soon the Populist crusade crested, then broke. Before long, many of its more modest proposals were enacted into
law, not by "hillbilly Marxists," but by businesslike urban
Progressives. "Reformism" was to triumph—not a genuine al-
teration of social and economic priorities in favor of the laboring
classes, but "moderate antitrustism, demands for public services, and moral crusades which did little to disturb the basic
social and economic order." [1]

Ahead lay the ambiguities of the twentieth century. There

---

1. Jack Temple Kirby, *Darkness at the Dawning: Race and Reform in the Progressive South* (Philadelphia, New York, Toronto: J. B. Lippincott Company, 1972), p. 2.

would be unprecedented technological and economic growth, as
well as world wars and depressions. Legalized racial and sexual
discrimination would end, while deep-seated social grievances
would be expressed as never before. Twentieth-century Americans welcomed a more open and apparently more intimate contact with their political leaders; they also experienced the horror
of nationally televised assassinations and presidential chicanery.
The nation's bicentennial seemed less a time for exultation and
self-congratulation than a moment of uneasiness about our condition and destiny. For once, social problems appeared to
overawe a nation of problem-solvers. The twentieth century
brought to bear the forces of "mass society." Americans are
promised a richer material life on the one hand, and threatened
with cultural homogenization, even dehumanization, on the
other.

For a long while, Kentucky maintained its pattern of withdrawal and passivity, a victim of stagnant economics, indifferent and uninformed public opinion, and selfish politics. The
Populist movement appeared to have ended before 1900, with
shattering finality, poisoning political relations and spreading
popular demoralization. The first thirty years of the new century
were marked by apathy, raids on the public trust, and reactionary moral crusades. Then new forces finally began to shake the
drowsing Promised Land: the trauma of depression and war,
federal legislation, and relentless economic changes. New men
have come to power over the past forty years, ambitious men,
hungry for recognition and power in a materially and culturally
impoverished state. The best of them saw that their reputations
would ultimately rest upon their efforts to diminish that same
poverty of body and spirit. But would the good and humane values embedded in Kentucky's rural heritage survive the coming
of modern times?

Throughout the 1890s, Kentucky's political and economic
power remained under the control of a familiar coalition of
regional forces. At its core lay conservative Bluegrass rural and
business interests, now aligned with the railroads and other corporate figures. With near-absolute control of state patronage and
contracts, this power center garnered votes from less affluent

country voters, mainly in the eastern and southeastern counties, to retain control at Frankfort. The rise of agrarian and urban discontent had challenged that rule, culminating in fierce internal Democratic factionalism and the startling Republican victories in 1895 and 1896.

A novel brand of issue-oriented politics was straining to be born in Kentucky. In such circumstances, personalities have often played a more important role than abstract ideals in arousing and holding together such reform coalitions. So it was in Kentucky. The attempt to organize an alliance of farmers and laborers and to do battle against conservative Democratic and Republican rule in the state became caught up in a storm of controversy that swirled around a single man, William Goebel. Goebel sought to create and ride the protest movement into power. Yet he was a strange and controversial figure whose personality and methods injected further discord into an already confused situation. Indeed, it was only because public affairs were so confused that such a man as Goebel was able to vault into prominence and power. Lauded and hated in life, praised and misunderstood in death, no man in the history of this state aroused more bitterly conflicting emotions. His tumultuous career brought a strange climax to one era as it raised the curtain on the next.

William Goebel was certainly an unusual candidate for the task of leading the Kentucky Democratic party into the twentieth century. What had been said of the Lexington "aristocracy" still held true for much of the state: "The controlling element consists of those who were born here of parents who were born here." [2] Goebel would have failed in that and in most other traditional tests for leadership. He was not a native Kentuckian, nor a member of a fundamentalist church; he was not a man of land and wealth, nor one who could show ties to the Confederacy. His parents were working-class Germans who had migrated to Pennsylvania, where William was born in 1856. His father had served in the Union army before settling in Covington, just after the war.

2. William A. Pusey, *A Doctor of the 1870's and '80's* (Baltimore: Charles C. Thomas, 1932), p. 12.

All his life, William Goebel was a man who stood apart from the customary nature of Kentucky political life. Seventy years earlier, during the bank-court wars, Amos Kendall told us that the key to success in Kentucky politics was to "drink whiskey and talk loud, with the fullest confidence." [3] Goebel was never short of confidence, but he was neither a drinker nor a fine orator. Though a good-looking fellow and undeniably brave, he was also cold, reserved, introspective; he evidently had few if any intimate friends. William Goebel saw himself as a man possessed of superior wisdom and will, surrounded by bombastic and lazy politicians. Yet even he did not realize how little time he had to accomplish his purposes.

Goebel unquestionably became the foremost figure in pointing Kentucky toward the regulation of corporate influence, the balancing of benefits of business growth against the state's obligation to protect the public interest. Before and after his election to the state senate, his private legal practice was heavily involved with suits against railroads and other large corporations. His experience on the committee to investigate lobbying abuses of the L & N, back in 1888, no doubt accentuated his populist instincts, for central to his entire career thereafter were his unyielding efforts to strengthen the Railroad Commission. Goebel was the first important Kentucky politician with an urban, working-class background and strong sympathy for the plight of industrial workers. He supported the idea of unions for workers in an age marked by unreasoning fear of that radical notion. He proposed limitations on working hours and supported bills requiring minimum safety standards and company-paid care for workers injured on the job—another "anarchist" idea opposed by the railroads. Goebel's reformist impulses carried him in other directions. He was a principal figure in the passage of a law making gambling and lotteries illegal in Kentucky. And he helped expand free public libraries and backed the controversial Chinn Textbook bill, which aimed at breaking the alleged monopoly of the American Book Company, the state's sole sup-

3. Hambleton Tapp, *A Sesquicentennial History of Kentucky,* edited by Frederick A. Wallis, 4 vols. (Hopkinsville, Kentucky: The Historical Record Association, 1945), 1:331.

plier of school textbooks. His legislative record alone made
William Goebel a link between urban and rural Kentucky, between the Old South and the New, between nineteenth-century
agrarian Populism and twentieth-century industrial Progressivism.

But strong political figures are never just the sum of their
legislative parts. Background, personality, use of language—
everything comes into play, as they project themselves and their
programs and seek public approval. Many groups in Kentucky
were apprehensive about Goebel's activities. But the extent of
deep polarization he generated suggests the presence of more
than policy disagreements or even the stirrings of class conflict.
A tension existed between Goebel's style and his public image,
and it tended to produce uneasiness about him among many citizens. He posed as a man of and for the people, utterly free from
"plutocratic" influence. Yet he was known to use individuals
ruthlessly, and he had gained a reputation as a political boss in
northern Kentucky. Lacking political grace, he prided himself
on using legal expertise and legislative skill to win votes for his
programs. Yet this same man, at the age of forty, had a pistol
fight on the streets of Covington, in which he killed John San-
ford, a local man, former Confederate hero, and a political
enemy of Goebel. That act won the undying hatred of many
who might have become Goebel's supporters. His contradictory
style and behavior created doubts in the minds of some about
his sincerity as a reformer. Where did honest motive end and
opportunism take over? Goebel was the quintessential *outsider*.
Was it that psychology that made him a powerful and reliable
enemy of the "interests"? Or was reformism simply the logical
route for such a man, a "foreigner" consumed with ambition
for respect and power in an essentially agrarian Kentucky?

For contemporaries and historians alike, this fascinating debate often turned on the issue of the famed "Goebel Election
Law." That measure—vociferously denounced as a cold-
blooded attempt to annihilate democracy in Kentucky and place
Goebel in the governor's chair—crystallized feelings against
him. Ostensibly, the bill was part of the Progressive movement's main thrust everywhere: to end partisan corruption at the
polling place. It was similar to bills in other states in setting up

an independent State Board of Election Commissioners. That board in turn appointed county boards of three commissioners who would oversee the polls and canvass and certify returns. The idea now seems mundane, but in those days, partisan debasement of the voting process was virtually a way of life in Kentucky and elsewhere.

The bill, however, was denounced, not by hacks, but by men of integrity in all political parties. What went wrong? The bill was plainly flawed, for equal party representation was not assured, nor could state and local boards of *three* have such balance. The legislature, now—in 1898—controlled by Democrats again would naturally appoint Democrats to the boards. Worse, it was believed that Goebel—who dominated the legislature—would dictate the selection of three State Board Commissioners. It seemed to many a ploy to destroy the Republican party and assure Goebel's election the following year. The genesis of the bill clearly lay in the narrow Republican victories of Governor Bradley and President McKinley, victories clouded by evidence of widespread vote-buying, especially in Jefferson County (Louisville). "The State was stolen from Bryan," Goebel had declared, "but, by God, it will not happen again." [4] Did it matter that Goebel was less responsible than his more partisan colleagues in the legislature for the flaws in the final bill? Did it matter that the State Board was not empowered to pass judgment on ballots cast in the gubernatorial elections, but merely to certify the votes from the counties? Did it matter that the commissioners named were in fact men of sound reputation? Possibilities for Democratic manipulation were still legion, and the odium fell on the controversial, apparently hypocritical reformer, State Senator William Goebel.

As the curtain rose on the 1899 elections, Kentucky's political scene was never more dense with acrimony and suspicion. There was a serious question whether a political solution lay down the road, or whether civil strife of a sort familiar to mountain and Bluegrass residents awaited the results of the fall contest. The Democratic nominating convention held in the last week of June at Music Hall in Louisville surely encouraged

4. *Louisville Courier-Journal,* April 15, 1896.

these fears. Only a great novelist or playwright could do justice to the incredible scene created during that meeting. It was no longer politics, but social conflict, organized intimidation, and personal treachery of a sort more familiar to readers of Shakespeare than state histories. There was no question that Goebel went into the convention with a minority of delegates pledged to him. The two leading contenders at the outset were "Wat" Hardin, whom Bradley had defeated four years earlier, and William J. Stone, a veteran of Morgan's Raiders and of countless political battles since. In platforms, there seemed little difference among the three, though Hardin privately was the conservative favorite of the L & N. But personal feelings had degenerated too far to let principle get in the way.

Amid a tragi-comic spectacle of noise and confusion, Goebel quickly moved to maneuver Hardin out of the picture by establishing an alliance with Stone. After that appeared to succeed, cries of betrayal erupted from Stone's backers, as Goebel men moved to grasp a majority. Louisville police first filled the aisles, then were removed by protesting delegates. A band played "Dixie," "My Old Kentucky Home," and other sentimental favorites in a vain effort to calm the furious assembly. Finally, after dozens of ballots, Goebel added enough to his urban-and-northern-county bloc to win the nomination. "The Louisville and Nashville Railroad must become the servant rather than the master of the people," [5] Goebel had exulted; but his moment of triumph was cut short when a faction of dissident Democrats bolted the party and launched their own ticket, dedicated to "freedom," corporate monopoly, and the destruction of William Goebel. Thus divided, the Democratic party went forth to battle William S. Taylor, the now-hopeful Republican heir to Governor Bradley, and a fourth contender representing the declining Populist party.

Week after campaign week, the atmosphere of distrust grew. Friends became bitter enemies; claims of fraud and deceit, warnings of retribution, and death threats filled the air. Election day itself was marred by the deaths of fifteen men killed at various polling places around the state, though not in a most

5. *Lexington Herald,* March 29, 1899.

dangerously uneasy and critical Jefferson County, where Governor Bradley had called out the militia to preserve order. Early returns favored Goebel, but as outlying county returns trickled in, his margin shrank, then vanished. Weeks more passed. Yet, with four candidates receiving votes, it remained unclear who had won. Not surprisingly, Democratic charges of corruption and improper voting procedure filled the newspapers. The State Election Board sat to review the returns—and hear charges that Bradley's militia had intimidated Louisville voters, that a trainload of white and black men had been brought in from Evansville, Indiana, to cast Republican votes in Hopkins County, and that (familiar story!) L & N money had been freely dispensed to bribe voters, election officers, and newspaper editors. An effort was also made to invalidate thousands of mainly Republican ballots cast in Eastern Kentucky, because they were written on thin tissue paper. Mass meetings were held in those staunch Republican strongholds when it appeared that the "Goebel Board" was going to try to repudiate voters in Jefferson and the eastern counties. The deadly rattle of old Civil War muskets and trustier hunting rifles began to be heard.

Finally, in a situation ominously reminiscent of the contested national presidential election of 1876, the State Board ended its hearings and went into closed session. Only a week before inauguration day, the board opened its doors and stunned Democrats by declaring, by a two-to-one majority, that William S. Taylor and the entire Republican ticket had been elected by some 2,000 votes. Taylor received 193,714 votes; Goebel, 191,331; "Goldbug" Democrat John Y. Brown, 12,140; and Populist John G. Blair, 3,038. The board correctly ruled that it lacked authority to adjudicate conflicting reports of fraud in the contests for governor and lieutenant-governor.

If the returns were accurate, it appeared that Goebel was defeated not so much by Republican voters as by the defection of thousands of Democrats in the Bluegrass and western counties—men who approved Goebel's reformist platform, but were hostile to the man and his Election Law. On December 12, 1899, Taylor was sworn into office, while Goebel announced plans to vacation in Arizona with his ailing brother. The election of 1899 seemed ended.

It had only begun. Two days later, Democratic leaders declared their intention to contest the results. Such a contest would be heard by two committees, one from each house of the legislature. The actual members of each committee would be chosen by lot, and since the legislature was once again strongly dominated by the Democrats, it was assumed that the two election committees would reflect that fact. Republicans were angry; but when the lots were finally drawn, they were outraged. Only two Republicans altogether drew their names from the box. Cries of "Goebelism" and fraud rang out. The predominantly Democratic committees nevertheless went ahead, and, by mid-January 1900, testimony concerning election fraud was being taken, most of which pointed toward a reversal of the election. Governor Taylor meanwhile had dispatched frantic letters to party friends warning of a usurpation and urging them to send help for his administration. Soon, the L & N was depositing hundreds of armed mountain men at the capital depot, a frightening Republican host supposedly organized by the new secretary of state, Caleb Powers, a young Republican leader from Knox County. These men mingled with companies of state militia called in by Taylor to quiet the little town of Frankfort, which by now trembled with rumor and tension. On January 29, the legislative committees retired, announcing that a decision was to come in a few days. Whether that report would signal a political response or something more deadly was unclear.

An answer was not long in coming. The next morning, as Goebel was walking toward the statehouse, a rifle was fired from the Executive Office Building, and the senator fell, shot through the abdomen. The news flashed across the town, and a mob quickly gathered, as Goebel was taken back to the Capitol Hotel. Governor Taylor at once retreated to the statehouse behind a cordon of troops, declared Kentucky to be in a state of insurrection, and ordered the legislature to convene in London, some eighty-five or ninety miles to the southeast, as the crow flies, in snugly Republican Laurel County. Democrats, rejecting this message, attempted to meet in the statehouse, but were barred by the militia. They hurried down to city hall, but found troops there, as well. Finally, the harried members convened in the Capitol Hotel itself, heard the news that Goebel's wound was almost certainly fatal, and hastily approved a report unseating Taylor and installing the dying Goebel as governor.

For the third time in a century, Kentucky had two conflicting governments, or parts thereof. The banking and court controversy of the 1820s had been resolved by ballot, while the struggle between Confederate and Union authorities was decided by bullets. Which way would the third crisis go? On February 3, Goebel died, and young Lieutenant-Governor John Crepps Wickliffe Beckham, a Bardstown native, was sworn in as his presumptive successor. Following an impassioned funeral for their dead and now altogether revered leader, Democratic legislators retreated to Louisville, leaving Taylor sheltered in the statehouse. The bubble, however, appeared to have broken. The thirst for blood seemed to have been quenched by that one tragic death. Taylor soon agreed to submit the entire case to the state courts. Democrats returned to Frankfort, which for the next few weeks was the farcical setting for two unhappy siamese-twin legislatures. Democratic and Republican members recognized only their own chamber leaders, rose and sat independently, met, gave speeches, and adjourned as if the other party were invisible. Fortunately, barbed words had replaced rifles.

The state courts upheld Beckham's claim, but it was not until the United States Supreme Court declined to hear the appeal in May 1900 that Taylor was at last unseated. Meanwhile, Taylor, Caleb Powers, and other Republicans were being indicted for conspiracy to assassinate Goebel. Taylor and several others managed to escape to Indiana, where they successfully resisted extradition on the reasonable grounds that a fair trial was unlikely; Taylor practiced law and later died in Indianapolis in 1928, still proclaiming his innocence. Less fortunate were Powers and others who were captured and repeatedly tried for the murder in Scott County court. They were convicted in trials marked by flagrant partisanship and emotional excess, but all later received executive pardons, and Powers was rewarded subsequently for his troubles by election to Congress. Who then fired the shot? Who hired the assassin? The state spent thousands of dollars trying to answer these questions. Perhaps Clay County marksman James Howard had been paid to pull the trigger, as alleged at the trials. It seemed so, But Kentucky historians may never be content merely to know who pulled the trigger.

The death of Goebel hurt Kentucky in many ways, for the man himself was deeply controversial, and the manner of his death was symbolic of the divisions and social pathologies that undercut the self-confidence and economic progress of the state. Only the Civil War itself approached the assassination for personal animosity—business partnerships ended, churches were disrupted, families divided, "no locality so remote, no circle so close knit, as to have escaped the evil influence." [6] Kentucky flared into national attention, its torments spread across a thousand newspapers, gaining negative publicity that could only damage pride and prospects for future investment. The state already suffered from inadequate sources of internal wealth and excessive dependency on external investment capital. Now potential developers were made still more wary because of the insecurity of public affairs. The political consequences were even more apparent. Goebel the man was missed, for his personal ambition and relentless pursuit of reform goals were the crucial catalysts in the political mixture of the 1890s. Then the shocking nature and timing of his death created an instant mythology, akin to the two Kennedy assassinations of the present day. While many Democrats tried to associate themselves with the Goebel myth of wisdom and purity of purpose, they soon fell into a pattern of nasty, scratching, personal hatreds, aimless factional strife, and notorious corruption.

It is misleading, however, to suggest that Goebel's death caused a basic shift in the fundamental character and direction of Kentucky politics and society. The guide word here should be *continuity,* rather than change. The real tragedy of the slaying and its aftermath was that it confirmed and intensified modes of thought and behavior, along with economic and other trends that had been forming for generations. These were now destined to continue in deepening channels well into the new century.

6. Samuel Hopkins Adams, "The State of Kentucky *vs.* Caleb Powers," *McClure's Magazine* 22 (1904):466.

The real meaning of the Goebel incident was that an opportunity
was missed to alter priorities and reinvigorate public morality
and public institutions. A road was not taken, and getting back
to it proved an incredible ordeal, not yet fully accomplished.

Many would-be reformers believed that that time of trouble
stemmed from Kentucky's overwhelmingly rural character—
well over three-quarters of her citizens lived in farm or small
town settings in 1920. More discerning critics, however, have
noted that the real source of Kentucky's vexations arose from
the persistence of "southern" cultural folkways and stateways,
rather than mere rural conservatism or provinciality. The bar-
barities of clan feuds, or moonshining in dry counties, the lawlessness of private homicide and continuing public vigilantism,
the abuse of prisoners and the pardoning power, the dominance
of self-serving courthouse-ring politics, one-crop agriculture,
suspicious Bible Belt fundamentalism, and the like, were un-
comfortably plain evidences of the persistence of nineteenth-
century (even eighteenth-century) cultural patterns. To those elements, add southern feelings of defeatism, persecution, and
fear of change, and the consequences were almost palpable.
Economic indicators show a steadily diminishing rate of growth
down to World War II, bespeaking a declining sense of initiative, self-confidence, diversity, and wealth. Where she had led
the southern states in such figures for a century, Kentucky was
now lowest in national per capita income, and nearly so in other
indexes of the quality of material life. The promised land had
become a place of penury for too many.

Gravest of the cruel social jokes Kentuckians played upon
themselves through most of the twentieth century concerned
public education. Muckrakers ranted over the desperate impov-
erishment of the entire system outside those few counties with
urban centers, the extremely low per-pupil expenditures, the
pitifully abbreviated school year. The evil was so plain—why
the resistance, or worse, the indifference to remedying it? Kentucky's great historian Thomas D. Clark reminds us that even
the single thread of education was part of a broad and complex
cloth of custom and attitudes. Crime, flaccid politics, economic
stagnation, illiberal views—Clark attributes these to the education problem. Yet, how to persuade a community of largely

poor, unschooled, complacent, or apathetic people to tax themselves more heavily to pay for better schools? And who was to
say, even were the revenues raised, that the money would benefit the children? For it was plain that courthouse cliques—often
individual families or clusters of families—frequently controlled
local school boards for the patronage they represented.[7]

Perhaps the only durable resolution to the conundrum lay in
the unspectacular processes of urbanization and economic
change. It is problematic whether a genuinely broad-based progressive movement could have flourished in such a doubtful garden. Bryan and Goebel had shown the potential for a new politics, but fate had undermined that effort. Kentucky in fact was
cursed by all the ingredients needed to create an unresponsive
political structure. It was a poor state: and in such places, patronage—government jobs and contracts, no matter how inconsequential—was vastly magnified in importance. In many
poverty-ridden counties, government was the only reliable employer. Indeed, that was a principal reason for the absurd mul-
tiplication in the number of counties, for each new one was a
sort of public welfare system for those fortunate enough to have
voted right or to have been born into the right local families.
Consequently, interest in the winner of the county school superintendent's race or an "in" with the current administration's
local contact man on patronage matters was infinitely more intense than interest in elections for president or senator. Some
might argue that all that was actually a homey and effective
means for transferring a portion of the state's unevenly distributed wealth to the less affluent counties. But the impact of such
a system on public morality was terrible, and politics became
little more than a contemptible series of tricks played on the
powerless.

"Issue politics" could hardly thrive in such a situation. Nor
was it likely to arise in a state generally dominated by a single
party. (Republicans won a few governorships and contested
most state elections very closely, but gerrymandering assured
almost absolute Democratic control of the legislature.) In such

7. Clark, *Kentucky: Land of Contrast,* p. 236.

instances, ruling parties tend to become large and unwieldy, breaking into factions concerned more with personality and the allotting of boodle than with the public interest. Popular attention to such meaningless struggles diminished except when some candidates specially gifted with stump oratory took to the hustings. The sovereign people had expressed their distrust by forbidding state officers from succeeding themselves in office. Nothing more positive seemed possible.

Perhaps the most disappointing aspect of it all was the intellectual bankruptcy of the Republicans. Apparently doomed to remain a stable minority bloc in the legislature, Republicans tended to develop a minority psychology and strategy. Instead of challenging incumbents and articulating alternative approaches to important questions, they were mainly supplicants; in the hope of gaining patronage in their own solidly Republican counties, they were generally obedient supporters of whichever Democratic faction controlled the state administration. The party, moreover, was a queer combination of inherently conflicting elements: whites from the highlands and the Knobs, central and western blacks from the Pennyroyal and the Purchase, federal pensioners and post office workers, and a growing urban contingent, especially in Louisville—all of them linked to a conservative, big-business-oriented national party. Small wonder that Republicans continued to offer so poor an alternative, so little leadership, even when they occasionally won state and federal offices.

These discordant patterns emerged quickly after 1900. Fate placed the power of the governorship in the hands of J. C. W. Beckham, a young, politically untested scion of a wealthy Nelson County family. Beckham proved most adept at getting reelected, winning the special election in the fall of 1900 and a full term in 1903. He therefore had an exceptional opportunity for leadership during a critical time. He did capitalize on the postassassination mood to gain repeal of the hated "Goebel Election Law"—though electoral fraud and violence were only partially diminished by bipartisan oversight of the polls. But in other respects, Beckham was a failure.

Perhaps it was his vacillating nature or his basically conservative Bluegrass philosophy that led to weakness and inaction. Many believed that more sinister motives were also at work. Beckham was only thirty when the oath of office was thrust upon him. In desperate need of political support, he appeared to emerge hog-tied to certain powerful men and interests. Would-be supporters in the western counties were soon accusing him of having sold out to the L & N. And an arrangement seemed to have been reached with Milton H. Smith, the brilliant president of that railroad, to block further antitrust action and stifle a proposed corrupt-practices act aimed at curbing corporate involvement in elections. " 'Shut them off—' " Smith was quoted as saying, " 'don't let them abuse the corporations,' " and criticism was squeezed off.[8] In a similar vein was Beckham's tender treatment of the Hargis-Cockrill feud in mountainous Breathitt County. This dispute between two rival coalitions of families and political factions was a classic example of mountain feuding and vigilantism, if such a word as *classic* can be used to describe organized, mean-spirited mayhem. The dispute supposedly originated in guerrilla battles waged during the Civil War, but by the time thirty-seven murders took place in 1901–1902, any semblance of ideological distinctions between the factions had long since disappeared. News of the bloodshed and anarchy was spread across newspapers and magazines nationwide, smearing the reputation of every Kentuckian. But the ridicule became mortifying when Governor Beckham pardoned nearly forty convicted murderers and assailants, allegedly for political favors he owed to the powerful Breathitt Democratic boss, Judge Jim Hargis. The old feudist had not long to savor his victory, however, for in February 1908, he was shot to death by his own violent son, Beauchamp.

Much more complicated was the vigilantism of disgruntled western Kentucky tobacco farmers. Predictably, Beckham's response was ineffectual. Discontent had been stirring there for years. Dark-leaf tobacco farmers were convinced that the true villain behind their economic woes was the American Tobacco

---

8. John H. Fenton, *Politics in the Border States* (New Orleans: The Hauser Press, 1957), p. 45.

Company trust, which, by 1902, had eliminated all competitive bidding and set a price that seemed a callous invitation to bankruptcy. Out of that came a remarkable demonstration of cooperation by fiercely independent families. The Dark District Tobacco Association was formed in 1904 and quickly gained allegiance from a majority of Tennessee and Kentucky growers. If all farmers had joined, the American-European purchasing conspiracy would have been broken. Unfortunately, a number of growers held back, choosing to sell their crop at extraordinary prices to buyers eager to break the new association. Despite urgings and threats, these so-called "Hill Billies" refused to join the association.

The stage was set for violence, and on December 10, 1905, vigilantism raised its ugly head again in Kentucky. A warehouse storing "Hill Billy" tobacco at Trenton in Todd County was burned. The effect was electric. All the pent-up emotion of present frustration and ancient populist grievance burst open to inaugurate a new era of anarchy. Quickly, a secret, semimilitary organization was put together, complete with passwords, handsigns, and lists of enemies. The "Night Riders" were on the warpath. Their techniques were familiar ones in southern culture, with innovations adopted from northern labor violence: the arsonist's torch, blasting powder, the whip and shotgun. Alongside those activities, the systematic destruction of tobacco plant beds seems almost incidental. Carefully planned cavalry raids were launched against some of the principal towns, such as Princeton, Russellville, and Hopkinsville, to demonstrate the brazen determination of the Riders and to destroy "enemy" warehouses. Racial violence—largely the work of the infamous Whitecappers (vigilante groups)—was also widespread in the lower South at the same moment, and so it was not surprising to see that black Kentucky farmers, especially tenants, became targets of a special campaign of terror. The danger was particularly bad in Trigg, Marshall, and Fulton counties.

Throughout Beckham's governorship, little was done to suppress the tobacco wars or to deal with the legitimate grievances of the growers. Local law was neutralized by sympathy or fear. There were state laws that could have been invoked, laws passed only a few years earlier to cope with the violence of

Bluegrass farmers in their vigilante battles against toll-gate operators. But Beckham was unwilling or unable to meet the emergency. By 1908, the peak year of the tobacco wars, Beckham was a private citizen again, and the problem had been dumped into the lap of the new Republican governor, Augustus E. Willson. Tobacco farmer vigilantism had spread into the Bluegrass burley belt by then, and the Harvard-educated Willson was only too eager to crush the insurrection of these mainly Democratic small farmers. Capitalizing on a mood of growing revulsion against the violence, he vigorously dispatched state militia from the northern and eastern parts of the state into the distracted counties, and the troops, together with prosecution in federal court, finally ended the meleé. Later, the American Tobacco trust was broken, and loose-leaf auctions restored at least the illusion of competitive bidding for the harvests of Kentucky's small tobacco farms.

These experiences alone would have widened fault lines in Democratic ranks and reinforced Kentucky's growing national image of lawlessness, provinciality, and insecure capital. But other stands adopted by Beckham made him even more sharply the focus of the new twentieth-century factionalism. His opposition to woman suffrage and his support of the infamous Day Law that ended forty years of harmonious biracial education at Berea College and instituted mandatory public school segregation throughout the state did not mark him as a progressive leader; neither did such views set him much apart from most white men. From the beginning, however, his stand on prohibition was recognized as a powerfully divisive issue.

The prohibition idea had been gaining converts since it burst upon the scene as part of the broad moral reform crusade, back in Andrew Jackson's America. Liquor was consumed at a stupendous per capita rate, and it was a simple matter for evangelistic reformers to seize upon prohibition as a potent weapon in their war against the sins of the flesh. The movement accelerated in the last decades of the nineteenth century, especially when many women's rights leaders (and many women otherwise opposed to feminist political agitation) added their strength to the cause. The alcoholic husband and father were a mortal threat to the sanctity of the family and to the physical and economic security of dependents. It is no surprise to learn that the notorious saloon smasher, Carry Nation, was a Garrard County, Kentucky, native.

There was much more involved in the "dry" crusade than fundamentalism or nascent feminism. Americans remained profoundly disturbed by widespread social change. Corporate industry and labor militancy, expanding cities, the influx of tens of millions of European immigrants of a new and troubling nature—Catholics and Jews—genuinely threatened the traditional character of the nation. The foundations of familiar moral guideposts were sunk in the soil of a small-town, agrarian society. How relevant were they in the new industrial age? How durable were the old-time values in an age that seemed bent on worshipping the "godless notions" of Darwinism, science, materialism, and bureaucratic efficiency? The promise of prohibition transcended mundane problems of drunkenness and abandoned children. It was sold by its true believers as a crucial weapon in the war to preserve native Americans not merely from a river of booze, but an ocean of unwanted change and immorality.

This mood of embattled traditionalism recognized no sectional boundaries; still, it was felt most strongly in the so-called Bible Belt states, of which Kentucky was most assuredly a part. Kentucky counties, or communities within them, had been going dry under a local-option law passed in 1874. It was a stroke of genius for Beckham to see the enormous political clout that might be gained by mounting the prohibition horse. Or perhaps the credit should go to Percy Haly, the principal advisor among those the young governor had latched onto in the wake of his sudden rise to prominence, and the guiding spirit behind the Beckham faction thereafter. Theirs was a strange political marriage, standing on a stranger platform. Haly was a brilliant, Runyanesque "boss," the Irish-Catholic son of a Lexington saloon-keeper; Beckham, the cream of Bluegrass Presbyterian society, was known to be well fond of his bottle, "a weak man and given to overindulgence," one WCTU lady wrote privately, but supported as leader of the drys because "he always votes right." [9] Together with Louisville's premier clean-government spokesman, Robert Worth Bingham, the Beckham-Haly group emerged as a potent new factor in state politics. Amidst charges of opportunism and deliberate intent to bury legitimate reformism under the "false" prohibition issue, the governor nevertheless succeeded in passing a County-Unit law through the legislature in 1906 as part of a drive toward drying out old Kentucky. What a victory that would be for the cause.

Injection of the new issue precipitated a tremendous struggle within the Democratic party. Anti-Beckham sentiment was already forming, but the liquor question gave it a distinctive identity. The wet faction, however, embraced even stranger bedfellows than their rivals. At the core were the reform-minded farmers of smaller tobacco acreages in the upper Bluegrass, the Pennyroyal, and the Purchase. Another major supporter was *Courier-Journal* editor Henry Watterson, somewhat frayed by two generations on the front lines but still an ardent industrial booster and friend of the distillers, the state's principal industry; Watterson's words and the distiller's dollars were indispensable ingredients in the anti-Beckham chemistry. Most ironic of all was the support that came from the still-powerful (and still corrupt) Democratic machine in Louisville, run by the passionately wet Irish Whallen brothers. With both wet and dry factions a confusing mixture of ideologies and conflicting interest groups, it was small wonder that, while Kentucky produced some outstanding Progressive-era spokesmen, the state was unable to develop a sustained and effective progressive *movement*. Not only did the culture and politics of the state nullify efforts to create a coherent reform coalition, but in the course of a few years, the Prohibition Amendment and the national Volstead Act would moot the wet-dry controversy. A great game of political musical chairs would follow, in which nearly everyone switched sides in a mad scramble for advantage.

It is inaccurate, however, to say that Kentucky was untouched by the spirit of progressive reform, even if prohibition

9. Hattie F. Moody to Alben Barkley, October 20, 1928, Barkley Manuscripts, University of Kentucky Library, Department of Special Collections, Lexington, Ky.

be omitted as an essentially reactionary crusade. And the voice most consistently urging Kentuckians to enter the twentieth century was unquestionably that of the congressman, governor, and senator from Henderson, Augustus Owsley Stanley. More than any faction could, Stanley represented a link connecting the western Kentucky reform spirit of the 1890s with Progressivism in the new century. Others—Scott County Congressman James C. Cantrill and Stanley's fellow westerner Ollie James, in particular—helped sustain the shrunken reform idea in an era of rampant Philistinism and demagoguery. But no Kentuckian accomplished more in spite of these obstacles.

On the surface, A. O. Stanley shared the characteristics of the stereotyped southern vote-monger. No Kentuckian, except perhaps only the golden-tongued Alben W. Barkley, surpassed Stanley as a stump speaker. In a state poor in most ways but blessed with a tradition of mellifluous oratory, that is saying quite a lot. For that was still an age that adored the spoken word, a land without television or radio, an intensely rural world lacking electricity, telephones, libraries. Really, until World War II (and even after, in more isolated regions), it was a world that revolved around the gossip of the country store, the local newspaper, and the resident Democratic or Republican old sage or inside dopester. Politics filled the information and entertainment gap, running in a perpetual cycle, never-ending, from the hopes of spring primaries to the winter plots of revenge. Politics meant humor, passion, and words spoken from the stump, the courthouse steps, or wherever an audience got together to be treated to Kentucky's classic stew—burgoo—her classic beverage—bourbon—and the melody of a political suitor courting voters.

In that setting, stories of comic incidents were passed along like precious charms, polished and enjoyed the more in the retelling. A classic one involved the marvelous gubernatorial race in 1915, between Stanley and the equally sonorous Republican from Somerset, Ed Morrow. The two traveled together around the state, debating, Lincoln-Douglas style—in appearance, if not substance. Morrow asserted that the principal issue facing the sovereign people of the commonwealth was a tax imposed on dogs at the insistence of Bluegrass-aristocrat sheep raisers. Free the mountaineer's "Old Dog Ring," Morrow cried in mock anguish. One day Stanley prepared himself for the fiftieth version of that piteous tale by consuming too much burgoo and liquor. The hot sun and Morrow's oratory did the rest, and Stanley suddenly got up and vomited off the rear of the platform. Chagrined, he begged to apologize to the stunned crowd. It could not be helped, Stanley explained, for "Every time I hear Ed Morrow speak, it makes me sick to my stomach." [10]

But Stanley was cuts above most of the windy, self-seeking men he dealt with. On a more serious occasion, he reminded his audience that the true purpose of government "is to make all men free, not a few rich," a clear expression of twentieth-century Jeffersonianism. [11] His own work did much to advance that radical notion in Kentucky. As a congressman, Stanley was an ardent supporter of federal regulation of railroads and of mine safety, a pure food and drug act, and the prohibition of child labor. He was best known for his relentless campaigns against the abuses of the United States Steel trust and the unlawful tobacco monopoly that had raised, in Stanley's phrase, the Night-Rider fury in his own congressional district. As governor, Stanley in a sense redeemed the long-postponed Goebel reform pledges. Prior to the 1960s, no period approached the years from 1915 to 1919 for progressive legislation in Kentucky. A Corrupt Practices Act and related measures were finally passed, theoretically ending heavy corporate contributions to candidates, free railroad passes, and the generosity of lobbyists in Frankfort. The workmen's compensation law was strengthened, and the first legislative redistricting in twenty-five years was approved. Among Stanley's most durable achievements was creation of a State Tax Commission; together with Kentucky's first modern budget system, it facilitated increased allotments to public schools, the penal system, state social welfare agencies, and the highway system. All of that may have been only a small gesture against the stronger current of control and power-

10. *Louisville Courier-Journal,* October 23, 1960.
11. *Address of the Honorable A. O. Stanley,* delivered at Glasgow, Kentucky, May 19, 1913 (n.p., [1913]), p. 1.

snatching, and Stanley himself was no saint. His experience in Frankfort did illustrate that enlightened leadership was as essential as it was rare.

The era of the 1920s was a time of ambivalence for Kentuckians who had been working in their own ways to improve the quality of public life. This is reflected in our popular images of that period between World War I and the Great Depression. Long celebrated as both a frivolous Jazz Age and as the twilight of the businessman-as-God, the decade is now recognized by historians as a period of major confrontation between rural and urban America, that conflict between modernism and fundamentalism symbolized by the Prohibition fight. The contradictions emerged only slowly, at the time. After all, the Great War had just made the world safe for democracy, and two of the mightiest crusades ever conducted had also ended triumphantly: Prohibition in 1919 and woman suffrage in 1920. John Barleycorn was dead, and the women of Kentucky were no longer classed " 'poetically with whiskey and horses' but 'politically with imbeciles and criminals.' " [12] The liquor-lobby dragon was slain, and the purifying touch of the feminine vote released from its spell.

Instead of a new millennium, however, the nation seemed besieged with Babbittry, urban and racial turmoil, and the waves of corruption that so often seem to follow great wars. There was no lack of simple solutions, but not all of them appealed to Kentuckians. Many agreed that the nation's problems would be eased by shutting off the influx of foreign immigrants. Others looked to a resurgent Ku Klux Klan and its direct action against Catholics, Jews, and other "un-American" influences; but to their credit, most Kentuckians found the new Klan of the twenties repulsive, and it never enjoyed the sort of popularity accorded to it in such neighboring states as Indiana.

Similarly, the campaign to end the teaching of Darwin's "atheistic" evolution theory evoked warm debate between liberal and fundamentalist Kentuckians. The 1922 state legislature

12. In the words of Kentucky's remarkable suffragist Madeline McDowell Breckinridge, *Lexington Herald,* December 4, 1913.

debated such a law, directed particularly at the commonwealth's most progressive institution, the state university at Lexington. Yet that was not to be the decisive issue for Kentucky that it soon became in Tennessee. The proposed bills were sharply criticized by the university's courageous president, Frank L. McVey, and he was soon joined by the editors of the *Courier-Journal*, the president of the Southern Baptist Theological Seminary in Louisville, and many of the state's respected ministers. Thanks to that defense of academic freedom, the principal "Monkey Law" was defeated in the house, 42 to 41. Two years later, young John Thomas Scopes graduated from the University of Kentucky and journeyed south to Dayton, Tennessee, and history.

The classic example of the way Kentucky blurred the question of its own future, however, took place in the gubernatorial election of 1927. Perhaps it was those contradictions in the reform constituency between moralistic and business-urban types that led to such a strange affair. Perhaps it was Kentucky's byzantine political history and structure and weak urban-labor base that led to confusion. Or maybe it was just foolish to pose such dangerous and unanswerable questions as "Who owns Kentucky?" The central issue of that election, astonishingly enough, was pari-mutuel race-track betting. And the principal antigambling candidate was none other than John Crepps Wickliffe Beckham, still relatively young (fifty-seven) and now the darling of the reform coalition and stalwart enemy of the "interests."

Actually, it was not altogether surprising to find Beckham in such a role, for ever since his early advocacy of prohibition, he had been looked upon by thousands of devoted rural followers as the true heir to the Goebel reform tradition. The antipari-mutuel betting issue had a briefer history, but one can see how it might become associated with the man from Bardstown. Gambling and prostitution had been rampant in sections of Louisville and in Newport, Kentucky, for a long time. The addition of bootlegging and associated vices only made matters worse. Opposition to these unfortunate realities of urban life and to political venality, generally, had principally come from the Louisville Churchmen's Federation, a coalition of Protestant ministers, professional people, and businessmen. The federation was the driving force behind efforts to throw out the Democratic machine, and it had actively supported prohibition. With that victory behind them, the federation resolved, in 1920, to attack not only petty local gambling, but the entire structure of legalized race-track betting in Kentucky.

The same moral indignation, evangelical language, and form of organization that had led to the prohibition victory were eagerly transferred to the new Anti-Gambling Commission. Now the wicked destroyer of soul, family, and community was not demon rum, but gambling and its attendent mischiefs. Now the power behind the throne, bending legislators and governors to do its bidding, was not the liquor lobby, but the still more clever and insidious monopoly known as the Kentucky Jockey Club. The club was, in fact, a group of wealthy Louisville and Bluegrass investors, horsemen, and political figures from both parties. Formed in 1918, it owned all the major race tracks in the state—Churchill Downs and Douglas Park in Louisville, Latonia in Covington, and the Kentucky Association course (now Keeneland) in Lexington. The club's peculiar strength also derived from the fact that its monopoly was in effect sanctioned by state law. The Kentucky Racing Commission controlled all tracks, all racing dates, and all betting; competition was not only unlikely, it was illegal. And—curiouser and curiouser—the president of the Jockey Club, millionaire horse-breeder Johnson N. Camden, was also chairman of the State Racing Commission. Here was a foe worthy of the best efforts of the Churchmen's Federation. The potential for making political hay was also not lost on such men as Beckham, for "the power of the Jockey Club, like the old power of the L & N, could easily be understood by the Kentucky taxpayer." [13]

The first man who attempted to ride the issue into the governor's seat, however, was the ambitious and talented congressman from Paducah, Alben W. Barkley. Long recognized as a brilliant Anti-Saloon League orator, Barkley made gambling

---

13. Robert F. Sexton, "The Crusade Against Pari-Mutuel Gambling in Kentucky: A Study of Southern Progressivism in the 1920's," *Filson Club History Quarterly* 50 (1976):55.

one of his chief planks in a bid for the 1923 nomination. In a style that mixed the wrath of a William Jennings Bryan with the antitrust progressivism of a Woodrow Wilson, Barkley stormed out of western Kentucky on a "Christianity, Morality, and Clean Government" campaign. No only did he promise to subdue the Jockey Club and other "trusts," but—more terrifying still—he intended to impose a severance tax on coal and other minerals to ease the property tax burden on the state's farmers. In linking these two ideas, Barkely gave the people a glimpse of something even more frightening than mere clubs: a bipartisan combine was operating, composed of gambling, coal, textbook, whiskey, and other interests acting in collusion to pervert and corrupt the political process, avoid regulation and fair taxation, and defeat hostile populist candidates. "You can't get a school bill through the Legislature without going to the race track or coal lobby," Barkley informed his audiences. "If you want a road past a schoolhouse you must see them. . . . I propose to take its filthy hands from the throat of Kentucky." [14]

Would that he could. Barkley was supported by a diverse collection of disgruntled "out" groups and leaders: Robert Worth Bingham, publisher of the *Louisville Courier-Journal* and a leader of the city's "good-government" elite; Beckham and Haly; the Churchmen's Federation; the Ku Klux Klan; and his faithful western dark-belt farmers. He was nevertheless defeated in the primary, largely because his opponent, J. C. Cantrill, was backed by the bipartisan combine and the urban machines in Louisville, Lexington, and northern Kentucky. Still, the political potential of the antigambling approach was manifest. Barkley's election to the U.S. Senate in 1926 cleared the way for the climax of old-style progressivism, the battle royal that would at last return Kentucky to the path not taken in 1900.

Or so the myth goes. The fact was that Kentucky's political and business leadership was by then so generally compromised by venality or narrow self-interest that any idea of genuine reformation and revised priorities verged on the preposterous. Perhaps Beckham was not engaging in demagoguery in the '27 campaign. There is no doubting his charge that the legislature

14. *Louisville Courier-Journal,* March 25, 1923.

and the current ruling faction were bought and paid for by an in-formal but powerful clique. Unlike her more affluent neighbor states, Kentucky had a less complex economic system and so-cial hierarchy. It was natural for a smaller, self-conscious elite to influence the decision-making process, insofar as one existed. It was done in Indiana and Tennessee; in Kentucky, it was only more apparent. Votes, pardons, state contracts, roads, slush funds to turn a district or stop a bill—in a culturally and materi-ally impoverished state, these were all too susceptible to ma-chine control.

But whether J. C. W. Beckham can be called the last man "who has genuinely challenged the position of the ruling oligar-chy of the state" is questionable, if only because Beckham was a tainted knight.[15] His moralism seemed honestly derived from prohibition days, but the rest was less than convincing. For one thing, many doubted that Beckham had ever swallowed the Bryan-Goebel reform ideology. It was under his administration that state-sanctioned racing began, in the first place, in 1906. A man's opinions could change with circumstances, but his record as a clean-government man was suspect. When he and his fac-tion were in control, it was understood that they exploited their control of the State Board of Valuations and Assessment to "encourage" corporate political contributions in behalf of their candidates. And besides, was the antigambling idea a fair test of reform sympathy? Certainly the Jockey Club was a corrupter. Still, it was exceedingly difficult to persuade tradition-loving Kentuckians to endorse what could be construed as an attack on the sacred horse and a major employer, the racing/breeding in-dustry. The gambling issue created an excessively moralistic, antimodernist tone that turned off potential urban supporters of Beckham in the campaign of 1927.

The crux of the story was appropriately bizarre. Beckham won the primary election handily, sparking a wholesale deser-tion from the Democratic party by the vanquished anti-Beckham administration faction and the combine. Then, in the general election, Beckham alone was defeated. Two million dollars was said to have been spent to secure Beckham's crushing defeat at

15. Fenton, *Politics in the Border States*, p. 55.

the hands of eastern Kentucky Republican Flem Sampson (whom one wit named "Flim-Flam"—accurately, as it turned out). At the same time that Beckham was going down, every other Democratic candidate running for state office with him was elected by wide margins—an amazing display of selectivity in ticket-splitting. Or was it proof of the bipartisan combine conspiracy? Even the pretense of reform seemed exhausted by that charade.

By this time, public and private affairs in the commonwealth seemed hopelessly demoralized. Reformism, either in its nine-teenth-century populist form or in the guise of the more recent business progressivism appeared dead, while the dreams of pro-hibition and woman-suffrage groups had proven to be naive. In Frankfort, a Republican governor sat surrounded by hungry Democrats, with various fat-cat lobbyists grinning quietly off-stage. Kentucky society had sown the seeds, and the trees were apparently bringing forth only evil fruit. However, the perspec-tive of nearly half a century reminds us that a long-static era was nearing its end during the 1920s. In fact, an economic and social metamorphosis of profound dimension was already beginning to make itself felt, a dynamic shift that was to re-shape Kentucky and create new political contours that have per-sisted down to the present day. Boom and bust in the eastern coal fields, militant unionization, city growth, shifts in black voting, dramatic changes in power balances between county, state, and federal government, new styles, new faces, and a vir-ulent new factionalism in the Democratic party—all had their roots in that era.

Signs of these developments were evident long before Gover-nor Sampson began his unhappy tenure. One such development that proved durable and consequential concerned highway con-struction—an area where the appetite for state action was insa-tiable; here taxes could be raised and spent, and the only com-plaint was where the road would go. The desire for all-weather roads and bridges was triggered by the popularity of new and cheaper automobiles, and the demand accelerated, once it was realized what a boon these roads could mean, both in towns eager for growth and in isolated communities. The best comparison is with the canal-and-railroad enthusiasms of the previous century, with similar results. Transportation of people and goods was facilitated, communication across Kentucky was enhanced, and parochialism somewhat reduced; school consolidation was now also possible in rural counties. At the same time, roads were built to open new coal mines and to facilitate timber-cutting in forests previously protected by inaccessibility, much as the railroads had done, decades before.

The political implications of the phenomenon went far beyond anything imagined by Milton H. Smith or William Goebel. Road construction and maintenance created a fantastic patronage bonanza, a cornucopia of state and county jobs and contracts so vast that it made everything that had come before look piddling. And who would control the flow? Many dominant courthouse cliques would be strengthened, but more important was the real source in Frankfort. The Highway Commission rapidly became the greatest single political power center in jobs-poor Kentucky. Theirs was the office in which the partisan machine and official state government met. The governor who controlled the commission not only commanded potential devotion from 120 eager county rings, he commanded campaign contributions (often wrung directly out of the pockets of state employees), he had a ready-made cadre of county political workers in the person of highway crews and allied figures, and he was in a position to handle the legislature as well.

The governor who lost control of the Highway Commission was practically impotent. That was Flem Sampson's dilemma. Accounts of those days tell us that Sampson's Commission was flagrantly corrupt, engaging in forced contributions, favoritism, and falsified contracts, all true enough. His commission was appropriately bipartisan, demonstrating that peculation was a contagious disease. That was sufficient to cause some men to favor a housecleaning. J. Dan Talbott, a Nelson County druggist, respected political advisor, and administrator extraordinaire was the most important of these. More critical to most state politicians than the issue of corruption, however, was the question of who was getting the benefits of commission largesse. Before long, a rebellion organized by the "outs" led to Sampson's being stripped of control over the Highway Commission. This resurgent Democratic faction, masterminded by Talbott, his mentor and father-in-law (and long-time congressman) Ben Johnson, and Billy Klair, party boss in Lexington, captured control of the party. In 1931, this rebellious clique nominated and helped elect Madisonville Judge Ruby Lafoon to the governorship.

The problems facing the new Lafoon administration were immense; so were its opportunities. The nation had begun a precipitous slide into the most severe economic depression in its history. Kentucky's prospects in the twenties had already made a mockery of the Republican "prosperity decade" theme. Prohibition had hurt the land of bourbon. Distilleries retained huge inventories, which they sold for "medicinal purposes," but thousands of their former employees were less fortunate. A boom in coal production had brought new wealth and increased population, especially to the traditionally isolated southeastern counties. But declining prices after 1927 created a powder keg of labor discontent, pitting evicted striking miners against armed company men deputized to suppress United Mine Worker efforts. These shameful scenes of collusion and desperation reached a peak in 1931. Harlan and Bell counties, among others, became hostile camps: workers were killed, their homes and meetings broken up, company property dynamited. Less spectacular but nearly as miserable, elsewhere in the commonwealth, were thousands of farm families who watched helplessly as prices of tobacco and other commodities fell steadily downward.

Yet an astute Lafoon administration vote-counter would have noticed, as early as 1931, that there were signs of a significant shift in voting patterns toward the Democrats. The eastern coal counties, for example, traditionally Republican, had grown more populous, and because of their labor troubles were becoming alienated from the strident Calvin Coolidge mentality of mine owners. In addition, Kentucky's cities had increased rapidly during the 1920s, more rapidly than at any other time in this century. Unlike rural counties whose voters usually demonstrate strong party loyalty and consistency of voting, urban voters tend to be in flux, more unpredictable, more literate, more issue-oriented, and more labor-conscious. Again, due to the world economic plight, both white and black (formerly staunch "Lincoln Republican") voters were beginning a swing toward the Democratic column that would become. pronounced with the election of Franklin D. Roosevelt in 1932. The key would be Louisville, whose shifts could and frequently did determine the outcome of statewide elections. Republican since 1917, the city would return to the embracing fold of Mickey Brennan's Democratic machine in 1933.

Under those circumstances, with the rascality of the outgoing Sampson administration added, the Lafoon government came into office amidst signs of promise. The party seemed uncommonly united and purposeful. Lafoon's principal supporter was Thomas Rhea, leader of a powerful faction in western Kentucky from his Logan County base. Rhea had nominated Beckham for governor, back in '27, and both were ancient enemies of Ben Johnson. Yet Johnson, forced out of the previous Highway Commission, was now restored as its chairman, while his son-in-law, Dan Talbott, was elected state auditor in the new regime. The guide word seemed to be harmony. Fresh new faces were also beginning to be noticed, as a new generation emerged from the political rubble of a failed era. One of the new generation was the incoming Lieutenant Governor Albert Benjamin Chandler, everlastingly nicknamed "Happy" by a Transylvania College friend. Chandler had been plucked out of the state senate and inserted on the Lafoon ticket at the insistence of Johnson and Talbott, and that proved to be a smart move. His bright manner and less ornate, staccato speaking style enlivened the campaign and represented that rising young group of college-trained, ambitious, optimistic leaders so badly needed.

All things considered, the Lafoon administration may have been the biggest flop in Kentucky history. Almost at once, a sense of resentment and betrayal began to poison relations between the governor and many of his erstwhile supporters. Since a Kentucky governor cannot succeed himself in office, his best hope for enacting his legislative program and making a decent mark for himself comes during the first biannual legislative session. In Lafoon's case, much time was lost before he finally proposed, during the end of that session, a 3 percent tax on all retail sales. Like many leaders across the nation (including Franklin Roosevelt campaigning for the presidency), Lafoon attempted, as a principal solution to the deepening woes of the depression, to balance the state budget with increased revenue from a new sales tax. Undoubtedly the state needed funds. Its treasury was empty, its credit bad, and matching funds would soon be needed to qualify for federal relief assistance. But a general sales tax alone was both political suicide and economic injustice. The proposal polarized the General Assembly. A majority, with Lieutenant Governor Chandler leading the attack, defeated the measure and instead passed a package of more selective taxes aimed at such nonessentials as beer and whiskey.

Lafoon was furious, and the battle lines between his people and those gravitating around the Johnson-Talbott-Chandler crowd were quickly etched in acid. In 1934 Lafoon finally succeeded in pushing a reduced sales-tax bill through the assembly by a one-vote margin. The power of the governor to influence recalcitrant legislators, especially in depressed times, was said to be evident here. Later that year, Lafoon, embittered by the treachery of the antitax group, struck back, using the device that had worked so well back in the Flem Sampson days. A "ripper" bill was passed, desiccating the powers of Talbott's office of state auditor, while others stripped Chandler of many of his normal powers as lieutenant governor and president of the senate. Ben Johnson was meanwhile removed as chairman of the crucial Highway Commission, and the trusted Tom Rhea was installed in his place. The governor and his friends were now riding high, but how fared Kentucky? Good government was hardly thriving in such a climate of personal vituperation.

Those forced out into the cold were not destined to remain there long, for the 1935 gubernatorial election season was fast approaching. The question of who is to succeed a governor is raised almost as soon as he is elected. How early Lafoon had determined on anointing Tom Rhea is not certain. Whether it was that decision rather than the sales tax issue or Lafoon's alleged incompetence that had inspired Talbott and the rest to disassociate themselves from the governor is debatable. So was the question of a candidate to match against the powerful Rhea. The lieutenant governorship is occasionally seen as a stepping-stone, but could the youthful Chandler win a statewide race on his own against the considerable force that an incumbent machine could muster? Chandler did have some things going for him: though a newcomer, he was a proven vote-getter; he had cultivated an image of being an enemy of machine politics; and lacking a strong base of his own, he would be obligated to Talbott and Johnson if elected. Other names were considered, Beckham for one, but in the end Chandler's fierce desire to make the race won out.

A more difficult hurdle was how to win the Democratic nomination. For thirty years that decision had been reached by primary elections. Then, in 1931, Lafoon was nominated by a Democratic party convention, supposedly to harmonize the differing factions. Lafoon and Rhea, unwilling to run the risk of a primary defeat, were determined to repeat the convention route. Talbott and friends were bitter but helpless, since the governor controlled party machinery. Then, on the afternoon of February 5, 1935 (according to Talbott's biographer), Talbott and Chandler conspired to pull off the zaniest gambit in Kentucky history. Talbott learned that the governor and Tom Rhea were going to Washington to, among other things, placate President Roosevelt, who was ill-disposed toward the "undemocratic" idea of nominating by convention. Roosevelt closely followed Kentucky affairs, in part because Kentucky's off-year election might be seen as a test of support for the New Deal. Talbott was in a state of high excitement and even sent a man down to the Frankfort depot to be certain that the governor had left, for, once the train crossed the state line and entered West Virginia, Chandler would lawfully be acting governor. On the morning of February 6 came the reason for this Machiavellian scheming. Acting Governor Chandler had summoned all members of the General Assembly to a special session, presumably to pass a bill requiring all party nominations by primary.

What bravado! At once, Lafoon and Rhea received telegrams frantically recalling them, with word that "Dan and Happy are playing hell with the machinery." [16] By the time the dust had

---

16. Orval W. Baylor, *J. Dan Talbott: Champion of Good Government* (Louisville: Kentucky Printing Company, 1942), p. 282.

settled, Lafoon was faced with a town full of wary legislators, men who recognized how much more popular the primary idea was than a "bossed" convention. Lafoon played every parliamentary card he held but was at last obliged to sign a bill authorizing a "double" primary, one requiring a second run-off between the highest finishers if no one received a majority in the first contest. He believed that that would guarantee Rhea's victory, considering his solid support in the courthouses of the state. When the popular vote sagged in the second primary—as all political history said it would—the machines would carry Tom Rhea into the governor's mansion.

But they had not reckoned with Chandler, the "crooner from Versailles." Introducing the sound truck to Kentucky town squares, the tireless Chandler put on an astonishing show, a "sweating, laughing, singing, hand-shaking, baby-patting dervish" the like of which Kentuckians had never before witnessed.[17] Denouncing "Sales-Tax Tom," Chandler promised less tax, more reform, and, above all, more of himself. He was convinced that he was a man of destiny, and in their desperation the people were glad to hear him and his renditions of "Sonny Boy." He trailed Rhea in the first primary but defeated him in the run-off, winning the governorship, thanks to an enormous voter turnout. The modern era in Kentucky politics had arrived.

Was the election of "Happy" Chandler and his first administration truly a watershed in modern state history? The man himself was so much bigger than life, bursting with ego and enthusiasm, that it is still difficult, forty years later, to distinguish glitter from substance. He certainly did not create Democratic party factionalism, for that had been its dominant characteristic since the later nineteenth century. But he did help to personalize and sharpen divisions for the next thirty-five years. He was not a brilliant organizer and really had depended on men such as Talbott to shove him forward at critical moments. But as a dramatic communicator, he was without peer. He had an uncanny ability to establish emotional rapport with crowds, to reach over the heads of hostile courthouse leaders and touch the thoughts

17. *Time,* August 1, 1938, p. 12. The reference was to Chandler's 1938 senatorial campaign, but the description was apt for all his campaigns.

and feelings of rural Kentuckians. Partly it was the times, sullen
and barren as they were. Chandler burst upon the scene, nova-
like, exuding limitless cheer and a dazzling sense of personal
destiny. And, of course, in Lafoon, Rhea, and the tax, he had
the perfect foils. The time and the man merged perfectly. In all
of that, Chandler was like Franklin Roosevelt and that master
politician's campaign against fear, Hoover, and depression. People could not be indifferent to such charismatic figures.

A certain ambivalence also surrounds Chandler's accomplishments as governor in the thirties. His economic program was
advertised as Kentucky's New Deal, but it was quite dissimilar
to the national program of legislation. Chandler was not a profound student of economic and social relations, nor was he noticeably introspective or self-critical. His approach basically reflected a simple, conservative ideology tempered by a measure
of populist spice gained in his western Kentucky, small-town
upbringing (Corydon, Henderson County). He parlayed his popularity to gain some modest social legislation—state child-labor
and old-age pension laws, for example. But social services generally were cut as budgetary moves, and the governor tended to
take credit for relief work and dollars actually funded by the
federal government. He removed the despised sales tax because
it was alleged that it placed too much of the tax burden on
lower-income groups. Instead, he sought to spread that burden
more equitably, employing a new progressive income tax, one
on inheritances, and—after a hard fight—a levy on cigarette
sales, whiskey, and beer.

Certainly such a revenue structure was superior to a high
sales tax alone. But the elimination of any sales tax has been
criticized. Over the next quarter-century, "the absence of a
sales tax and the prevalence of Chandler's pay-as-you-go philosophy" curtailed construction of public facilities, and, most fatally, helped to starve public school education; that in effect
helped deprive generations of Kentuckians of the intellectual
nourishment needed for state economic growth and decent in-
comes for individuals.[18] In short, the commonwealth continued
its unfortunate slide toward the lower end of scales comparing

18. Neal R. Peirce, *The Border States South: People, Politics, and Power in the Five Border South States* (New York: W. W. Norton & Company, Inc., 1975), p. 239.

state expenditures in education and health, in taxes raised, in personal income, and in length of schooling. "Happy" Chandler can hardly be held accountable for these attitudes toward schools, libraries, and taxes, for they were endemic to Kentucky and the South. Reform began only in the 1950s and gained ground in the sixties, when a sales tax was finally re-adopted under the administration of Governor Bert Combs; local school taxes also began to be collected at levels commensurate with twentieth-century student need. These combined with substantial federal assistance to begin the long-postponed process of upgrading education and other basic public services.

Chandler's most unvarnished piece of wisdom was in bringing into his new government a cadre of brainy, energetic men and having the good sense to let them do their best to modernize the antique structure of Kentucky's executive government. The Reorganization Act of 1936 was a great step forward in introducing sound administrative principles, clear lines of authority, and much better oversight of expenditures. Much later, additional progress was made in that direction under Governor Wendell Ford (1971–1974) in consolidating myriad agencies and boards into more manageable and responsive program departments. Incidentally, by producing a capacity at least for more efficient and intelligent state government, these changes have hastened the erosion of the power of the county court, its judge and sheriff. State control of patronage and access to federal programs have enhanced the inevitable ebbing of the prestige and influence of local government. Urbanization has contributed to that; and the 1975 Judicial Article (which virtually eliminates the judicial authority of county justices, transferring it to new district judges), will also further reduce the authority of the county court and improve the quality and statewide consistency of justice.

Nevertheless, there was no way that any Reorganization Bill in the thirties was going to end all the traditional ways of getting things done in Frankfort and the counties. Human nature being what it was, the channels might be narrowed, but the water would still flow. Certainly one of the reasons Chandler supported the bill was that it tended to increase the powers of the governor—indeed, created an unprecedented concentration of authority over administrative, personnel, and financial matters in his hands. No governor, particularly none as ambitious and strong-willed as Chandler, could find that objectionable. In truth, prior to 1936, Kentucky had never enjoyed such effective administration of its public affairs as it did under the reorganized system. Thanks must go to Chandler, because he used his prestige to get the bill adopted and because he appointed many good department heads and left day-to-day affairs largely in their hands. It is also fair to say that it was a happy instance where Chandler's interests and the interests of Kentucky coincided.

Yet the possibilities for abuse were also enriched. One former state legislator recollects that Chandler and his program were so popular "You just couldn't afford to be against him." [19] That was meant figuratively, but often had a literal dollars-and-cents meaning, as well. The focus of corruption was in the new Department of Finance, which had budget, purchasing, and personnel responsibilities. That department, as one contemporary political observer noted, "missed perfection by a wider margin than it should have." [20] Evidence of favoritism in hiring and in awards of contracts, of padded state employment rolls, and of direct levies imposed on state employees to fill the coffers of the Democratic party and the pockets of certain individuals were common then and thereafter. The comprehensive merit-system law passed under Governor Combs in 1960 drastically reduced jobs available for patronage, and that number continued to decrease as more positions went under the merit system. Perhaps, as some say, that has diminished popular interest and participation in government, but the alternative of organized venality is hardly preferable. Also, the modern Kentucky governor is not without his resources, whether they be unskilled highway jobs, gravel roads, personal-service contracts, or administration backing in upcoming elections. Though it is scarcer and sometimes

19. Ollie J. Bowen interview, March 30, 1974, A. B. Chandler Oral History Project, Department of Special Collections, University of Kentucky Library.

20. J. E. Reeves, in J. B. Shannon et al., *A Decade of Change in Kentucky Government and Politics* ([Lexington]: Bureau of Government Research, University of Kentucky, 1943), p. 29.

comes in less apparent forms, patronage remains "the currency of politics in Kentucky." [21]

The experience of the people of Kentucky in the last quarter of their bicentennial century has been marked by tension between the forces of change and continuity. The equilibrium of the state's economic and social life has been jarred by momentous developments affecting agriculture, industry, mining, race relations, the flow of population toward cities and suburbs, and our relationship with the fragile physical environment. Small wonder that Kentuckians and their national brethren have often exhibited a sense of confusion and malaise. Modernization, call it progress or not, has come faster than most people can cope with.

Certainly the state's structure of politics did not keep pace with the sudden arrival of the twentieth century since World War II. From the moment of Chandler's "revolution" in 1936 down through the 1960s, state politics was caught up in an ennervating three-party struggle between Chandler's devoted faction, one associated chiefly with Governor Earle Clements (1947–1951) and Governor Bert Combs (1959–1963), and—almost incidentally—the Republicans. The squabbles, dirty tricks, narrow victories, and bitter charges of fraud delighted the Kentuckian's love of the game of politics. Not even registration laws and voting machines could subdue the spirit of election finagling. "Used to be that with paper ballots there had to be some work done, ballots copied and marked, stubs torn off," one Republican noted wryly. "Now, all you have to do is throw the switch on the voting machine as many times as you want, as fast as you can, so that the curtain is flapping like a flag in high wind." [22] Needless to say, that skill is no Democratic secret.

As comic opera, such shenanigans make us laugh. As an arena for balancing real-life demands between private citizens, pressure groups, and an enlightened sense of the broad public

21. Malcolm E. Jewell and Everett W. Cunningham, *Kentucky Politics* (Lexington: University of Kentucky Press, 1968), p. 43.

22. *Louisville Courier-Journal and Times Sunday Magazine,* November 28, 1976, pp. 6–7.

interest, Kentucky politics "missed perfection" by a disheartening margin. It was no accident that the two politicians who achieved the most noteworthy reputations from this state did so in part by disassociating themselves from local realities. Both Democratic Senator and Vice-President Alben Barkley ("the Veep") and Republican Senator John Sherman Cooper cultivated an image of independence and integrity, of concern with large national and even international questions. State and county leaders cannot afford such luxury. One can only hope that, in the post-Watergate era, expectations regarding the performance of public officials will produce if not better legislation then at least better legislators.

The state certainly will need both to cope with the profoundly complex changes introduced into Kentucky economic life. While the agrarian dream continues to nestle at the core of its popular mythology, changes in Kentucky's agricultural and industrial sectors over the past two generations have been astonishing. Since 1940, for example, cropland harvested has declined by nearly a million-and-a-half acres; the number of farm families has decreased by 50 percent, and nearly half of those remaining are now small, part-time farm operations. The agribusiness center is slowly shifting toward the relatively large-scale grain, soybean, and livestock farms of the western counties. Where all that leaves the principal support of the smaller farmer—burley tobacco—is unclear. Despite the use of tractors and fertilizers that sustain high-production levels on fewer acres, harvesting the tobacco crop still requires much of the same hard hand labor of cutting and stripping that it did three hundred years ago. Fewer men relish that kind of toil, even on their own land, much less as tenants or day laborers. Kentucky retains its rural character and significant human investment in agriculture. But the issues of tobacco and health and tobacco and labor appear intractable. With the industry printing bumper stickers urging the public to "Enjoy Smoking," the future of Kentucky's number-one crop remains uncertain.

These agricultural developments did not occur in a vacuum. The farmer who deserts his ancient acres by choice or by economic compulsion is also being drawn into the city by the magnet of better pay and more leisure. There is no doubt that the industrial revolution has reached Kentucky, though its character is markedly different from the sort that rewrote the history of northern big cities. Since the boom generated by World War II, industry has migrated southward into the state at a considerable rate. There are more than twice as many manufacturing plants today as in 1940, and four times as many Kentuckians earn wages in industry now as did on the eve of that war. The nature of work in these plants has also undergone a sea-change. Even traditional industrial operations now demand a more literate, skillful worker, as employees at the mammoth General Electric or Ford plants in Louisville or Rockwell International in Clark County could attest. Just as striking has been the influence of still more sophisticated assembly plants that have created or expanded local communities of white-collar, managerial, and highly trained technical employees. The phenomenon is familiar to residents of Paducah, Bowling Green, and the many growing towns along the northern tier of counties.

But nowhere has it been as remarkable as in Lexington, which was changed from a static, farming-trading-college town into one of the fastest-growing metropolitan areas in the country. The arrival of the prestigious International Business Machines plant in 1956 marked the beginning of the transmutation; a more productive, affluent, and troublesome day had arrived. New industries, coupled with the rapid expansion of the University of Kentucky brought an expanded tax base and a more demanding urban clientele, including a substantial migration of hopeful job-seekers from nearby eastern counties. The traditional banker-lawyer-horse set elite has managed to retain control, but Lexington's adoption of a pathbreaking (for Kentucky) urban-county government and massive downtown reconstruction may eventually yield payoffs in the form of enlightened traffic- and land-use planning not yet in evidence. City boosters tell us that states like Kentucky can profit from the examples of northern urban blight. One cannot tell that from Louisville's graphic tripartite race-class neighborhood segmentation surrounded by a ring of petty suburban principalities; nor does Lexington's haphazard "Sunset Strip" commercialization or Ashland's smog-obscured face give promise of a better day. The price for economic progress still seems very high.

Attractive or not, however, Kentucky's towns and cities retain the charm of employment, and that will probably sustain the state's most pronounced population trend over the past half-century: a movement away from the rural areas of the southern and western counties and back toward the original centers of settlement along the Ohio River and the Bluegrass region. Such a shift has already begun to recontour the social and political face of Kentucky. In time, reactionary courthouse cliques and school boards may yield. State-imposed property-tax assessment rates will translate into improved public services. From larger cities to smaller towns eager to diversify and avoid fossilization, people are concerned about the negative effects of new industry on air, water, sewage disposal, streets, and schools. The economic motive will no doubt triumph. Whether such economic "progress" improves or erodes the quality of our lives will depend upon our developing an alert and educated citizenry and political leadership.

One can measure these economic developments by charting the ebb and flow of Kentuckians out of their native state. For most of this century, Kentucky's over-all population has grown negatively—that is, more slowly than the national average. The state has been a seedbed, exporting her sons and daughters, or worse, forcing them out from a lack of educational and industrial opportunity. In recent years, that outflow has fortunately been stopped, perhaps even reversed. These whites—principally eastern Kentuckians—expanded a path originally blazed by black Kentuckians back in the frustrating post-Civil War years. From those decades until the 1950s, Kentucky's Negro population fell precipitously, and only in our own times have modest increases been recorded. Indeed, during the bicentennial year, this state had approximately the same number of black residents as lived here on the eve of the Civil War.

We can hardly call *de jure* discrimination in schooling, jobs, and housing encouraging. Yet Kentucky has had at least a mixed record on race relations in this century. Blacks never lost the suffrage, as they did in all states to the south. And there have been dramatic instances in which governors have provided praiseworthy moral leadership. In 1917 and 1920, for example, Democratic Governor Stanley and Republican Governor Ed

Morrow personally intervened to prevent lynchings and subdue racist mobs. In 1954 Governor Lawrence Wetherby signaled the state's uniquely positive response to the Supreme Court's *Brown* v. *Board of Education* decision. It may have been tokenism by later standards, but measured by the climate of the day, it was an act of courage. Two years later, Governor Chandler, serving his second term (1955–1959), went the next step by defending school integration with state police and the National Guard. The state also made a decent record in acting to overturn Jim Crowism generally. During the progressive Combs administration, legal discrimination was prohibited under the new state merit system, and a Human Rights Commission was established. After a frequently bitter six-year struggle, the commission was given enforcement teeth with a Civil Rights Act adopted in 1966 with support from Governor Edward Breathitt.

Everyone recognizes that such legislation, though important as law and symbol, must be followed by a metamorphosis in public attitudes. Leadership is important here, but it need not always come from high officials. The more blatant forms of race fears and stereotypes are susceptible to change when thousands of employers, clergymen, educators, journalists, and parents speak against them. For all his word antics, heavyweight boxing champion Muhammed Ali (baptized, ironically, as Cassius Clay) has played a role in the drama of black cultural sensitivity. In a quite different way, Whitney Young, Sr., president of black Lincoln Institute, as well as his remarkable son Whitney Young, Jr., director of the Urban League until his untimely death in 1971, both contributed mightily to the cause of racial justice in Kentucky and the nation. Significantly, all three men were natives of Louisville, the center of black leadership in the state.

Black education, employment, and income prospects remain circumscribed by limited opportunity, white prejudice, and black self-doubt. The school-busing controversy has bedeviled and confused people of both races. Working-class whites and blacks in Louisville tend to see busing as class discrimination, since wealthier East Enders apparently remain less affected by it. Many other blacks, meanwhile, interpret integration to mean that black schools are closed and their school spirit and athletes swallowed up in largely white, amorphous public schools. We no longer need the sort of physical courage shown by Stanley and Morrow when they stood before crowds howling for a Negro sacrifice. What is needed now is wisdom, perseverance, and mutual good faith, and these have ever been in short supply.

Public concern with issues of poverty, education levels, cultural or genetic deprivation, and other strayings from the path of middle-class progress have, however, taken a unique turn in Kentucky. Except during isolated moments of racial turmoil, the focus of attention has not been on black conditions but on white—on Eastern Kentucky, specifically. No other aspect of life and culture in this state has evoked half the notoriety and political activism. By the later 1960s many Americans might have been surprised to learn that Appalachia was not confined to Kentucky and that Kentucky was not exclusively Appalachian. For a time, the entire region was a-swarm with concerned sociologists, anthropologists, economists, federal antipoverty agency representatives, Community Action people, socially-minded ministers, family planners, bright-eyed VISTA volunteers, and horrified environmentalists. Poverty had been rediscovered by a pudgy and affluent middle class.

The devastating 1957 flood and regional studies that followed were a catalyst in shocking Eisenhower-era Americans into a dim realization of the existence of vast islands of people left behind in the postwar economic boom. Television and journalistic coverage of John F. Kennedy's West Virginia campaign in 1960 sharpened popular awareness of the quiet tragedy. Soon, tens of thousands were reading a book entitled *Night Comes to the Cumberlands* by a Letcher County attorney named Harry Caudill. The book is a painfully truthful indictment of economic oppression and impending human and ecological disaster in the mountains. The spirit of social reform reached one of its periodic peaks, pushed there in part by the assassination of President Kennedy. The nation went to war on poverty. Technology was going to put men on the moon in the sixties. The triumph of American social engineering could hardly be less successful. Time passed, dollars were spent, commissions created, reports filed. Mutual frustration between official "benefactors" and mountain (or urban black) "patrons" increased. There was some heartening progress, but the over-all challenge proved less tractable than hurling men into outer space. Locals entrenched in official positions or businesses threatened by change (as well as some state politicians who saw an opportunity for cheap personal gain) combined to counterattack with xenophobic charges of "Communism!" Social scientists shook their heads and spoke of a resistant "culture of poverty." And in the case of both the white and black poor, this resurgent mood of fatalism and despair led to uninformed talk of innate inferiority, "genetic factors," a biological determinism that would doom all redemptive schemes to failure.

Social problems as immense as those presented by Appalachia (or the inner city) have always tended to generate cycles of exaggerated optimism and pessimism. This is not to minimize the dimensions and complexity of the situation. Natives of the numberless valleys and hollows of the Cumberland Plateau experienced a traumatic history that created a distinctive culture ill-suited to meet the forces of modernization. Their ancestors' prolonged devotion to an essentially eighteenth-century hunting-grazing economy, the terrible impact of the Civil War, local feuds, incompetence and corruption in county and state politics, and the exhaustion of thin soils washed by fierce mountain deluges would have been enough to stunt the growth of a progressive tradition. But these were the least of the traumas. By the later nineteenth century, the immense riches of the plateau were recognized, not by natives as much as by agents of industrial capitalism. Fine hardwood timbers were needed, and here was God's loveliest expanse of mixed forest, soon denuded of its best stands. Coal was needed to heat homes and stoke the ever-hungry steel furnaces. And the blight that coal mining brings to every place it touches came to the coal-rich fields of Appalachia.

Over the past seventy years, bust followed boom, and the sequence was repeated; mechanization created the paradox of high production and unemployment; deep mining, with its high human costs, yielded to strip-mining, with its despoliation of the ancient mountains. Billions in tons and dollars have poured out of the hills, by now an economic colony of Bethlehem Steel, Kentucky River Coal, the Tennessee Valley Authority, Ashland Oil, the Mellon family, Consolidation Coal, et al. All of this wealth should have helped to improve the quality of life in the regions from whence it was taken, but that is rarely the case with extractive industries controlled by distant corporations imbued with a quasi-imperialist mentality. Low prices, puny tax assessments and rates, and the exemption of coal-industry equipment from the state sales tax combined with a shameful lack of local and state political responsibility to produce a bitter harvest: not wealth, but widows and orphans, broken bodies, weak public services, and widespread suspicion, anxiety, and welfare dependency.

The experience of the past fifteen years, however, indicates that the old stereotypes are contradictory and are increasingly false. For example, there has always been more variety in the people and culture of Eastern Kentucky than the popular myth of homogeneity would have one believe. Many counties are without the benefits and penalties of coal deposits; poverty contrasts with wealth much as it does in every region, and mountain people live in a bewildering range of circumstances, from the more remote few still living far back up the hollows, through small rural communities and the remaining coal-camp towns, to the growing regional cities. The old nemesis of physical isolation has been reduced by new and better roads—which, one hopes, will not be pounded back into dust by overweight coal trucks. The influence of radio and television cannot be overstated. The idea that Eastern Kentucky is changeless never has been tenable, and certainly is not true now. The birth rate, long the highest in the nation, has fallen significantly as the economic and cultural benefits of large families decrease. More and more mountain women have found useful and satisfying activities aside from raising babies and keeping house. Out-migration—the safety valve that was also an open door through which hundreds of thousands of the most discontented, desperate, ambitious, and able young people left the state—has also been slowed and even reversed in most counties, in the 1970s. Per capita income has grown faster than the national average, though the gap remains large.

Obviously, the coal boom, which peaked again during the energy crisis of 1974, was the decisive factor in some of this, along with the work of the Appalachian Regional Commission and other agencies. Since the boom, employment figures and the number of smaller truck mines in operation have declined, but coal mining will doubtless remain the state's leading industry until the liabilities of nuclear energy safety and waste disposal and solar energy costs are mastered. Kentucky is now the nation's leading coal supplier, and this immense resource will become even more significant in an increasingly energy-starved world. In the meantime, the local benefits of economic growth have not been confined to displays of Cadillac and Rolls Royce automobiles, but have been felt among a broad segment of the population in the form of better home conditions, new appliances, and the use of the long-delayed coal severance tax for community improvement.

A large segment of Kentucky's Appalachian population seems unwilling to accept the notion that their part of the universe is in a condition of irreversible pathology. Even the angriest native critics cling to the fact that the region still has abundant resources and potential—coal, oil, gas, timber, clean air and water, electric power, and a splendid base for natural recreational facilities. The real problem, as regionalist Harry Caudill reminds us, is political: how to gain effective control of these resources to construct an alternative future for Eastern Kentucky and for the state, one in which this great wealth may benefit Kentuckians at least as much as it enriches a few local and national corporate developers. Yet the problem is something of a "Catch-22," for the political structure of the region and the attitudes of its natives militate against concerted, progressive planning. The traditional emphasis on rugged individualism, lack of familiarity with the notion of community interests and actions, suspicion of "outside" ideas, cynicism toward politics and bureaucracy (well-justified), and a disproportionate influence of older, more conservative men have all made adaptation to changing times more difficult.

If we will step back and consider the entire state here, in the beginning of its third century, we can see that the problems and

opportunities of Eastern Kentucky are only different in degree
from those of Kentucky as a whole. What are the good things
worth preserving in the commonwealth's cultural heritage? Can
they be preserved? Do we value personal warmth and loyalty, a
sense of rootedness, a productive but slower, less competitive
life-style? Can the state enter the mainstream of modern mass
society and sustain these values? Even if we go about the task of
defining humane and cautionary goals, will it matter, in the face
of the legitimate pressures for material improvement that have
led most American communities toward the suburban life-style,
impersonal neighbors, and commercial strips with their inevitable Kentucky Fried Chicken stands and "Golden Arches"? We
know that some of the values and behavior distinctive to the
South and the southern mountain area have proved remarkably
resistant to the homogenizing effects of mass culture—the stric-
tures of "thou-shalt-not" orthodox Protestantism, respect for
family authority, back-to-the-wall defensiveness and "ethnic"
pride, among other traits. Perhaps acquisitiveness can be balanced against values rooted in a rural past. A new constitutional
convention, long delayed and badly needed, might be an effective forum for clarifying community goals and developing a
more responsive political climate.

The difficulties in the way of establishing responsible policies
are well illustrated in the problem of strip-mining and environmental preservation. Energy is fundamental to economic growth
and prosperity. Coal is fundamental to Kentucky's sharing in
that prosperity. Unprecedented improvements in the efficiency
of earth-moving machinery have combined with the voracious
appetites for fuel of industry and the TVA to wreak havoc on
the western coal fields and worse than havoc on the steeper
slopes of the Cumberland Plateau. Attempts to stop or even to
temper the pace of this self-destruction were repeatedly thwarted
by State Court of Appeals decisions more concerned with corporate development than with a reasonable regard for the circumstances of native Kentucky residents and the future of our
precious landed heritage. TVA, for example, has accomplished
great things in promoting rural electrification; at the same time,
its impact on the environment deserves criticism. Cannot a balance be struck to avoid the false equation between more jobs

and a better material life, on the one hand, and fouling our nest and the nest for our children's children, on the other?

The evidence is not all negative. Back in 1929, for example, a tremendous victory was won over the Kentucky Utilities Company and its owner, Samuel Insull. Their plan to turn majestic Cumberland Falls into a hydroelectric dam was thwarted when industrialist T. Coleman du Pont offered to buy the land and donate it to the state as parkland. Fortunately, Insull was supported by Governor Flem Sampson, and Democratic legislators were persuaded to follow a vocal public opinion and accept du Pont's offer. There is a lesson here worth noting. Doubtless few of those men in the General Assembly had ever seen Cumberland Falls. Luck and politics happened to save it. But today we have a better awareness of our interdependency. We are all in the same boat, and while regional variety is fine, the state must act under an enlightened sense of a general public interest. Cities will sink if made to sustain rural welfare and educational systems indefinitely. Country people can see the value of balancing agriculture with industry, prosperity with ecology. The farmer with a two-thousand-acre spread in Fulton County does have a common interest with the Louisville merchant who loves to fish in clear streams, and with the Pike County miner who has a new mortgage. Ultimately, they will all rise or fall together. The impressive system of state and federal highways is a vital factor, but knowledge is as essential as mobility. If we remain strangers to one another and share no higher value than self-gratification, the conclusion will not be in doubt.

The idea of community, a statewide community of interests, needs to be cultivated. For too long, the principal things that gave Kentuckians a sense of unity have been the flimsy reeds of sports. It is easy to see why sports is popular. College and schoolboy basketball and football are grand entertainment. They build local school spirit. They are innocuous and take one's mind off the reality of personal or social problems. In the symbolic battles waged on court and field, there is a release of tension and energy, the illusion (and sometimes the reality) of violent aggression. Basketball in particular has worked against state sectionalism because of the amazing record compiled by the University of Kentucky's long-time coach Adolph Rupp.

Thanks to "the Baron's" forceful coaching and recruiting, Kentuckians experienced the vicarious thrill of national victories—a sensation that helped blur their feelings of cultural inferiority in other respects. But the exaggerated celebration of school athletics has had less fortunate consequences, as well. For a half-century, precious resources have gone into inflating coaches' salaries, constructing immensely inelegant stadia, and creating the illusion that schools exist so that teams can have cheering fans. The question again is one of proportion, of priorities, and of developing a wise sense of what is important. If Kentucky schools produce top-ranked national teams while the state remains forty-ninth in money spent on public school education, as it was in 1975–1976, the real losers will continue to be Kentucky children.

This is Kentucky's bicentennial celebration, as well as America's. Birthdays are a good time to look back and recall the successes and the failures, to see what is valuable and worth preserving of a culture whose economic underpinnings are being altered before our eyes. Everywhere there is a yearning for freedom, for personal security and dignity, for a deeper understanding of who we are and what to make of our lives. As state and nation stand on the threshold of their third century, the future remains unpredictable, but not without hope. We are reminded of that nineteenth-century vision of progressive Kentucky held by Henry Clay, Cassius Clay, and others: diversified industry providing meaningful work and fair wages, public education encouraged to teach and able to hold onto its best teachers and most promising students, an atmosphere where toleration and open-mindedness flourish, instead of sectionalism, racism, and class suspicion. Perhaps Kentucky's border-state heritage will give us leaders with the wisdom to chart a path between the rocks of private ambition toward these modest goals.

Suggestions for Further Reading

In most states, the challenge of writing critical state and local history has evoked an uneven response. Genealogy has its role, and the celebration of leading families, homes, and county events by ardent locals has always flourished alongside entertaining and superficial biography. More serious analysis has been daunted by the inadequate preservation of official and private source materials and by a widespread indifference to the value of supporting a thoughtful evaluation of the state's history. Only one compelling lesson will be learned from honest and professional histories, namely that we are wholly our fathers' children—our present and future shaped by their acts.

There are no better introductions to the deeds that created Kentucky's present character than Thomas D. Clark's writings. Readers will certainly appreciate the colorful and episodic *Kentucky: Land of Contrast* (New York: Harper & Row, 1968). The early period of state history has elicited the greatest volume of historical scholarship. A brief survey rich with detail and opinion is Robert S. Cotterill's *History of Pioneer Kentucky* (Cincinnati: Johnson & Hardin, 1917). No one interested in the origins of Kentucky mythology and its class distinctions should miss Arthur K. Moore's *The Frontier Mind: A Cultural Analysis of the Kentucky Frontiersman* (Lexington: The University of Kentucky Press, 1957), for it is one of the outstanding studies in Kentucky history. An obvious way to approach the formative period is through the experiences of Daniel Boone; John Bakeless, *Daniel Boone, Master of the Wilderness* (1939; reprint edition, Harrisburg, Pa.: Stackpole Co., 1965) is a readable and reliable biography. Also valuable is Charles Gano Talbert's *Benjamin Logan, Kentucky Frontiersman* (Lexington: University of Kentucky Press, 1962).

Aspects of eighteenth-century culture and politics that influenced the life of the state into contemporary times are nicely described in John B. Boles's *Religion in Antebellum Kentucky* and Robert M. Ireland's *The County in Kentucky History,* both published in Lexington by the University Press of Kentucky, in 1976. Agriculture, land, and horses

213

have also been part of the Kentucky experience and imagination since the beginning. Good accounts, all published in Lexington by the University Press of Kentucky, include W. F. Axton, *Tobacco and Kentucky* (1976); Henry G. Crowgey, *Kentucky Bourbon: The Early Years of Whiskeymaking* (1971); James F. Hopkins, *A History of the Hemp Industry in Kentucky* (1951); and Kent Hollingsworth, *The Kentucky Thoroughbred* (1976).

The history of nineteenth-century Kentucky has yielded some excellent studies. Two older works that remain useful are J. Winston Coleman, *Slavery Times in Kentucky* (Chapel Hill: The University of North Carolina Press, 1940), and E. Merton Coulter, *The Civil War and Readjustment in Kentucky* (1926; reprint edition, Gloucester, Mass.: Peter Smith, 1966). Biographies provide an invaluable approach to the period. The best short study of Kentucky's foremost statesman is Clement Eaton, *Henry Clay and the Art of American Politics* (Boston: Little, Brown & Co., 1957). Albert D. Kirwan's *John J. Crittenden: The Struggle for the Union* (Lexington: The University of Kentucky Press, 1964) is a prize-winning study of Clay's would-be successor as savior of the Union. William C. Davis, *Breckinridge: Statesman, Soldier, Symbol* (Baton Rouge: Louisiana State University Press, 1974) is a brilliant life of John C. Breckinridge, congressman, senator, vice-president, Confederate general and war secretary, and postwar railroad promoter. Standing above them all in vision and vexatious contradiction was Cassius M. Clay; the most reliable biography remains David L. Smiley's *Lion of White Hall: The Life of Cassius M. Clay* (1962; reprint edition, Gloucester, Mass.: Peter Smith, 1969). Readers will also want to learn about Clay's remarkable family, and Paul E. Fuller's *Laura Clay and the Woman's Rights Movement* (Lexington: The University Press of Kentucky, 1975) is a beginning.

In most respects, the history of Kentucky in the later nineteenth and twentieth centuries remains to be written. Issues and personalities of vast importance—circumstances that have shaped the character and quality of our lives—await critical examination. Hambleton Tapp and James C. Klotter, *Kentucky: Decades of Discord, 1865–1900* (Frankfort: Kentucky Historical Society, 1977) is an important start. Malcolm E. Jewell and Everett W. Cunningham's *Kentucky Politics* (Lexington: The University of Kentucky Press, 1968) throws some light on that Byzantine subject. Neal R. Peirce, *The Border States South: People, Politics, and Power in the Five Border South States* (New York:

W. W. Norton & Company, Inc., 1975) surveys the contemporary scene.

Eastern Kentucky has been treated more effectively than any other region of the state. The work of Harry M. Caudill has attracted national praise. His study *Night Comes to the Cumberlands: A Biography of a Depressed Area* (New York: Little, Brown & Co., 1962) remains his most substantial and eloquent work. Virgil C. Jones, *The Hatfields and the McCoys* (Chapel Hill: The University of North Carolina Press, 1948) describes that unhappy saga, while Jack E. Weller's *Yesterday's People: Life in Contemporary Appalachia* provides a sympathetic analysis. Conditions are changing rapidly, and David S. Walls and John B. Stephenson, two sociologists at the University of Kentucky, edited a valuable collection of more recent views in *Appalachia in the Sixties: Decade of Reawakening* (Lexington: University Press of Kentucky, 1973).

Index

Abolitionism, 98–100 *passim,* 104–105, 108. *See also* Emancipation; Freedmen; Negroes; Slavery; Slaves

Adair, John (governor), 80–81

Agriculture: colonial practices, 5–6; soil, value of, 43–44; changing patterns, 44, 77, 90, 95, 96, 157–159, 201–202; crops, 78–80, 95; slaveholders dominate, 95, 96; sharecropping and apprenticeships, 137; agrarian discontent, 158; Grangers, 159; economic decline, 157–158. *See also* Crops; Livestock industry

Ali, Muhammed (Cassius Clay), 204

American Colonization Society, 98, 99

American Protective Association, 161, 163

American Tobacco Company, 159, 161, 178–180 *passim*

Ancient Cultivation Law, 40–41, 43

Anti-Gambling Commission, 187. *See also* Kentucky Racing Commission

Appalachian Mountains: settlement in, 4; exploration of, 7; Unionism in, 123; and war on poverty; 205; social problems, 206, 207; mentioned, 10, 29

Appalachian Plateau, 58, 91

Appalachian Regional Commission, 208

Appellate Court controversy: fight to remove justices of, 82–85; and relief party actions, 83; Old Court party, 84–85, 87; New Court party, 84–85, 87, 88

Appomattox, 136, 138

Bank of Commonwealth, 80–81

Banks: and inflation, 77–79, 85; failure of, 80–81. *See also* Kentucky—economy

Barkley, Alben W. (vice-president), 187–188, 201

Barry, William: and Appellate Court controversy, 88

Beckham, John C. W. (governor), 173, 177, 186

Berea College, 108, 180

Birney, James G., 99–100

Bingham, Robert Worth: and clean government, 182; publisher, *Courier-Journal,* 188

Bluegrass, 22, 144, 145, 165

Blue Licks, 30, 35

Boiling Springs, 17, 26

Boone, Daniel: teamster and blacksmith, 9; legends about, 11; first Kentucky explorer, 12–13; role in settlement, 13, 17; returns to Yadkin, 14–15; and Shawnee captivity, 30–31; land acquisition, 42; mentioned, 14, 18, 20, 44, 74

Bourbon coalition: and economic development, 148, 149; and public services, 153; and "New South" creed, 156; breaks up, 160–161. *See also* Kentucky—politics and government

Bourbon whiskey. *See* Whiskey

Bowling Green, 121–122, 123

Boyle, John: and Appellate Court controversy, 82–84

Bradley, William O'Connell (governor), 161, 169–170

Bramlette, Thomas (governor), 131–132, 134

Breathitt, Edward (governor), 204

Breckinridge, John C.: member, proslavery faction and Congress, 107, 113, 115–116; in Confederate army, 117–118; leads C & S railroad lobby, 147

Cameron, Simon: abolitionist and secretary of war, 129–130

Camp Charlotte: treaty of, 19

Cantrill, J. C. (governor), 188

Carlisle, John G.: and Cincinnati railway bill, 150–151

Centre College, 101

Chandler, Albert B. ("Happy"): governorship, 193, 194–200 *passim*

Cherokee, 4, 11. *See also* Indians
Cincinnati, O., 77–78, 86
Cincinnati and Southern Railroad: political involvement, 146; proposal for, 146, 150, 151; defeat of bill for creating, 147
Civil Rights Act, 138, 204
Civil War: coming of, 75–76, 88, 92; prosperity prior to, 77; secession, 77, 109–110, 114, 115; impact of, 88, 120; Confederate States of America, 114; state involvement, 117, 126; Battle of Shiloh, 123–124; "Morgan's Raiders," 124–125; Battle of Richmond, 125; partisans and guerrilla bands, 127, 139; free blacks as soldiers, 130–132
Clark, George Rogers, 27, 32
Clay, Cassius Marcellus: emancipationist, 49, 105, 106, 108, 211; progressive vision, 105, 108, 133, 211
Clay, Cassius M. (nephew of Cassius Marcellus Clay): and railroad lobby, 159
Clay, Green: and state constitution of 1799, 48; in War of 1812, 48; and investments in early economy, 49, 53
Clay, Henry: and economic diversification, 49; secretary of state under Adams, 87; and American Colonization Society, 98; defeated by James Polk, 100; and anti-slavery issue, 104; death, 107; vision of progress, 211; mentioned, 56
Clay, Laura: early leader, women's rights, 156
Clements, Earle (governor), 200
Coal mining, 88–89, 146, 206, 207, 208
Colleges and universities. *See* by name
Combs, Bert (governor), 198, 200
Compromise of 1850, 110
Confederate States of America, 114. *See also* Civil War
Congressional Reconstruction Acts, 120
Constitutions of Kentucky: of 1792, 66–71; of 1799, 72–73; convention of 1849 and constitutional changes, 89. *See also* Kentucky—politics and government
Corn: as food and drink, 52; surplus, 59; value to economy, 96, 112
Cornstalk (chief, Shawnee), 19, 25
Cotton: prices after 1815, 78, 79; and slave labor, 96
Corrupt Practices Act, 184
Court of Appeals. *See* Appellate Court controversy

Calhoun, John C., 110
Crittenden, John J., 113–114
Crops: hemp, 49–51, 59, 78, 95–96, 112; tobacco, 49, 50–52, 63, 144–145, 158–159, 179–180, 184, 201; corn, 52, 59, 96, 112; rye, 59; cotton, 78, 79, 96; prices, 78–80; grains, 95; value to economy, 95; wheat, 96
Cumberland Gap: named by Walker, 8; and "Path Deed," 21; "Kaintuck hog road," 54; in Civil War, 121; mentioned, 7, 17, 25
Cumberland River, 20, 52

Danville: founded, 17; and first convention for statehood (1784), 60
Dark District Tobacco Association, 179. *See also* Tobacco
Darwin, Charles: theory of evolution debated, 185–186
Davis, Jefferson: president, Confederate States of America, 114–115, 124
Debt: imprisonment for, 69; increase in, 78–79. *See also* Banks; Kentucky —economy
Demaree, T. B., 162
Democratic party: and slavery, 107; break-up of (1860), 111; post-Civil War, 135–136, 143; and states' rights, 147–148; governor's race (1871), 150–151; and rural discontent, 159; and "Statehouse Ring," 161; bested, 162, 163, 166; Louisville machine, 182; mentioned, 169, 170–171, 176
Desha, Joseph (governor), 83
Dinwiddie, Robert: governor of Virginia, 8, 9
Distilleries. *See* Whiskey
Dragging Canoe: prophecy of, 21–22, 24, 25, 57
Duke, James B.: and American Tobacco Company, 159
Dunmore's War, 18, 25

Emancipation: programs of, 97, 129; and proposed constitutional amendment, 104; proclamation issued, 120, 128, 129, 130; 13th Amendment, 134, 136; opposition to, 135. *See also* Freedmen; Negroes; Slavery; Slaves
England: exploration, dominance in North America, 7, 10–11, 29; and Indian as-

England (*Cont.*)
    sault forces, 29, 33; keeps forts on Great
    Lakes, 61

Farmers' Alliance, 159, 166
Fayette County, 57
Feuds, 153, 178
Fifteenth Amendment: passage of, 148–149
Finley, John: adventurer-explorer, 9–13
Ford, Wendell (governor), 198
Fort Ancient: pathology, early inhabitants, 23, 24
Fort Boonesborough, 26
Fort Donelson, 123
Fort Duquesne, 9
Fort Henry, 123
Fort Nelson, 32
Fort Pitt, 18
Fort Stanwix: treaty of, 11
Fourteenth Amendment: and Civil Rights Act, 138
France: early exploration in North America, 5, 7, 9
Frankfort: site of new statehouse (1799), 72
Freedmen: question of rights, 97; repatriation proposed, 98; during Civil War, 129; as soldiers, 130–132; problems of, 137. *See also* Emancipation
Freedmen's Bureau, 138, 140

Garrison, William Lloyd, 98
Goebel, William: investigation into railroad lobbying, 159–167 *passim;* early life and characteristics, 166–168; "Goebel Election Law," 168–169, 171, 177; runs for governorship, 170–171, 173; assassination and aftereffects, 173–175; mentioned, 176
Governor's Neutrality Proclamation (1861), 116. *See also* Civil War
Grangers, 159
Grant, Ulysses S., 117, 120–121

Haly, Percy: advisor to Governor Beckham, 181
Hardin, Wat: and 1895 governor's race, 162, 170
Hargis-Cockrill feud, 178
Harlan, John Marshall, 150–151
Harrod, James: and Harrodstown, 16–17

Harrodstown: convention, 27; seat of county government, 28–29
Hatfield-McCoy feud, 153
Hemp: early manufacture of, 49, 50, 59; Kentucky chief producer of, 50–51, 78; factor in slavery, 50–51, 96; prices of, 78–80; mentioned, 75, 79, 95, 112
Henderson, Richard: founder, Transylvania Land Company, 19; early life, 20; sends Boone to Kentucky area, 24; illegal land operations of, 26; and land compensation, 28
Highway Commission: and politics, 191
Horses: breeding of, 50, 54, 56, 75; racing, 54, 56; increase in numbers, 59; and pari-mutuel race-track betting, 186–187, 188. *See also* Kentucky Jockey Club; Kentucky Racing Commission; Livestock industry
Human Rights Commission, 204

Indians: hostile to whites, 10; and boundary for white settlements, 11; as British assault forces, 29; attack on northwestern frontier, 63. *See also* Cherokees; Iroquois; Shawnee; Wyandottes
Industry, 54, 86, 202
Iroquois: claim to territory, 11
Iroquois Confederacy, Six Nations of, 11, 22, 23

Jackson, Andrew, 87, 88, 99
Jefferson, Thomas, 28, 71
Johnson, Ben: and Highway Commission, 192–194
Johnston, Gen. Albert Sidney, 121–124
Johnston, George W.: governor, "shadow-Confederate" government, 124

Kendall, Amos: and Appellate Court controversy, 88
Kentucky: name, 4, 57; images of, 4, 6–7, 44; river boundaries, 20, 57, 62; key role in westward movement, 39; mystique, 36–37, 76–77, 153; first western slave state, 46; first frontier state, 67, 70; provincialism, 72, 74; first transmontane state, 74; position as slave state, 95, 100, 111–112, 114–115; position during Civil War, 114, 116–117, 118, 120–121, 123,

Kentucky (*Cont.*)

127–128 *passim*, 129, 135–137; and Reconstruction, 136; growth rate, 175; border-state heritage, 211

—economy: during Revolution, 41; taxation, 41, 73; early diversification, 49–50; influence of slavery on, 50, 51, 95–97, 105; economic patterns, 56, 91, 157–158; growth and diversification, 71; overexpansion and inflation, 77–79; currency printed, 78, 79–80, 81; new banks chartered, 79; deflation, 79–80; panic of 1819, 79; depression, 80–81, 87, 88; financial relief measures, 80–83, 88, 97; dominant cities, 86; rebound after 1819, 88; urbanization and economic change, 92, 111, 143, 152, 176, 202–203, 206–210; exploited, 152–153; declines, 157–158; panic of 1873, 158; growth rate decreases, 175; growth and change since World War II, 202–203; war on poverty, 205

—education: poorly supported, 69, 75, 86, 89, 90, 175–176; quality of enhanced, 86; advances in, 89; state school fund provided, 90; public education lags, 120, 154, 155–156; public education for Negroes, 137; Common School Law, 155–156; segregation and integration, 180, 203–205 *passim*; mentioned, 93, 210, 211

—immigration: origins of immigrants, 5–7 *passim*, 39, 91; and Proclamation of 1763, 10; increases, 32, 42, 59, 77; first census (1777), 30; reasons for, 37–38; in 1820s, 77–78; high rate of, 97; few Europeans, 156; outmigration, 203, 207

—land: geographical divisions, xiii–xiv, 177, 182; speculation, sale, settlement of, 4, 7, 8, 19, 38, 41–42; Virginia claim to, 27–28, 40–41; and Transylvania Co., 27; myths of, 36; land acquisition problems, 40–41, 71, 96; faulty surveys and land claims, 40–44, 46; law of 1779, 41, 57; prices, 78–79

—politics and government: vendetta style of, 26; courts established, early counties created, 57, 73; constitutions and conventions for, 66–67, 69–71, 72–73, 89, 90, 107, 159–160; voting and voters' rights, 68, 69, 149, 156–157, 161–162, 185, 203; local government, 72–74, 75;

court controversy, 73, 77, 82–85, 87; corruption at local levels, 73–74, 89, 154–155, 184, 188–189; relief measures after panic of 1819, 80–88; two-party competition, 89; slavery and political issues, 100, 104, 106, 107, 113; Civil War aftermath, 138, 144; Civil Rights Act, 138, 204; public affairs demoralized, 165, 190–196 *passim*; "Goebel Election Law," 168, 171, 177; Progressive movement, 168, 182, 184; Reorganization Act of 1936, 198. *See also* Democratic party; Political parties; Republican party;—statehood

—population: increases, 5, 39; growth rate, 5–6; first census (1777), 30; ranked sixth nationally, 77–78; in slavery, 95; federal census of 1860, 95; population shifts, 102; decreases, 145; outmigration, 203, 207

—settlers: drawn by new lands, freedom, 4–7, 38–39; origins of, 5, 39, 91; early settlers, 19, 37–39; immigrants and squatters, 42, 49–50; and "western destiny," 38

—social life and customs: religious beliefs and manifestations, 5, 37, 75, 92–93, 156, 185, 209; adoption of Virginia life-style, 45, 48; violence and aggression, 39, 138, 141, 143, 153, 175, 203–204; social patterns, 44–47 *passim*, 56, 75, 92–93, 109, 156–157, 165, 200, 205; rural characteristics, 61, 74–75, 88–91 *passim*, 143, 156–157, 175; urbanization and economic change, 92, 143, 152, 176, 202–203, 206–210; social problems, 205–210

—statehood: issues of, 56; agitation for, 60, 64–65; origins as separate state, 56–57, 160; separation from Virginia, 58, 60, 62, 63–64; conventions preparing for, 60, 61, 62, 65, 66; state constitution drafted, 67; statehood achieved, 70–71; agitation for constitutional revision, 71–72; state relationship to Union, 77, 93, 114–115

Kentucky County, 28, 39, 40, 41

Kentucky Jockey Club, 187, 188, 189

Kentucky Racing Commission, 187

Kentucky River: early land boundary, 20, 57; trade route, 88; mentioned, 17, 25

Kentucky, University of, 186, 210–211

Kentucky Utilities Company, 210
Ku Klux Klan, 140, 142–143, 185

Lafoon, Ruby (governor), 192, 194
Lee, Gen. Robert E., 122–123
Lexington: and 1825 financial crisis,
    85–86; slave market, 103; growth, 152;
    "aristocracy," 166; industrial growth
    and change, 202; mentioned, 188
Lincoln, Abraham: presidential nominee,
    110; early life, 115; deems Kentucky
    vital area in Civil War, 114–115,
    123–124; pledges intentions, 128; call
    for emancipation, 129; mentioned,
    130–132
Livestock industry: horses, breeding of, 50,
    54, 56, 59, 75; cattle, sheep, hogs, 54,
    59; work animals, 54, 59, 112; men-
    tioned, 95, 96
Logan, Benjamin: pioneer leader, 26, 44
London Company, 19
Louisville: prospects of, in 1820s, 77–78;
    economic dominance of, 86–88, 112;
    accelerated development, 133; principal
    city, 144–145, 155; growth, 152; and
    L & N railroad, 153; industrial growth
    and change, 202; mentioned, 161, 188
Louisville and Nashville Railroad: in Civil
    War, 117, 123; postwar expansion,
    144–147 *passim;* interests, 150; and un-
    regulated competition, 152–153; and
    railroad commission, 159, 167; and elec-
    tions of 1899–1900, 170, 172, 178;
    mentioned, 163, 167

Magoffin, Beriah (governor), 116
Manufacturing: beginnings, 49; and trade,
    77, 85–86; decline of, 88; use of slave
    labor, 96; growth and change since
    World War II, 202
Marion Regulators, 141, 142–143. *See also*
    Vigilante groups
McClellan, George: presidential candidate,
    133
McKinley, William, 162, 169
Mills, Benjamin; and Appellate Court con-
    troversy, 82–84
Mississippi River: land boundary in 1763
    Treaty of Paris, 9; western boundary of

Kentucky, 35; trade route, 59; in Civil
    War, 117, 121
Mississippi Valley, 4, 22, 38
Morgan, John Hunt: and Morgan's Raiders,
    124–125
"Monkey Law." *See* Darwin, Charles
Morrow, Ed (governor), 183, 202
Murray, John: Royal Governor of Virginia,
    16

Negroes: rights as freedmen, 97; repatria-
    tion proposed, 98; during Civil War,
    129, 136; as soldiers, 130–132; public
    education and civil rights of, 137–138;
    establish black communities, 138; pros-
    pects and limitations, 140, 203–205; and
    racial violence, 140–141; migrate
    northward, 142, 203; suffrage, 149, 203;
    and Republican party, 161; as farmers,
    179. *See also* Freedmen; Slavery; Slaves
New Orleans, La.: importance to western
    trade, 51, 64, 66; port closed, 59, 62–63;
    Spanish control, 66
Nicholas, George, 68, 69, 70
Nicholas, Samuel (judge), 105
Night Riders, 179, 184. *See also* Vigilante
    groups
Northwest Ordinance, 69–70

Ohio Company, 8
Ohio River: Falls of the Ohio, 8, 17, 32, 51;
    entirely within Kentucky boundaries, 62;
    slave territory boundary, 70; mentioned,
    16, 19, 23, 24, 30, 123
Owsley, William: and Appellate Court con-
    troversy, 82–84

Path Deed: negotiation of, 20–21
Pitt, William, 9
Point Pleasant, Battle of, 18
Political parties: Court party, 64; Relief
    party, 82; New Court party, 84–85, 87,
    88; Old Court party, 84–85, 87; Free-
    Soilers, 110; Whigs, 110, 112, 148;
    American (Know-Nothing) party, 110,
    148; Constitutional Union party, 113;
    Greenback party, 159; Populist party,
    160–165; Prohibition party, 162. *See
    also* Kentucky—politics and govern-
    ment; Democratic party; Republican
    party

Powers, Caleb: secretary of state, 172; election to Congress, 173
Prohibition, 180–182
Prohibition Amendment, 182, 192

Railroads: construction and improvements of, 86, 89; economic impact of, 89, 112; expansion in 1850s, 144, 152; railroad commission, 159, 167; mentioned, 91, 120. *See also* Chesapeake and Ohio; Cincinnati and Southern; Transportation and trade routes
Reconstruction Acts, 136
Reformism, 164
Relief party, 82, 85
Republican party: rapid rise of, 110; abolitionism and sectional appeal, 111, 112; majority in Kentucky, 133; and social change, 135; radicalism, 146; and governor's race (1871), 150–151; growth and gains, 161–163, 166; mentioned, 114, 149, 169, 170–171, 177
Rhea, Tom: and Highway Commission, 194
Richmond, Battle of, 125. *See also* Civil War
Roads, 39, 89. *See also* Transportation and trade routes
Roosevelt, Franklin D., 193–194

Sampson, Flem (governor), 190, 191
Schools. *See* Kentucky—education
Sevier, John: and State of Franklin, 63
Shakers, 37–38
Sharecropping, 137. *See also* Agriculture
Shawnee: towns, 8; hunting parties, 14; attacks by, 14–15, 17, 18; as British forces, 29; and Old Chillicothe, 30, 33. *See also* Indians
Shiloh, Battle of, 124. *See also* Civil War
Shelby, Isaac (governor), 53, 71
Slavery: Kentucky first western slave state, 46; fact and fantasy, 47, 94–97, 100–103; influence on economy, 50–51, 95–97, 105; abolition proposed, 68; and state constitution of 1792, 69–71; and westward expansion, 70; debate over, 77, 93, 111; spread of, 94–95, 112; antislavery movement, 97, 102; abolitionism, 98–100 *passim*, 104–105, 108; and political issues, 100, 104, 106,

107, 113; 13th Amendment, 134; ends, 136; apprenticeships, 137; mentioned, 45, 46, 72. *See also* Emancipation; Freedmen; Negroes; Slaves
Slaves: population growth of, 46, 94–95; prices and selling of, 79–80, 102–103, 132; in factories, 96; runaway, 100; treatment of, 101–103; mentioned, 44, 75, 79, 112
Stanley, Augustus Owsley (governor), 183, 202
Steamboats: development of, 51. *See also* Transportation and trade routes
Sycamore Shoals, 24

Talbott, J. Dan, 191–192, 193
Taxation, 73. *See also* Kentucky —economy
Taylor, William S. (governor), 171–173
Tennessee Valley Authority, 207, 209
Tobacco: eastern market, 45; production, manufacture, growth of, 49, 50–52; transportation problems, 51, 63; Kentucky top producer of, 52, 158; prices, 79–80; varieties, 144–145; and panic of 1873, 158–159; wars, 179–180; uncertain future, 201; mentioned, 79, 95, 96
Tories, 32, 38
Trade: early routes, 39, 59, 89, 112; Kentucky desire for, 77; interstate, 113; Mississippi embargo on, 117. *See also* Manufacturing; Transportation and trade routes
Transportation and trade routes: Cumberland Gap, 8, 17, 21, 25, 54; Mississippi River, 35, 59, 117; overland roads and trails, 39, 89; trade routes, 59, 112; turnpikes and railroad connections, 86, 90; Kentucky River, 88; river traffic and canals, 89, 144; railroads, 89, 91, 112, 120, 144, 152; boom and improvements, 89. *See also* Railroads
Transylvania Company: founded, 19; impact on state, 20; and early settlers, 26; illegal operations of, 27
Transylvania University, 86–87
Treaty of Paris (1763), 9–10

United Mine Workers, 192
United States Constitution, 67
United States Steel Trust, 184

Vigilante groups: Marion Regulators, 141–143; Night Riders, 179; Whitecappers, 179
Virginia: movement into Kentucky, 16, 40; powers of in statehood, 28; land acquirement traditions, 40; governs Kentucky, 57
VISTA, 205
Volstead Act, 182. *See also* Prohibition

Walker, Thomas: and Loyal Land Company, 8; on Frontier, 9
Washington, George, 8, 9
Watterson, Henry; editor, *Courier-Journal,* 147; advocates new departure, 149–150; and "wet" faction, 182
Westward expansion, 38, 46, 100
Whig party, 110

Whiskey: early manufacture of, 50, 51, 59; bourbon created and developed, 52–53; early distillers, 53; principal industry, 182; mentioned, 54, 78, 112, 183, 185
Whitecappers, 179. *See also* Vigilante groups
Wilderness Congresses, 11
Wilkinson, James: separationist, 61, 63; dalliance with Spain, 64; decline and death, 66
Willson, Augustus E. (governor), 180
Women's rights, 156–157, 185
Wyandottes, 29. *See also* Indians

Young, Whitney: president, Lincoln Institute, 204
Young, Whitney, Jr.: director, Urban League, 204